Challenging Research in
Problem-based Learning

SRHE and Open University Press Imprint

General Editor: Heather Eggins

Current titles include:

Catherine Bargh *et al.*: *University Leadership*
Ronald Barnett: *Beyond all Reason*
Ronald Barnett: *The Limits of Competence*
Ronald Barnett: *Higher Education*
Ronald Barnett: *Realizing the University in an age of supercomplexity*
Tony Becher and Paul R. Trowler: *Academic Tribes and Territories (2nd edn)*
Neville Bennett *et al.*: *Skills Development in Higher Education and Employment*
John Biggs: *Teaching for Quality Learning at University (2nd edn)*
Richard Blackwell and Paul Blackmore (eds): *Towards Strategic Staff Development in Higher Education*
David Boud *et al.* (eds): *Using Experience for Learning*
David Boud and Nicky Solomon (eds): *Work-based Learning*
Tom Bourner *et al.* (eds): *New Directions in Professional Higher Education*
John Brennan *et al.* (eds): *What Kind of University?*
Anne Brockbank and Ian McGill: *Facilitating Reflective Learning in Higher Education*
Stephen D. Brookfield and Stephen Preskill: *Discussion as a way of teaching*
Ann Brooks and Alison Mackinnon (eds): *Gender and the Restructured University*
Sally Brown and Angela Glasner (eds): *Assessment Matters in Higher Education*
James Cornford and Neil Pollock: *Putting the University Online*
John Cowan: *On Becoming an Innovative University Teacher*
Sara Delamont, Paul Atkinson and Odette Parry: *Supervising the PhD*
Sara Delamont and Paul Atkinson: *Research Cultures and Careers*
Gerard Delanty: *Challenging Knowledge*
Chris Duke: *Managing the Learning University*
Heather Eggins (ed.): *Globalization and Reform in Higher Education*
Heather Eggins and Ranald Macdonald (eds): *The Scholarship of Academic Development*
Gillian Evans: *Academics and the Real World*
Andrew Hannan and Harold Silver: *Innovating in Higher Education*
Lee Harvey and Associates: *The Student Satisfaction Manual*
David Istance, Hans Schuetze and Tom Schuller (eds): *International Perspectives on Lifelong Learning*
Norman Jackson and Helen Lund (eds): *Benchmarking for Higher Education*
Merle Jacob and Tomas Hellström (eds): *The Future of Knowledge Production in the Academy*
Peter Knight: *Being a Teacher in Higher Education*
Peter Knight and Paul Trowler: *Departmental Leadership in Higher Education*
Peter Knight and Mantz Yorke: *Assessment, Learning and Employability*
Mary Lea and Barry Stierer (eds): *Student Writing in Higher Education*
Ian McNay (ed.): *Higher Education and its Communities*
Elaine Martin: *Changing Academic Work*
Louise Morley: *Quality and Power in Higher Education*
Moira Peelo and Terry Wareham (eds): *Failing Students in Higher Education*
Craig Prichard: *Making Managers in Universities and Colleges*
Michael Prosser and Keith Trigwell: *Understanding Learning and Teaching*
John Richardson: *Researching Student Learning*
Stephen Rowland: *The Enquiring University Teacher*
Maggi Savin-Baden: *Problem-based Learning in Higher Education*
Maggi Savin-Baden: *Facilitating Problem-based Learning*
Maggi Savin-Baden and Kay Wilkie (eds): *Challenging Research in Problem-based Learning*
David Scott, Andrew Brown, Ingrid Lunt and Lucy Thorne: *Examining Professional Doctorates*
Peter Scott (ed.): *The Globalization of Higher Education*
Peter Scott: *The Meanings of Mass Higher Education*
Michael L. Shattock: *Managing Successful Universities*
Maria Slowey and David Watson: *Higher Education and the Lifecourse*
Anthony Smith and Frank Webster (eds): *The Postmodern University?*
Colin Symes and John McIntyre (eds): *Working Knowledge*
Peter G. Taylor: *Making Sense of Academic Life*
Richard Taylor, Jean Barr and Tom Steele: *For a Radical Higher Education*
Malcolm Tight: *Researching Higher Education*
Penny Tinkler and Carolyn Jackson: *The Doctoral Examination Process*
Susan Toohey: *Designing Courses for Higher Education*
Paul R. Trowler (ed.): *Higher Education Policy and Institutional Change*
Melanie Walker (ed.): *Reconstructing Professionalism in University Teaching*
Melanie Walker and Jon Nixon (eds): *Reclaiming Universities from a Runaway World*
David Warner and David Palfreyman (eds): *Higher Education Management of UK Higher Education*
Gareth Williams (ed.): *The Enterprising University*
Diana Woodward and Karen Ross: *Managing Equal Opportunities in Higher Education*

Challenging Research in Problem-based Learning

Maggi Savin-Baden and Kay Wilkie

Society for Research into Higher Education
& Open University Press

Open University Press
McGraw-Hill Education
McGraw-Hill House
Shoppenhangers Road
Maidenhead
Berkshire
England
SL6 2QL

email: enquiries@openup.co.uk
world wide web: www.openup.co.uk

and Two Penn Plaza, New York, NY 10121–2289, USA

First published 2004

A catalogue record of this book is available from the British Library

ISBN 0335 21544 0 (pb) 0335 21545 9 (hb)

Library of Congress Cataloging-in-Publication Data
CIP data applied for

Typeset by YHT Ltd, London
Printed in the UK by Bell & Bain Ltd, Glasgow

Learning is but an adjunct to ourself,
And where we are our learning likewise is...

Shakespeare, W.

Love's Labour's Lost IV, iii

For our children ... Anna and Zak Savin-Baden, David and Neil Wilkie, whose challenging questions about life help us to learn more about both them and ourselves.

Contents

Contributors

Terry Barrett is Programme Leader at Waterford Institute of Technology, Waterford. She works as an education developer with staff on problem-based learning initiatives. Her doctoral research is entitled 'Lecturers as problem-based learning students: the dialogue and the praxis of a staff development module'.

Brian Bowe is a Lecturer in the School of Physics at Dublin Institute of Technology and, having undertaken a PhD in physics, is currently working towards a master's with a research project in qualitative evaluation that involves the investigation of the effects collaborative assessment has on student learning and contribution to the group process. Brian led the staff team that introduced problem-based learning into the physics element of the degree in applied science course in September 1999. He also developed a virtual learning environment and integrated it into the problem-based learning physics course to provide students with on-line learning resources, feedback, methods of communicating remotely and course information. His particular research interests include problem-based learning, on-line learning and assessment strategies involving self, collaborative and peer assessment.

John Cowan is a Professor Emeritus of the Open University, a visiting professor at three other British universities, an honorary graduate of two Scottish universities, a member of the SEDA Roll of Honour, an Honorary Fellow of EIS and the recipient of awards at home and abroad for innovative teaching. He was the first Professor of Engineering Education in the United Kingdom, during a career with Heriot-Watt University which saw him pioneer resource-based learning, self-directed learning, self-assessment, education for capability and the use of reflective activities to develop personal and professional capabilities. He is in frequent demand as a keynote speaker, as a provider of staff development in a range of areas, but especially in respect of innovation and quality enhancement, and as an educational consultant, both at home and abroad. He is the author of the well regarded text *On Becoming an Innovative University Teacher*.

Erik de Graaff trained as a psychologist and holds a PhD in social sciences. From 1989 to 1990 he was involved in the development of the problem-based curricula of medicine and health sciences at the University of Limburg in Maastricht. Since 1990 he has been attached to Delft University of Technology as an Educational Advisor and he was appointed as Associate Professor in the field of educational innovation in 1994. He was appointed part-time Guest Professor attached to the Videncenter for Læreprocesser (VCL), University of Aalborg, Denmark, in 1999. He has published on problem-based learning, project organized learning, assessment of learning, evaluation and educational innovation. He is also an active member of several professional bodies in higher education and engineering education.

Roisin Donnelly completed a teaching and research fellowship at the University of New South Wales in Sydney and then commenced working in the Learning and Teaching Centre in the Dublin Institute of Technology in 1999, where she designs and delivers the postgraduate certificate, diploma and master's in third level learning and teaching. She is currently completing a doctorate in education (EdD) at Queen's University, Belfast. Her teaching and research interests include on-line and blended learning, computer-assisted assessment, interactive teaching methods, creative curriculum design strategies and implementing action research in class settings in higher education.

Chris Hockings took up the post of Learning and Teaching Co-ordinator for the University of Wolverhampton in 2003, having spent ten years as a Senior Lecturer in business. She continues to work closely with lecturers, mentoring them through the process of changing to problem-based learning. Her doctoral research focused on the conditions under which lecturers can and do change to alternative approaches to learning and teaching and on the effects of problem-based learning on staff and students.

Bill Hutchings teaches eighteenth-century literature at the University of Manchester. He has published on, among others, William Cowper, Thomas Gray and Samuel Johnson. In 2000 he was awarded one of the first UK National Teaching Fellowships (NTFS) in the scheme administered by the newly founded Institute for Learning and Teaching in Higher Education. His NTFS project is to research the applicability of problem-based learning models to the teaching of literary studies.

Dan Jacobsen is Associate Professor at the Norwegian University of Science and Technology, where his main obligations are university pedagogy and staff development. The activity is organized in the Unit for Higher Education Development. Jacobsen is the former leader of this unit and is also a member of the university's Committee for Quality in Learning. In addition, Jacobsen is affiliated professor with special responsibilities for staff development at Molde University College. Dan Jacobsen has a PhD in education and his main research interests are in higher education pedagogy, problem-based learning and theory development relevant to learning and group learning assistance.

Peter Kandlbinder is a Lecturer at the University of Technology, Sydney, whose main responsibility is academic staff development in assessment. Over the past ten years Peter has been involved in staff development in distance and flexible learning in Australia and the South Pacific, most recently focusing on developing flexible learning programmes for academic staff. Peter's broad research interests are in innovations in teaching and learning, the evaluation of learning technologies and academic decision-making.

Sharron King is a Lecturer in the School of Health Sciences, University of South Australia. She is currently completing a master's by research, investigating the impact of implementing major educational reform on educators. She played an instrumental role in the introduction of a fully integrated problem-based learning curriculum in the medical radiation programme.

Ranald Macdonald is Head of Academic Development in the Learning and Teaching Institute at Sheffield Hallam University. He is a previous Co-Chair of the Staff and Educational Development Association and currently chairs the SEDA Research Committee. Ranald has run problem-based learning workshops and consultancy sessions throughout the UK and in countries such as Ireland, the Netherlands, Sri Lanka, Singapore, Sweden, the USA and Australia, as well as presenting many conference sessions. His problem-based learning research interests include the student and staff experience and intercultural aspects of using this approach.

Claire H. Major is an Assistant Professor of Higher Education at the University of Alabama. Her research focuses on issues related to university teaching, problem-based and collaborative learning, and faculty knowledge. She teaches courses in university teaching, academic cultures and academic programmes. Her service involves helping college and university faculty to improve teaching.

Yves Maufette was formally Director of the undergraduate programme in biology and he is currently associate dean at the Faculty of Science at Université du Québec à Montréal. He is responsible for the development and supervision of undergraduate and graduate programmes in science. Over the past ten years, Yves has actively participated in the development and has coordinated the implementation of a new problem-based learning programme in biology. The change to problem-based learning was begun in September 1996, and the first graduates from this new programme received their diploma in May 1999. At present, approximately 300 students are in the problem-based learning programme in biology. He is also an active field biologist specializing in plant–insect interactions in forestry and former Director of the research group GREFI (Research Group in Forest Ecology).

Karen O'Rourke is a Research Associate, and is responsible for investigating current problem-based learning methods and systems at the University of Manchester. In her previous post as Student Enterprise Officer, Karen was proactive in encouraging students to act as partners in their learning experience. She supported a wide range of innovative student-centred projects as well as implementing cost-effective teaching and learning innovations through involving students in the development and promotion of their ideas.

Betsy Palmer is currently an Assistant Professor in the Adult and Higher Education programme at Montana State University. Her research interests include college student learning, university teaching and diversity issues in post-secondary education. She uses a variety of active learning strategies, including problem-based learning to teach courses in higher education, research design and statistics.

Maggi Savin-Baden is a Principal Lecturer at Coventry University, who first began using problem-based learning in 1986 and commenced research into it in 1987. Maggi's early research focused on staff and students' experiences of problem-based learning in four universities in the United Kingdom. Over the past ten years Maggi has consulted widely on problem-based learning and she has been funded to set up a problem-based support network that promotes good practice in this field. She was an invited keynote speaker at the Asia Pacific Conference on Problem-based Learning, Australia, in December 2001 and also at the problem-based learning 2002 Conference, Baltimore, USA, in June and is a popular keynote speaker throughout the UK.

Charlotte Silén is Associate Professor and Head of the Unit for Educational Development and Research, Faculty of Health Sciences, Linköpings Universitet. The faculty is responsible for nine study programmes within health care where problem-based learning has been the basic pedagogic approach in all programmes since 1986. Charlotte was one of the pioneers in planning and implementing problem-based learning at the Faculty of Health Sciences and since then she has been practising and developing problem-based learning across Linköping University. She acts as a consultant for universities in Sweden and the other Nordic countries. The developing projects that Charlotte has been in charge of include examinations within problem-based learning, qualitative criteria assessing understanding, learning plans in clinical practice, the tutorial processes and problems used in tutorials. Her research has focused on the tutorial processes, the tutors' role, self-directed learning and students' responsibility and independence in learning.

Alexandre Soucisse is a former graduate from the problem-based learning programme in biology at Université du Québec à Montréal. He worked for two years at the Université Catholique de Louvain la Neuves (UCL) as a developer for a new student-centred programme in engineering. Alexandre is presently a lecturer at the Université de Montréal in the department of education.

Kay Wilkie is Director of Learning and Teaching at the School of Nursing and Midwifery, University of Dundee. She coordinated the implementation of problem-based learning in the pre-registration nursing and midwifery diploma programmes within the school. Her research focused on the lived experience of nursing lecturers making the transition to becoming problem-based learning facilitators.

Acknowledgements

Thanks are due to a number of people: Graham Gibbs and Gina Wisker for their endorsements of the book and Shona Mullen, Publishing Director, Open University Press for her support and guidance during this project.

We are grateful to all those who have participated in our research over the past ten years and agreed to be quoted here. Our grateful thanks are also due to Bob Rankin for the design and permission to use the cartoon on the front cover.

Finally, our thanks are due to John Savin-Baden for his support, patience, proofreading and indexing and to Tom Wilkie for clearing off and giving Kay space to write.

Introduction

Maggi Savin-Baden

Problem-based learning is an approach to learning that continues to grow and develop and the variations in its use still tend to cause much debate in higher education. The idea for this book emerged out of discussions with colleagues about the need for the problem-based learning community to illustrate such variety in a research-based text. It is a book that does not present a single view about what counts as problem-based learning, nor does it offer ideal ways of undertaking it in a module, course or programme. Instead it presents chapters from academics in a range of disciplines and countries who have not only implemented problem-based learning but also researched their own practice and the practice of others. Since the book focuses on individuals' own courses and modules and their disciplinary interests, much of the research here is qualitative. This is a feature of the book that we feel should be celebrated since it offers a different perspective from much of the current published work that tends to omit staff and student voices. Thus our argument for producing this book and assembling it in the way that we have done stems from four important issues that we see being played out on the global stage, which are that:

1. Arguments about problem-based learning continue to rage institutionally and globally.
2. Comparisons between problem-based learning and traditional curricula remain problematic.
3. The nature and process of facilitation still occurs largely behind closed doors.
4. The impact and complexity of change in this field over the last ten years has been underplayed.

We use this argument to set the scene for the book as a whole. However, the text is divided into four parts and at the beginning of each part we locate the studies in the wider context of the problem-based learning literature, summarize each chapter, provide links across the studies and offer some practical suggestions for future research and practice.

Arguments about problem-based learning

One of the difficulties in presenting a text such as this is that it raises questions about what counts as problem-based learning. There remains diversity of opinion about what does and does not count as problem-based learning and broadly speaking we seem to have three camps.

The first are the evangelists for problem-based learning who argue that it can only be done one way, across a whole programme and thus a course in, for example, physiotherapy does not comprise modular segments of anatomy, manipulation and physics but instead the focus for learning is clients and their problems. The first camp thus argues for an integrated curriculum where one problem builds upon another semester-to-semester, and year-to-year.

The second camp tends to be where those implementing problem-based learning believe in the essential principles of the problem-based learning approach rather than the content driving the learning, but who believe that there are disciplinary considerations that need to be taken into account. We believe it is the people who belong to this camp that are represented in this book. What this group of tutors and researchers suggest is that it is the nature of the discipline that affects the possibilities for implementation in terms of the rules and expectations implicit within that discipline. For example, Hutchings and O'Rourke (Chapter 13) argue that contestability is central to the discipline of literary studies, whereas Bowe with Cowan (Chapter 12) argue that students are used to solving problems rather than seeing them as a means of learning. The introduction of problem-based learning in these two disciplines has therefore meant adapting the original problem-based learning process (Barrows and Tamblyn 1980) to encompass disciplinary differences.

The third camp comprises those who believe that problem-based learning is just another strategy, merely another piece of equipment in the toolkit for lecturers. Thus it tends to be used within a subject or as a component of a programme or module, where other subjects may be delivered through lectures. This means that problem-based learning may just be used for a few seminars or half a module and in fact the students do not realize that they are doing problem-based learning, or if they do they do not really see the differences between it and other seminars they are undertaking.

For us problem-based learning remains different from problem-solving and problem-solving learning. We believe that in problem-based learning the focus is in organizing the curricular content around problem scenarios rather than subjects or disciplines. Students work in groups or teams to solve or manage these situations but they are not expected to acquire a predetermined series of 'right answers'. Instead they are expected to engage with the complex situation presented to them and decide what information they need to learn and what skills they need to gain in order to manage the situation effectively. It is:

an approach to learning that is characterized by flexibility and diversity in the sense that it can be implemented in a variety of ways in and across different subjects and disciplines in diverse contexts. As such it can therefore look very different to different people at different moments in time depending on the staff and students involved in the programmes utilizing it. However what will be similar will be the focus of learning around problem scenarios rather than discrete subjects.

(Savin-Baden 2000a: 3)

Comparisons of problem-based and traditional curricula are problematic

There are still many academics who suggest that it is not possible to say that problem-based learning is any better than lecture-based learning because there have been no quantitative studies that have proved this. Boud and Feletti (1997) argued that comparing traditional and problem-based curricula was virtually impossible because what was being compared was so radically different that it was almost impossible to have common variables to measure. It seems that, certainly in the UK, this has proved to be exactly the case. Newman (2003) attempted to undertake a randomized controlled trial that compared two curricula, one problem-based and the other traditional. The difficulty he found was in establishing common variables and in finding and developing appropriate measurement tools. Yet it seems it was questionable whether the curriculum that was alleged to be problem-based was any more than the implementation of problem-based learning as an instructional design strategy. Students and staff on the problem-based programme seem to have been ill prepared and the findings indicate large-scale dissatisfaction with the approach. What are needed instead are mixed method studies that use validated measurement tools such as The Student Course Experience Questionnaire (University of Sydney 1999) and learning inventories, along with narrative inquiry which explores the staff and students' experiences. A study that compared problem-based learning with traditional programmes would need to be undertaken with large student numbers over at least a five-year period to be able to demonstrate significant differences.

Facilitation still occurs largely behind closed doors

The debates about what counts as facilitation in problem-based learning are still under debate but one of the main challenges is that it is very difficult to know what really goes on in problem-based seminars. Much of the research into facilitation begins not only from the standpoint of the teacher but also from that of the researcher. For example, Gijselaers (1997) examined contextual factors on tutors' behaviours and the effects of departmental affiliation on tutoring. Quantitative analysis of data indicated that overall the level of stability in tutor behaviour, which was examined across different problem-based learning teams, was low, as was the generalizability. What was apparent from the study, although Gijselaers did not couch it in such terms, was that both the learners and the learning context affected the team facilitator. Earlier studies by Dolmans *et al.* (1994a,b) have also sought to quantify team facilitator behaviours and effectiveness.

Staff and students' voices are still largely unheard in the literature on problem-based learning and there are very few quantitative studies that have looked at students' experience. In this book we open the doors on several institutions in Part 2 and begin the process of exploring what really does happen in terms of rhetoric and reality, the process of becoming facilitators and the personal and pedagogical cost to lecturers.

The impact and complexity of change is underplayed

The nature of problem-based learning and its use within complex and diverse curricula has evolved considerably in the past ten years. In the 1970s and 1980s the majority of academics used the McMaster model (Barrows and Tamblyn 1980) and adapted it minimally to suit their discipline and institution. New models emerged in the 1990s and more still seem to appear. However, there appears to have been little evaluation or documentation of the changes made over time. I have argued elsewhere (Savin-Baden 2000a, 2003) for different models and modes of problem-based learning. Those I speak with around the world say that these delineations have been useful but it is only in an edited text such as this that we can begin to see the types of problem-based learning on offer and the ways in which they do and do not fit with disciplinary cultures. Certainly many of the chapters here explore not only the triumphs but also the struggles of implementation and thus offer a signpost to those wanting to implement problem-based learning in terms of barriers to implementation and the complexities of managing change.

Conclusion

We hope that in this book you find much that is helpful and that stimulates you to consider implementation of problem-based learning in your subject. Alternatively, it may prompt a reconsideration of the way in which you have implemented it or perhaps it will confirm what you have achieved. The book has been written to stimulate debate within the problem-based learning community not only about the nature of problem-based learning and the positioning of students' voices within it, but also about the kinds of research the problem-based learning community itself believes should be undertaken. There are many discussion lists that relate to problem-based learning and it is my hope that the problem-based learning community will develop this debate so that we can continue to challenge research and undertake more challenging research into problem-based learning.

Part 1
Curricula Concerns

This part unpacks some of the many curricula concerns that emerge when problem-based learning is used. The recent debates about what counts as a curriculum and the arguments about the position of problem-based learning within a programme are still of concern to many tutors in higher education. The notion of curriculum remains problematic because although we talk about the concept of and construction of a curriculum, in many ways we do not, as it were, *have* a curriculum, since it is constructed with and through our students. To date there has been little in-depth discussion about the design of problem-based curricula. Instead the discussions have tended to centre on what counts as problem-based learning, ways of implementing it and types of problem-based learning (for example, Boud 1985; Barrows 1986). More recently Conway and Little (2000b) have suggested that problem-based learning tends to be utilized as either an instructional strategy or a curriculum design. Instructional design is where problem-based learning is largely just seen as another teaching approach that can be mixed in with other approaches. Thus it tends to be used within a subject or as a component of a programme or module, where other subjects may be delivered through lectures. By contrast, in an integrated problem-based learning curriculum there is a sense of problem-based learning being a philosophy of curriculum design that promotes an integrated approach to both curriculum design and learning. Here students encounter one problem at a time and each problem drives the learning.

There have been a number of other discussions about types of problem-based learning, the most basic being that there are two types: the pure model and the hybrid model. The argument is that either the whole curriculum is problem-based and is modelled on the McMaster version of problem-based learning, whereby students meet in small teams and do not receive lectures or tutorials, or it is the hybrid model, which is usually defined by the inclusion of fixed resources sessions such as lectures and tutorials which are designed to support students. Lectures may be time-tabled in advance or may be requested by the students at various points in the module or programme. The so-called pure model is often termed the Medical School Model, and is invariably defined as necessarily having a dedicated facilitator for small teams of eight to ten students, being student-centred and being seen to be a good choice for highly motivated experienced learners in small cohorts (see, for example, Duch *et al.* 2001). The difficulty with this notion of there only being two types, a pure model and a hybrid model, is that, given the current number of forms of problem-based learning in existence, is it actually possible to distinguish when and if a model is hybrid or not? It is interesting to note that McInnis (2000) in a study of Australian universities found that 74 per cent of academics claimed to be using problem-based learning in their teaching. This would imply not only that many academics are changing their approaches to teaching but also that problem-based learning continues to be implemented as an instructional approach rather than being seen as an approach that requires embedding as a curriculum philosophy and design.

The difficulties of designing problem-based curricula are affected by both cultural and institutional constraints but issues that do tend to differ across disciplines also affect them. In this part of the book the authors explore four different curricula issues. Maufette *et al.* begin in Chapter 1 by exploring the nature of problems in problem-based learning. To date there has been little research that has explored the impact of the different types of problems on students' experiences of problem-based learning, nor has there been much exploration of the use of the different types of problem at different levels of the course. Maufette *et al.* present the findings of a survey into the quality of different problems experienced by students throughout the three years of a problem-based learning programme in biology at the Université du Québec à Montréal. They found that three motivational qualities of problems, namely the structure, variety and challenge, impact upon students' learning and the team dynamics within a tutorial. These three qualities can also enable an assessment of the nature and quality of the problems to be made. For example, they argue that the first set of problems experienced by students should not focus on specialized learning objectives but instead provide an overview of how the material will be learned. Throughout the sequence of the tutorial, the problems need to support the shift to the last phase, where the problems are more complex and relate strongly to interrelationships between the basic concepts in the field of study.

In Chapter 2 de Graaff examines the impact of problem-based learning on the process of problem-based learning itself. The impact of assessment on student learning, in both traditional and problem-based curricula, has been the subject of much debate and education research (Boud 1990; Gibbs 1992). For many tutors assessment is still seen as having two aims: it provides students with the results of their performance and gives them an award of intellectual or vocational competence. Yet this performative approach is too narrow for problem-based approaches where the process of learning is also seen as important. Students here need to be enabled to assess how they learn and equipped so that they know how to provide evidence of this learning. De Graaff begins by examining assessment paradigms in problem-based learning and exploring the nature of self-direction in relation to assessment. He then presents the findings of his study that explored the impact of assessment on the process of problem-based learning and suggests ways in which it is possible to use assessment to enable and improve the learning process for students.

Macdonald also explores students' experience and in Chapter 3 presents the findings of a study that used participatory action research to examine and change problem-based learning on a business and management course over a period of four years. The student experience of problem-based learning has received more attention than in former years. There are a number of authors who have discussed the importance of learner experience in the context of problem-based learning. For example, Ryan (1993) sought to identify whether students felt that it was important to be self-directed as learners and Dolmans and Schmidt (1994) studied the extent to which various elements of problem-based learning curricula influenced students' self-study patterns. Taylor and Burgess (1995) documented the findings of an illuminative evaluation undertaken into a problem-based learning course in social work. This study showed that students arriving on the course were at different stages of readiness for self-directed learning. The students, with the benefit of hindsight, felt that four areas could usefully have been included within an orientation programme to facilitate their introduction to problem-based learning. These were the lecturers' expectations of self-directed learning, the role of the facilitator, the principles and practices of learning in groups, and issues of time management. Macdonald builds on such studies and argues that by using an action research process it was possible to identify issues related to specific blocks and tutors and address them in a more focused way than previously. He suggests that evaluation of practice, reflection on the basis of timely feedback from students and the opportunity to make changes can have an immediate impact on the student experience. The findings of his study also indicated that such feedback proved uncomfortable for some tutors, while others welcomed the opportunity to obtain such specific feedback – both positive and negative – about their teaching and facilitation skills. Providing continual educational development support to enable staff to reflect and learn from the research led to a culture among many tutors of continually looking for ways to improve the student experience.

The final chapter in this part explores curricula concerns raised by a tutor running an on-line problem-based learning programme. On-line learning and distance education have been huge areas of development since the late 1980s. There are modules and programmes that use different forms of on-line learning to support problem-based learning but few, if any, to date are wholly problem-based. On-line education continues to be a growth area in education but many of the frustrations in universities seem to stem from the expense of new equipment, the speed of change and the need for continual updating. Universities have tight budgets and securing funds for new systems to support on-line learning seems to be a constant battle-ground. Donnelly undertook an evaluation of an on-line teaching envir-onment that adopted problem-based learning as its primary learning approach. She discovered that the participants in the study found that the problem complexity, the role of the tutor, the relationship between the individual and the team and the way in which language was used in on-line learning environments raised challenges not highlighted in terrestrial problem-based learning. Her findings indicate that a blended approach to on-line problem-based learning which included face-to-face encounters facilitated cohesiveness, good dialogue, quality tutorial input and indivi-dualized support. Furthermore, the key to promoting team collaboration was in giving the participants the opportunity to experience on-line learn-ing first as an individual, then in a pair with one participant in a mentor role and finally in a series of on-line group and reflective activities.

Part 1 includes a diverse collection of studies that address issues in dif-ferent contexts and countries but that all explore curricula concerns from staff and students' perspectives. Many lecturers' experience of designing problem-based curricula stems from a tendency to focus on content and outcomes. There are arguments about the order in which content should be covered and how much time each discipline is going to be allowed to have, so that there is an underlying sense that the greater the length of time given to the particular discipline, subject or topic, the more it is valued. What seems to be missing in these discussions is a concern for the learner and the learning. Instead what we see in these chapters is a focus on just that, so that curricula concerns about such issues as the types of problems, the impact of assessment and the experience of problem-based learning, both terrestrially and virtually, have been addressed to reflect students' concerns and to improve students' learning.

1

The Problem in Problem-based Learning is the Problems: But do they Motivate Students?

Yves Mauffette, Peter Kandlbinder and Alexandre Soucisse

Introduction

The growing interest in problem-based learning comes from the integration of sound educational principles into a single, consistent teaching and learning approach. This approach commonly consists of aspects of self-directed and life-long learning, with problem-solving and critical thinking skills developed through facilitated group learning. A basic premise of problem-based learning is that students take greater responsibility for their own learning, with the benefit that they develop a wider range of transferable skills such as communication skills, teamwork and problem-solving. At the same time problem-based learning students perform just as well in examinations, but develop slightly better reasoning ability and have consistently higher levels of satisfaction (Norman and Schmidt 2000).

In considering ways to improve problem-based learning most of the effort has focused on the role of the tutors (Barrows 1985, 1988). Margetson (1997), however, suggested that it is now necessary to rethink the nature of the problems used to trigger student learning. Margetson's argument is based in a belief that problem-based learning has a distinctive identity, which he proposes is centred on the problem (Margetson 2000). Within the problem-based learning context, problems are invariably defined as 'ill-defined' and 'real-world', pointing out that they are artificial abstractions specifically constructed to facilitate student learning. Despite the success of problem-based learning in health and medicine, there has been a tendency for other disciplines, like science and humanities, to argue that this focus on 'problems' renders problem-based learning impractical for their particular knowledge domain. While it might be the case, as Margetson (2000) argued, that the use of problems is what helps to define problem-based learning, the very nature of how problem situations assist student learning is not well enough understood to make it helpful to lecturers in all disciplines. Van Berkel and Schmidt (2000) described a strong, direct effect on the students' interest in the subject matter and the quality of the problems, highlighting the importance of research on what makes a good problem. Authors who have previously attempted to determine the nature of problem-based learning problems have relied on factor analysis to categorize a number of possible attributes, which has been useful in providing a taxonomy for the classification of problems (Schmidt and Moust, 2000a,b). In an alternative approach, Marchais (1999) used a panel of experts to develop criteria for judging problems.

Several authors have addressed motivation in different educational environments, although mainly for traditional classrooms (Pajares 1996; Eccles *et al.* 1998; Viau 1999; Wlodkowski 1999). As problem-based learning is taken to be inherently motivating, few authors have considered the motivating factors for problem-based learning (MacKinnon 1999). The motivation literature offers explanations of the factors influencing students' performance without exploring the implications for principles of design. Similarly, guidelines for constructing problems from the problem-based learning literature generally do not draw significantly on the motivation literature. Much of this advice comes from generic suggestions for good writing such as clarity and relevance (for example, Barab and Landa 1997). Authors who have considered both the process of writing problems and the choice of key elements that constitute a good problem (such as White 1995; Duch 1996; Guilbert and Ouellet 1999) provide excellent examples of well written problems and insights into how they were written. Chapman (2000), for example, offers guidance for writing motivating problems based on stylistic issues observed in well written problems.

There is a considerable body of advice on writing good problems, though it is rarely evidence-based and does not start from the views of the students. It is this lack of specific research on the motivating factors of problems that has led us to embark on a study that aims to provide a conceptual understanding of how problems develop in a particular field or context to motivate student learning. In this chapter we report on the findings of a survey into the quality of different problems experienced by students throughout the three years of their problem-based learning programme in biology at the Université du Québec à Montréal (UQAM). Based on these survey results we describe how problems can be used to engage the interest of students. We conclude this chapter with a discussion of the implications of using the motivating aspect of problems for problem-based learning.

Motivating students to learn

Constructivism emphasizes that it is what the students do rather than what the teacher intends that leads to student learning (Larochelle *et al.* 1998). Translated to the learning situation, research has shown that the quality of learning depends on the approach students take to their studies (Biggs 2003). Ramsden (2003) describes high quality student outcomes as the result of students taking a deep approach to learning whereby they actively attempt to develop a meaningful understanding of the topic. Students adopt a surface approach to learning when they passively focus on the reproduction of isolated facts without trying to get to the topic's underlying structure or meaning. Students who adopt a deep approach report greater fulfilment through their studies, construct better assignments and achieve higher grades (Ramsden 2003: 57). Deep approaches to learning are related to a student's interest for its own sake and to a sense of ownership of the subject matter.

Creating an environment that encourages a deep approach to learning is a complex undertaking. As Ramsden (2003) demonstrates, it is not a simple process of telling students the best way to approach their learning. It is not possible to train students to be deep learners, though it is possible to create an environment in which a deep approach to learning is rewarded and, in turn, encourages intrinsic motivation. When students are naturally motivated to complete a task, external rewards have been shown to reduce their intrinsic motivation (Deci *et al.* 2001). Rather that concentrating on extrinsic rewards in decontextualized settings, more recent contextual studies of motivation suggest that the learning environment needs to be structured in such a way that it supports the student's intrinsic motivation (Järvelä 2001). The contextual view of motivation sees it as the interplay between the individual and their environment so that the student's beliefs interact with cues present in the classroom. According to Paris and Turner (1994) academic tasks that motivate students have four characteristics. These are the freedom to choose among alternatives, challenge that is moderately difficult, control over the task and collaboration through peer commitment. Cordova and Lepper (1996) argue that students are more likely to become deeply involved in activities when they are embedded in meaningful and appealing contexts that are personalized for the students or where the students have some degree of choice, even over incidental aspects of learning.

Research clearly demonstrates that providing an environment that encourages interested and engaged students results in higher quality student learning. Interest-focused problems from the student's perspective would begin to develop more interesting learning activities, provide more choice and ensure the tasks are optimally challenging. Neither the motivational literature nor the problem-based learning literature addresses the challenge of designing interest-driven problems. To provide guidance for constructing problems by drawing on the motivational literature, we will now turn to a survey of student responses to their experiences of different problem situations, which describes the kind of environment that is authentic and interesting to the students as the basis for describing the characteristics of problems that motivate learning.

What students do in the classroom depends on how they appraise their learning context (Boekaerts 2001). Each student experiences this context differently, often making the students' responses to this environment unpredictable. The key function of a problem is to bring some predictability to the problem-based learning environment. Problems in problem-based learning structure the students' learning by providing the trigger for their interest in the topic as well as providing the boundaries of what will be studied. Narrowly defined problems restrict the proportion of the curriculum that gets considered, leading to a lower element of choice for the students, with the danger of reducing students' intrinsic motivation. Whenever motivation drops students choose to ignore some parts of the course, progressively falling behind in their studies and working only to meet deadlines. As a result students put less time into studying and study less of the course in depth (Donald 1997: 90).

The context of the study

To build on students' intrinsic motivation requires starting from the students' perspectives and understanding the students' perceptions of the problems they encounter. A study undertaken in the problem-based learning biology programme at UQAM (Mauffette and Poliquin 2001) surveyed the students' perceptions of problems to determine the common elements that impact on the students' interest (see Soucisse *et al.* 2003 for complete details of the survey and questionnaire). The original survey was conducted in 1999, with a total of 117 students out of 130 electing to complete the questionnaire. All participants were students enrolled as full-time biology students and were distributed in the first three cohorts of this programme that commenced in autumn 1996. Sixty-seven students were in year 1, who had completed approximately 30 problems, 24 in year 2, who had experienced about 90 problems, and 26 in their final year, who had experienced approximately 130 problems. The questionnaire had a total of 50 questions and was completed by students during the winter semester of 1999. The questionnaire was divided into three sections with a series of related questions focusing on:

1. Sociological data and contextual information.
2. Interest in and appreciation of the problems that the student encountered.
3. Style and structure of the problems and related information for the problems.

Students were asked to use a four point scale (1, absolutely not; 2, a little; 3, reasonably; and 4, completely) to rate the extent of their agreement for questions pertaining to sections 2 and 3. Students were also invited to provide written comments.

Findings

The qualities reflected in the students' responses to this survey indicated that a measure of the quality of a problem is the degree to which it stimulates the students' desire to learn. The two features of problems highlighted by the study were the levels of variety and challenge perceived by students. Our findings suggest that the style used in the writing process, such as being discursive or explicative, does influence the students' interest. From the students' response it was concluded that one should be cautious with a more directive problem because it can restrict the students' ability to explore issues and as a consequence decrease the students' intrinsic motivation. Further, students appreciate problems that deal with realistic or actual situations. They appear not to want to be distracted from the substantive learning issues by flights of fancy or gratuitous humour. At the same time, students wanted to explore a diversity of contexts to avoid the repetition in which they became caught up by continually using the same pattern of expression, which may form a barrier to them extending their learning. This led us to argue that when writing problems educators should make a proper use of the language through short and simple sentences that have been shown to be appreciated by students. Overall, problems exhibiting a discursive style will lend themselves to the problem-based learning format and lead students to engage in group discussions and enhance group dynamics.

A second issue addressed within this questionnaire dealt with the level of challenge inherent in the problems. The question on directed and non-directed problems asked students what their choice would be between problems with ill defined (non-directed) learning issues compared with those where the learning issues were more structured and less flexibility was given (directed). As might be expected, first year students favoured having mainly directed problems while senior students preferred the contrary. This shows that the levels of student experience have a twofold implication when developing problems. First, inexperienced students rely much more heavily on the details of the problem to identify the challenging aspects of the learning objective. This could simply be the result of students in their first year having experienced fewer non-directed problems and therefore suggests that the range of problems needs to be extended from time to time to ensure students experience sufficient variation in their learning environment. Second, the confidence and the competency levels of the students increase through time and senior students require less detail in order to be challenged. A similar trend was reflected in the students' preference for having reading material assigned to the problems. First year students demonstrated a preference for receiving the appropriate lectures ascribed to them when compared with senior students, who favoured less direction in their reading assignments. We would expect that the increasing knowledge of and familiarity with the problem-based learning method would progress throughout the years.

Table 1.1 Criteria for motivational problems

	Introductory	Intermediate	Advanced
Educational goals	Goals are clearly stated relating to specific student actions	Goals are identified and relate to suggested approaches for learning	Goals are not identified in the problem
Background information	Draws on one source of data	Draws on two or more sources of data	Draws on many sources of data from current practice
Setting	Complete information provided without any details omitted	Most information provided with some details omitted	Information provided with key details omitted
Problem	Clearly identifies and summarizes the problem	States the problem and places it in a wider context	Does not clearly state the problem and emphasizes the wider context
Content	The content is sharply focused, supported with a variety of significant details	The content is structured with a clear focus and supported by relevant details	The content covers a number of areas and is supported with a few general examples
Resources	Includes self-contained independent materials like handouts and worksheets	Includes list of bibliographic references	Includes vocabulary and key concepts
Presentation	Tightly written with limited specialist vocabulary	Clearly written with a range of vocabulary used	Fluid writing style using extensive specialized vocabulary

Problems do not have to be a piece of literature, but our study shows that style does impact on students' learning. What this study indicated was the link between challenge and variety, so that, as the students' self-efficacy and competence levels increase, they rely less on the structure of the problems and look for learning challenges elsewhere. Table 1.1 summarizes general criteria for judging the appropriate level of the resulting problem. In each case the focus is on what is written and provided to the student. Of the three levels suggested here, the most complex problem to write is the advanced level. Introductory problems have all the details of the setting (see Appendix 1.1), while more advanced problems have fewer details and rely on more inferences (see Appendix 1.2). Advanced problems are closely related to practice and require subtle decisions of what details the students are able to provide themselves. In line with the students' survey responses the advanced problems would be more flexible, less directive problems without extensive reading lists. In many cases literature directly related to the problem may not exist and students would be expected to find their own information when formulating their solutions. Similarly, they may not have the educational goals described in the problems themselves but this is not to suggest that these goals do not exist. They are more likely to be stated in the tutor's guide than written directly in the problem.

As we have discussed elsewhere (Soucisse *et al.* 2003), our survey indicates that students must first perceive the problem's value (perceived task) and then the problem must allow for the appropriate level of structure and challenge to support their learning. Viau (1999) argues that the level of competence is determined by the students' past performances, emotional and physiological reactions to the task to be accomplished, how the students will be observed by their peers and the encouragement given by their associates. A further source of motivation in the problem is the perceived control by the student. In a situation with a low degree of perceived control, students would feel that everything is imposed upon them. In contrast, high control is where students feel that they completely master the situation (Deci *et al.* 1991; Viau 1999). It is clear from the student responses to our survey that self-efficacy is a particularly important factor for senior students.

Designing motivating problems

In this section we turn to the question of designing problems based on our understanding of what motivates students to learn. Our study of motivating problems demonstrates that problem-based learning problems are double-sided in nature. They stabilize and structure the learning experience, yet the same problem changes in meaning for each student group. When it comes to writing problems that motivate students, it is necessary to emphasize these two characteristics to ensure that students have the variety and challenge needed to maintain motivation, as well as to receive the kind of support they need for learning just at the time that they need it. This support, like scaffolding, selectively diminishes over time, so that first year students receive greater explicit guidance from the structure of the problem, while senior students would be expected to draw on their more extensive prior knowledge of problems to structure their own learning during an open-ended exploration of the topic.

Many problems used in problem-based learning programmes come from actual events that are rewritten to make them into a trigger for learning. The challenge in problem construction is to take a story that describes a 'normal' event and turn it into an effective learning activity. This involves a number of stages beginning with documentation of the original case material, analysis of its salient points to draw out the problem's themes and rewriting the problem to provide a structure for the students' learning. Our survey suggests that one of the secrets to constructing a motivating problem would be to identify a situation that students might actually encounter which will develop the knowledge, skills and behaviours required by a practitioner in this situation. It is not the case that each problem needs to be set specifically in the role of the practitioner as long as the students can discern the relevance of the problem. This link between prior experience and future application will help students to perceive the underlying value of the problem. This will change with the students' experience, so that the common cases would be studied before introducing the more exotic topics. A schematic view of the key motivational elements that should be incorporated in a problem is presented in Figure 1.1.

Sources of motivation

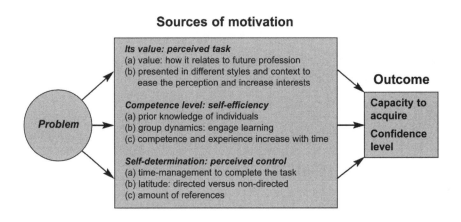

Figure 1.1 Key motivational elements that should be incorporated in a problem.

Generally, problems concentrate on a setting that consists of the location, the problem's actions and the time that they occurred. It is this description of a particular place that the students will use as the basis for determining what happened. The original story of a situation will include all the details of the context, such as the setting, who is involved in the situation and what events took place. This situation would need to be analysed to determine the underpinning major concepts that can be drawn upon for student learning. One of the key tools for making the transition from story to problem is the *problem map*, which identifies the central themes of the story (Skinner *et al.* 2001). This is a visual representation of the many concepts, topics or associated ideas in the story and an analysis of the nature of the relationships between them.

While there are many ways to develop a problem map, the intention is to create an alternative, less complex way of looking at the problem, stripped of the detail of the setting. It is then possible to identify any gaps that exist between the problem map and any concepts that are appropriate to the intended objectives of the problem. It could also indicate that one story may well provide the source material for a number of problems, as different elements of the setting are progressively revealed to the students. It is this mapping of the problem that also indicates the level of challenge or the students' competency level within the problem. Challenge has a complex relationship to student performance. Csikszentmihalyi (1975) describes optimal performance as a path between anxiety and boredom. Not enough challenge and students are indolent and uninterested in learning. Student performance increases with increased challenge until a point where it plateaus. When it becomes clear to students that they are unable to meet the problem's challenge, their performance dips once again as they give up.

An earlier study on tutors' perceptions of problem-based learning (Kandlbinder and Mauffette 2001) provides some guidance in how we can design progressive problems to challenge the students. In this study we found that student-focused tutors in problem-based learning courses have four primary descriptions of the basic concepts they wanted their students to learn. This knowledge of a discipline was portrayed as an interconnected network of views that define the discipline. Each description emphasized a different aspect of the knowledge valued by the discipline, increasingly emphasizing the relational aspects between concepts. Less complex problems would be those that handled discrete concepts that would be quantitatively built up over a number of problems. The most complex problems would be those that contained a series of concepts but emphasized their interconnections, as tested against the reality of various situations.

The analysis of the story is completed with the review of the problem map and selection of parts of the situation that best allow the objectives to be achieved. The story is then rewritten as a problem that ensures the students encounter each of the branches of the map, emphasizing the conditions or constraints that will be met. Problems intended for earlier years might have single concepts that are built up sequentially over a number of problems. More advanced problems would contain a wide range of concepts that define the boundaries of the discipline. It is also here that it is possible to provide the cues and hints that will help the students to formulate learning issues and learning questions for hypothesis testing. As suggested in Table 1.1, introductory problems would have more straightforward hints written as part of the problem. The most advanced problems might contain almost no clues for learning but emphasize the interconnections between the basic concepts.

Throughout this rewriting stage it is essential to consider the two factors that we identified to influence the motivational characteristics of problems, namely variety and challenge. In problem-based learning it is the theme within the topic that is intended to teach; however, the theme is never presented directly to the student as otherwise it becomes a simple exercise-solving activity. Students extract the theme of the problem from the characters, action and setting that make up the problem. Although the particulars of the problem may be different from the details of the original story, the problem writer's task is to communicate the general underlying concepts behind the story with increasing levels of ambiguity.

Consequences of motivating problems for problem-based learning

The role of the problem is to serve as a stimulus for learning. Not all difficulties in student learning will simply disappear by ensuring that well designed problems do not undermine intrinsic motivation. Each problem is delivered in a context and that context also needs to be planned to support the motivating nature of the problems. A clear case in point is the question of a student's workload and its influence on a student's capacity to control his or her learning. It is well known that an excessive workload is a demotivating force. The time allotment students reported for their personal studies in the biology programme at UQAM were between eight and eleven hours per problem. However, the students also indicated that they would have liked to invest an even greater amount of time. This information could be taken to indicate that the problems set were too demanding at that level or that the students could not afford more studying time because of their extracurricular activities (70 per cent reported having part-time jobs).

In either case this clearly indicates the important role tutors play in ensuring that the students are adequately prepared to tackle a problem. Too many problems, even when they are well designed, do not provide students with sufficient time to take a deep approach to their learning. Students in our survey clearly found it difficult to gauge the learning objectives from the problems themselves. This becomes a major issue for students' motivation if they perceive they cannot reach the learning objective in the given time period. More importantly, in the context of problem design, it clearly demonstrates that problems are not appropriate for managing a student's time on a learning task. Only tutors working with the student groups can ensure their expectations and workloads are appropriate so that students do not become alienated from group discussions or become frustrated because they are inadequately covering the supporting reading.

The outcomes of our survey have a number of implications for tutors' facilitation of problems. Van Berkel and Schmidt (2000) reinforce the importance of the three-way relationship between the quality of problems, group function and tutor performance. In their analysis, the quality of problems had the greatest effect on group functioning, which in turn impacts on the students' interest in the subject matter. The third variable that impacts on the group functioning is the tutor performance. How the quality of the problem is related to the performance of the tutors is a question for another study. A clue to the answer lies in the study by Reeve *et al.* (1999), which found that autonomy-supporting tutors reinforced the students' intrinsic motivation by listening more, holding instructional material less and resisting providing solutions, while also endeavouring to discover student wants, answering students' questions and volunteering perspective-taking comments that support the internalization of educational values.

In any case, this triangular model proposes a simple and idealistic view of the facilitation process, but accords with issues we have observed in the tutorials of the biology programme at UQAM. The well written problem assists the facilitation by structuring the learning so the tutor is able to focus on group dynamics. The dynamic processes found within tutorials are similar to those that govern traditional methods of teaching and we will not go into any greater detail here. However, we suggest that within the problem-based learning environment, the interactions between students, tutors and problems adapt and change through time. During the first phase when problem-based scenarios are first given, the student-centred philosophy of problem-based learning suggests that interaction between students and tutor must be enhanced to install a sound working relation within the group. The second stage is when all three components approach an equilibrium. As the motivation literature shows us, tutors should not overshadow students but neither should they neglect acquiring the knowledge necessary as part of their learning process. In the final stage students need to be sufficiently motivated to learn by themselves, with an enhanced interaction between students and knowledge promoting self-learning. The role of the tutor in this last phase is as counsel to perfect the students' methodological skills in the acquisition of information and knowledge (see Figure 1.2). In addition to the role the tutor must play, we cannot overlook his or her pedagogical stances, because as Savin-Baden (2000a,b) has reported, they are contributing factors that can also strongly influence the students' learning experience.

The three motivational qualities of problems – structure, variety and challenge – help us in part to understand the dynamics within a problem-based tutorial but also offer us guidance in assessing the nature and quality of the problems necessary to establish an appropriate sequence related to the pedagogical focus of the three-way interaction. Clearly the first set of problems experienced by students should not focus on specialized learning objectives but provide an overview of how the material will be learnt. Throughout the sequence of the tutorials, the problems need to support the shift to the last phase, where the problems are more complex and relate strongly to interrelations between the basic concepts in the field of study.

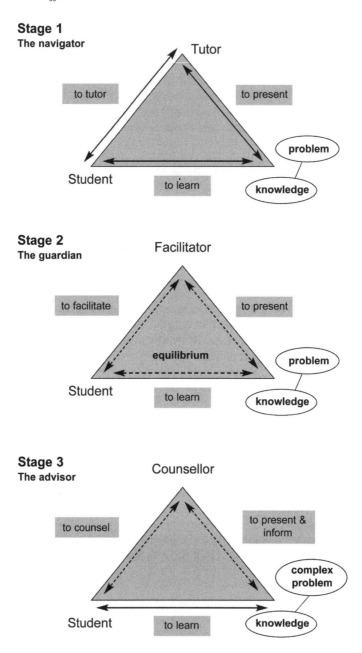

Figure 1.2 Problem-based learning environment, set within three stages.

Conclusion

In this chapter we explored the potential application of effectively designed, motivational problems for student learning. It has been known for a long time that motivated students learn better than unmotivated students, but it has always been assumed that motivation is an individual characteristic of students. Recent research into student motivation demonstrates that contextual factors like the quality of the problem and the lecturer-tutor's performance impact on the quality of the group functioning, which in turn impacts on interest in the subject matter.

While the role of facilitation has been a central theme in problem-based learning (Burgess and Taylor 2000), problems are the stable component of any problem-based learning course. We suggest that a major factor in increasing the effectiveness of problem-based learning through relatively minimal changes may have been overlooked. The students at UQAM quite clearly viewed some of the features of problems as key to the quality of their learning experience. Our study indicated that key elements of problems do sustain student motivation. Problems that can be decoded in a step-by-step manner will lead to a surface approach to learning. This bears out what the literature on motivation would predict. With some of the basic principles of reported motivational research confirmed by our survey, we have used those aspects of motivational theory to comprehend the nature of the sources of motivation found in problems. Our conclusion permits us to portray what elements should be included, and why, in the design of any new problem.

Appendix 1.1: problem 1

John must collect ten different plant species. The following weekend he travels to northern Quebec in the Abitibi region to visit his parents. At the same time he decides to collect his plants. Upon his return during a meeting the herbarium taxonomist points out to John that he only has nine species of plant, two being the same species. Going back to his field notes he realizes that he collected one of these phenotypes in a field near an abandoned mine. Even if the taxonomist says that these different forms could be due to a random process, John thinks it could instead be an adaptation phenomenon which evolved. John considers that it could even be the residues from the old mine that have led to a mutation to protect the plant against toxic effects.

This is the first problem given to students in the biology programme at UQAM. It is a short problem with some new words students must learn but it also aims towards more directed learning outcomes in biology such as natural selection and mutation. However, the context for the students is real because in their first year they are requested to collect ten plants; hence it is a situation they may experience and will be perceived as a realistic task. The problem should also lead students to initiate hypothesis making, but it has the potential of three 'solutions' (a mutation, the process of natural selection or even both). Such a structure can be challenging for the student because he or she should realize the biological complexity or it can be frustrating because no right or wrong solution may emerge. The problem will therefore challenge their competence level ('Does the student have the prior knowledge to deal with it?') but also their self-determination ('Can the student achieve the learning issues?'). In summary, the problem does address basic concepts in biology but is structured to include our three main sources of motivation.

Appendix 1.2: problem 2

24 February 1998

Dear cousin,

This winter I imagine you saw on TV the impacts of our famous ice storm that occurred during the month of January. You probably saw that numerous cities and many individuals greatly suffered during this crisis but I think it is my sugarbush that suffered the most.

During this storm many of my maple trees lost considerable amounts of branches taking away a fair proportion of buds. I am certain that I will not harvest any sap this spring. In some instances, I had to rebuild my sap collecting system leading to additional investments I had not planned. Our old timers say that we should cover the wounds with tar to prevent sap losses and protect the trees against parasites and fungi. The foresters from our government have advised us to tap only the trees which have less than 50 per cent damage. I think I should cut down all the trees that have been wounded because I sense they will soon die, it is not a forest anymore it is a battleground.

I know that you are completing a degree in biology and worked for many summers with foresters. Have you encountered such problems and what would you do? Your suggestions would be highly appreciated because our experts do not know much.

Best wishes,
Peter

This is a problem set for senior students principally in the ecology option. The context is a major storm that did occur in 1998. These students have prior knowledge pertaining to issues in plant science and ecology. However, the problem does include multiple possibilities in engaging in applied sciences, relating to the industry or its economy (will the owner be compensated for his investment?), in the sense of despair of the owner and in the potential actions of restoration or remedy. The problem may therefore take alternate discussion paths rather than focusing principally on plant ecology and the role of perturbations in forest ecosystems. Senior students will be asked to consider the numerous ramifications relating to biology, but also to research through the existing literature potentially to justify what actions must be taken. Based on past experience, when students engage in this problem they often perceive it to be simplistic and consider that the literature should rapidly point to a direct answer. Hence, frustration does not occur in establishing their learning objectives, but when seeking information and realizing the complexity of the issues whereby no simple solution can be presented. The challenge lies within establishing, throughout their reading and reasoning, the elements of a sensible action that their cousin must take and also why it must be taken. The basic factors that should motivate students, such as the value of the task or prior and lacking knowledge, are easily addressed. However, it is the perceived control that underpins the motivation. For the students to grasp a full understanding of the situation they must take control of their learning and then act upon it responsibly. This problem is an example of the complexity relating to written problems, whereby motivation often emerges when students seek information and construct their knowledge to establish an understanding of the action to be undertaken.

2

The Impact of Assessment on the Problem-based Learning Process

Erik de Graaff

Introduction

Assessment forms an integral part of a curriculum, usually with examinations at the end of each part of the course (De Corte *et al.* 1981). It is generally recognized that the impact of assessment of learning outcomes on the behaviour of students is considerable. Sometimes teachers even utilize this 'didactic function of assessment' to give the students a sort of beacon indicating what performance level is to be expected by the end of a course (Wesdorp 1979). In the case of problem-based learning, however, the directional effect of assessment on the student's behaviour is potentially counter-productive. In a problem-based curriculum students are expected to define their own learning goals, within the broad scope of the course. When they know in advance what knowledge will be in the test, the risk is substantial that their learning choices will be limited to those aspects.

In order to deal with this problem an alternative approach to assessment of student learning has been developed for an undergraduate programme course in applied physics at Delft University of Technology (De Graaff and Kruit 1999a, b). The model for alternative assessment was investigated in a study into the effects of assessment procedures on self-direction of the learning process within a framework of different measurement paradigms. Data from different sources, including interviews, a questionnaire and test scores, were analysed and related to the model. Based on the analysis, this chapter makes recommendations for improving assessment methods in problem-based learning courses.

Assessment of learning results in relation to problem-based learning

Assessment paradigms

The foundation of a paradigm consists of a set of axioms, assumptions that cannot be proved or disproved. Traditionally, assessment operates within the boundaries of a paradigm characterized as 'scientific measurement' (Hager and Butler 1994; Hager *et al.* 1994) or 'rationalistic'. The cornerstone of the rational or scientific measurement paradigm is static. In order to measure something it has to remain constant, at least for a reasonable period of time. In this view, a process is treated as a series of successive events, much as in a cinematic film the illusion of movement is created by rapidly displaying a succession of pictures. However, within this static framework reliability could be defined in terms of repeated measurements and validity in terms of prediction of future performance. Objectivity is the second hallmark of the rational paradigm. Naturally it makes sense, within this framework, to focus on the object being measured. If you want to predict performance on a fixed set of external criteria, you need absolute qualifications.

Despite its domination of the scene, the rational paradigm is not the only one that applies to educational measurement. The evaluation literature features a multitude of evaluation models, such as 'naturalistic evaluation', 'illuminative evaluation', 'responsive evaluation', 'adversary evaluation' and 'judicial evaluation' (Noll 1961; Stufflebeam *et al.* 2000; Walberg and Haertel 1990). The choice of paradigm is obscured by the implicit dominance of the values of the rationalistic paradigm. For example, the quality of assessment employing multiple judges in the scientific measurement paradigm is defined in terms of intersubjective agreement among the judges. Using such a criterion amounts to paying lip service to objectivity (Norman *et al.* 1991; van der Vleuten *et al.* 1991). The true value of a verdict by a human judge could very well be determined by the individual attention for a case, resulting in different outcomes depending on the personal attributes of the judge. The quality of such 'sensible interpretations' is being recognized in a process-oriented paradigm. Table 2.1 summarizes the assumptions of the traditional scientific measurement paradigm with the process counterparts in the sensible interpretation paradigm.

The basic assumptions of a problem-based learning curriculum appear to fit best with an alternative assessment paradigm that focuses on sensible interpretation. The element of self-direction by the students implies that there is no one best way to study. Students will reach equally valid but different outcomes as a result of this personally tailored learning process. Appreciation for these unique learning results fits best in a dynamic paradigm. As a consequence at least some of the instruments used for assessment will be subjective in nature. This chapter presents an example of a blended approach combining assessment strategies from both paradigms.

Table 2.1   Assessment paradigms

Scientific measurement	Sensible interpretation
Quantitative	Qualitative
Static	Dynamic
Repeated measures	Unique moments
Prediction of future performance	Description of on going change
Objective	*Subjective*
Absolute	Variable
External criteria/responsibility	Internal criteria/responsibility

Learning objectives

In both the rationalistic and the sensible paradigms, educational objectives play an important role. Traditionally, Bloom's taxonomy is widely used. This taxonomy distinguishes three main categories: the cognitive domain, psychomotor skills and attitudes (Bloom 1956). However, in a rationalistic paradigm, detailing learning objectives in such categories can easily result in fragmentation. The link between a particular element of knowledge and competence in practice gets easily lost. In a problem-based curriculum this link constitutes the core of the learning process. When a small group of students analyses a problem from professional practice, they test their combined knowledge regarding the subject at hand. At the boundaries of their understanding they stipulate their own learning goals. Naturally, the ensuing learning process is different, depending on the specific competencies of the individuals involved. As a consequence, the procedure of teachers defining the desired outcomes beforehand is counter-productive.

In the design and choice of measures to use within a problem-based curriculum the specific demands in relation to the learning objectives must be taken into consideration. What is needed is a dynamic framework allowing students to set their own goals. However, this does not necessarily mean that instruments that were originally designed to operate within the scientific measurement paradigm, like multiple-choice tests, are not suitable. The pertinent question is how the measures are used for decision-making and information. A good example is the Maastricht Progress Test. This test method was designed within the context of the medical problem-based curriculum at the University of Maastricht. Even before the graduation of the first students in 1980 it was discovered that the usual practice of summative assessment, by means of a test at the end of each block period, obstructed the problem-based learning objective of self-directed learning

(Verwijnen *et al.* 1982). That is, the students tried to figure out what they needed to study in order to perform well in the test. In order to prevent this test-directed study behaviour the educational staff in Maastricht developed a test that could be administered independently of the curriculum. A progress test consists of a large number of objective type items aiming at the end level of the curriculum (van Berkel *et al.* 1993). Several times a year, a parallel version of the Progress Test is administered to all students, in all year groups. The gain in knowledge takes the shape of a growth curve as the students make progress through the curriculum. Since the test is developed separately from the curriculum, there is no way students can prepare for this examination, except to study as best as they can.

The problem-based learning course in applied physics

Design of the problem-based learning module

The professional practice of engineers consists of organizing, computing, cost estimation, problem analysis, simulation research, attending meetings, advisory work and so forth. The element that distinguishes physicists from other practitioners in engineering is that they have to find solutions for technical problems with a physics component. Hence, knowledge of physics is a prerequisite. The work on technical problems in practice is usually done in teams and involves brainstorming, task division and reporting to each other. A real life simulation of these conditions would be a good introduction in applied physics. Bearing this in mind, the renewed introduction course for first year students was developed according to the principles of problem-based learning. Following the Maastricht example, students analyse problems in order to define their own learning goals, working together in groups of eight, supported by a process-oriented tutor. The model method of problem-solving handed out to the students mirrors the engineering problem-solving process in practice. Next to the ability to analyse physics problems, the learning objectives defined by the problem construction team emphasize teamwork and communication skills. Most important is that students develop a feeling for applied physics. In other words, they experience the challenges of physics, which motivated them to choose to study the discipline in the first place. The learning objectives of the course in applied physics were defined at a general level, above the concrete contents of the course:

1. Given a problem in applied physics, the student must work towards a solution in a structured manner. It must be possible to defend that solution as the best one possible. The student must find the balance between conviction of the correctness of their own solution and openness to criticism.

2. Given a problem in applied physics, the student must activate, select and judge relevant prior knowledge.
3. In the group a student must judge critically the information and knowledge supplied by other students.
4. In the group the student must be able to communicate effectively technical ideas and suggestions, using formulae and sketch diagrams.
5. Given a problem in applied physics, the student must be able to identify lacking information, to decide on priorities and to search for missing information and knowledge.
6. In a multitude of information the student must quickly retrieve the relevant aspects and be able to understand the technical information (tables, graphics, construction drawings, etc.).
7. In the group problem-solving process all members must contribute equally.
8. Given a problem in applied physics, the student must develop 'feeling' for the relevant units, and be able to play with it: how far can you bend something, how much is 1 kW, when does something melt, is 1 T a strong field?
9. After completing the course the student must have developed a sense for applied physics (orientation leading to self-selection during the first year programme).

The problem-based learning course in applied physics covers the four major research fields of the faculty. Staff members from these four fields each prepared a case for the students:

• Acoustics: design of an acoustic device to measure wind velocity.
• Nanotechnology: vibrations in a scanning tunnelling microscope.
• Optics: retinal scan display.
• Particle optics: X-ray tube for medical diagnosis.

The project-team developed a problem-solving model suited for the engineering problem-solving process. The methodical approach to learning from problems consists of the following five steps:

1. Analysis.
2. Brainstorm.
3. Action plan.
4. Independent study activities.
5. Report and conclusion.

During a period of seven weeks groups of eight students met for two afternoons per week to work on the problems. Each group was assigned a staff member who had the task of facilitating the learning process. To support the problem-based learning group work, a plenary session with all groups together was organized at the end of each week. Four of these sessions were set up as poster sessions, where the groups could display the result of their work. The staff member who had constructed the case commented on the students' work and presented an analysis of the problem. The other three plenary sessions were reserved for specific topics relevant to the group work, like how to draw a sketch to communicate a technical idea, strength and stiffness of constructions and forces and principles of technical drawing. As a rule these topics were addressed after the students had tried to deal with them by themselves.

Methodology

The study on the problem-based learning experiment in applied physics aimed to establish the degree of realization of the objective of raising the attractiveness of the curriculum and to gather suggestions for further improvements to the module. In the course of the investigation, data were gathered by means of various instruments and procedures:

- observation of the group sessions (an unsystematic sample);
- observation of the lectures;
- interviews with students (an unsystematic sample);
- interviews with the teaching staff;
- intermediate ratings of student participation in the group work;
- a questionnaire, taken just before the final examination;
- the final test results;
- the final group performance ratings;
- a student evaluation session after the conclusion of the course.

The data consisted of experimental data reflecting the experiences of the individuals involved as well as measurements indicating the learning results. The research design aimed to combine the data from these sources.

Outline of the assessment model

The assessment methods of the newly developed course Introduction to Applied Physics were designed to reflect the pre-defined learning objectives. These objectives emphasize students' ability to solve technical physical problems in a structured manner. The students must be able to identify relevant knowledge and to analyse possible solutions, working together in small groups. The focus of learning objectives on competence is in line with the educational model of problem-based learning (Hager and Butler 1994; Hager *et al.* 1994).

The objectives are designed partly to produce individual learning in the domain of general physics, and partly to reflect the ability to contribute effectively to the group work. Accordingly, the assessment is divided into two parts. Half of the mark pertains to the contribution the students have made to the group work. The other half of the mark is based on a written test, measuring the student's individual ability to apply knowledge to physics problems.

The 'participation in the group work' element is rated by the group facilitators. As a first step they have to complete a checklist for each student, matching the learning objectives. The checklist is used as a support for the overall performance rating. This rating is expressed as a mark on a scale from one to ten. This scale is used throughout Dutch education and ranges from absolutely insufficient to excellent. A mark of less than six is considered unsatisfactory. The facilitators complete this procedure twice for each student. Midway through the module the results are discussed with the students in a formative manner. At the end of the period the overall rating for participation in group work represents 50 per cent of the mark for the course. It was recognized that this type of marking might suffer from systematic differences between judges; for example, differences in leniency. In order to check for the occurrence of such effects, the overall group average was equated with an overall group rating of the group performance by the coordinating professor. This judgement was primarily based on the poster presentations. The final score for the students was decided by negotiation between the two judges.

A few weeks after completing the course the students had to take a *written examination*. The format of the examination was a written test consisting of 13 open-ended questions. The questions aimed at the level of understanding physics, expressed in the learning objectives. An example of a question is: 'Explain how you can calculate the floor deviation when an unbalanced ventilator is running.' The open answer format was chosen in order to focus on producing answers rather than on recognizing a correct formulation (Frederiksen 1984). The task division in the groups could result in differences in the proficiency of students in relation to specific topics. As a consequence a test with fixed items could unjustly favour some of the students. In order to compensate for this effect, students were allowed to select ten questions to answer from a test consisting of thirteen questions. All questions represent a basic level of understanding of the respective topics. The room for choice was thought to allow for the differentiation in emphasis that groups could have placed when studying each of the topics. The end result of the test is calculated as a mark ranging between one and ten (one point for each correctly answered question).

Findings

Experiential findings

The members of the project team carried out informal observations during the whole process. All team members always tried to be present at the plenary sessions. The educational advisor of the team conducted the interviews with students and staff members. Throughout the project, two weekly team meetings were held where the observation reports and interview results were discussed. In some cases immediate action was taken to address evident mistakes. The picture emerging from the interviews was that of a general sense of support and enthusiasm. The results from the student evaluation at the end of the module supported this general picture. The students' comments indicated that they liked the way the course was organized, in particular the variety of the cases. The support from the group tutors was appreciated. The value of the lectures explaining core concepts became clear to students by the end of the module, at which point they realized they should have followed the suggestion to make notes regularly.

Findings from assessment

The programme started with 77 students, allocated to ten groups. During the course two students dropped out. The remaining 75 students received a mark for their contribution in the groups (see Table 2.2 for the average rating per groups). In the overall judgement of the participation in group work element, the judgement of the coordinating professor deviated in two cases from the judgement of the group facilitator. In the first case (group 1) it was decided to raise the marks of the group members by 0.5 points. In the second case (group 9) the group facilitator argued that the higher marks at the end of the module reflected improvements during the process. Therefore, the higher marking was considered justified (see Table 2.2).

Table 2.2 Mean rating of the contribution to the group work

Group	No. of participants	Group judge	Overall judge	Final score
1	8	7	7.5	7.5
2	7	8	8	8
3	7	8	8	8
4	8	7	7	7
5	7	8	8	8
6	8	8	8	8
7	6	7	7	7
8	8	7	7	7
9	8	8	7	8
10	8	8.5	8.5	8.5

The students' mean score overall was 7.5 and the standard deviation 0.9. In four cases students received an unsatisfactory mark (below 6). A total number of 75 students participated in the written examination. The mean score was 7.4, standard deviation 1.4. Ten students received an unsatisfactory mark (below 6).

In a questionnaire taken at the time of the examination the students were asked (among other things) to estimate the mark they expected to get for the examination. The mean of the expected scores was 6.4, standard deviation 0.9. The relationship between the different marks was investigated by means of correlational analysis. Table 2.3 displays the correlations between the mark for the contribution to the group work, the mark on the written examination and the expected mark. None of the correlations reported above was statistically significant.

Table 2.3   Correlations between different marks

	Examination	Expected
Group work	0.18	−0.12
Examination		0.19

A questionnaire consisting of 45 items to be rated on a five-point scale and two open-ended questions was completed prior to the final exam. All but three of the students present completed the questionnaire ($n = 68$). The results from the questionnaire indicated that students appreciate the methods of assessment as being suitable for the course (M = 3.70). They thought that the intermediate assessment was useful (M = 4.08) and they thought that it was justified to weight the group performance with as much as 50 per cent of the overall mark (M = 4.16). The students' answers indicate that the general objectives of the innovated course are being met. The statement that the course has raised interest in the study of applied physics reached an average score of (M = 3.73). A clear majority of students also indicated that the course contributed to a clearer picture of the study of applied physics (M = 3.84).

Conclusions

The objectives of the course stress that the ability to deal with problems in applied physics depends on two factors: some basic understanding of the main concepts of applied physics and the ability to share these understandings in teamwork. These two aspects were operationalized by means of a written examination and a rating of group performance. The agreement between the two judges on the performance rating was high, suggesting that the reliability of this judgement is acceptable. The mean of the scores on the performance rating was slightly higher than the mean of the scores on the examination (not statistically significant). The total number of unsatisfactory scores was very low (four and ten respectively). Surprisingly, combination of the two parts resulted in even fewer unsatisfactory scores, thus reducing the number of failed students. Eventually only students who failed to show up for the examination failed the course. This result is consistent with the low correlation coefficients, indicating that the rating of group performance measures something different from the examination. It also suggests the students have low accuracy in predicting their scores. Apparently these students in applied physics prefer not to overestimate themselves. Such carefulness could be interpreted as a valuable quality for future scientists in this field.

Discussion

The educational model of problem-based learning recognizes the validity of a differentiation of learning outcomes. Within the globally defined objectives of a course, students are free to choose and define their own learning goals. Consequently, the relationship between the learning goals and the assessment methods has to be looser than in a conventional course. Further, the general objectives in a problem-based course tend to highlight process aspects, like personal development, communication skills and professional attitudes. With a traditional approach to assessment, within the scientific measurement paradigm, it is quite impossible to fulfil the necessary measurement conditions.

The example of the first year problem-based course in applied physics demonstrates that it is possible to design an alternative assessment model focusing on sensible interpretation of the study results. The model distinguishes both learning results in terms of knowledge and process variables. The first aspect is measured by means of an almost traditional paper-and-pencil test. The effect of differentiation in specific topic-related knowledge was countered by allowing students to choose ten out of thirteen questions. The relevant process variables were measured by means of ratings by the group facilitators. A comparison between the markings of an overall judge and the group facilitators indicated little difference.

The approach to assessment in the problem-based course described in this chapter is only one attempt out of many possibilities to do justice to the differentiation of student learning results. In fact, this experiment does not depart that much from the traditional models, utilizing a quite traditional written test for half of the mark. Some may want to go further by allowing students to set their own criteria, for instance (De Graaff and Cowdroy 2002).

A most interesting aspect of the data from this experiment is the low correlation between the two measurements. This can be interpreted as an indication that the traits 'knowledge and understanding regarding the topics' and 'contribution to the group process' differ systematically. Apparently the students who know best do not contribute most to the group process and vice versa. When we assume that such an effect also exists in traditional curricula, with assessment based on the scientific measurement model, students with highly developed process skills have been disadvantaged for a long time. If that is the case, the introduction of problem-based learning and accompanying assessments methods will result in the emergence of a completely new breed of graduates excelling in process skills.

3

Researching the Student Experience to Bring about Improvements in Problem-based Learning

Ranald Macdonald

Introduction

This chapter is concerned with how we can use research and evaluation to bring about improvements in the use of problem-based learning and, perhaps more importantly, improvements in the student experience of learning through problem-based learning. Too often data from questionnaires and interviews used to elicit feedback from students are not employed to bring about perceptible improvements in the student experience or, at least, are not seen as doing so by the students. The students' experience of problem-based learning is both varied and individual and much of its evaluation aggregates responses and ignores the richness of individual students. The intention of this study was to explore and respond to the major issues concerning students, through the use of an action research approach and an outside facilitator in a 'process consultancy' role (Carr and Kemmis 1986) in a form of consultancy style action research (Beaty *et al.* 1997).

The study was concerned with how to 'close the loop' in evaluation of the students' experiences by bringing about changes that should improve that experience. For most tutors the immediate feedback from students and the opportunity to discuss it with an experienced educational developer, as well as their peers, has provided a stimulus for further improvement in their practice, as well as providing greater personal satisfaction. In a sense the study has been modelling problem-based learning by working from the experience of the learners, providing evidence of the effectiveness of practice and creating the opportunity to learn from experience and planning for further action. It was recognized in the study that the 'learners' in problem-based learning were not just the students, but also included tutors, managers and the institution. Consequently, this chapter represents a snapshot at a particular point in time (August 2003) of an ongoing evaluation.

The chapter begins by describing the context in which the study took place and the approach to problem-based learning adopted. The research methodology used was the action research cycle of planning, introducing change, observing the results and reflecting on the impact and need for further change.

The context

The International Business School Breda (IBS Breda), as part of a vocationally oriented institution (Breda Business School, Hogeschool Brabant, The Netherlands), provides an undergraduate education preparing its graduates for a range of management positions in business and commerce. All students have to study three foreign languages and the programme is a partner in a number of exchange programmes with students from most European countries, the USA and mainland China. English is the medium of learning, teaching and assessment on the programme.

Students studying the full four-year programme begin with a 'propaedeutic' year (year one), which, among other things, has a diagnostic purpose to ensure that they progress to the most appropriate programme and have the ability to succeed on it. On successful completion of this year, or on entry through a partner exchange programme, they may proceed on to the International Business and Management Study Programme in IBS Breda. In certain circumstances those for whom Dutch is their first language may change to another programme in the Business School.

A previous study (Macdonald 1996) examined the experiences of students studying in different countries before the change to problem-based learning at IBS Breda. The main differences or difficulties encountered when studying in different countries included differences in assessment methods, adapting to a different educational system and environment, unfamiliar expectations and information, the role of the tutor or lecturer and the teaching and learning approaches used. These issues may be exacerbated for students studying at IBS Breda because of the use of problem-based learning as the curriculum model and the fact that it is unfamiliar to most students. With such a high proportion of students coming from outside the Netherlands there is a difficulty in isolating the impact of problem-based learning from factors such as having to adapt to a different country, culture, language and student cohort.

The use of problem-based learning

In 1996/7 the IBS Breda moved the second year of its programme to a version of problem-based learning, which structured the curriculum according to 'themes'. The approach adopted was based on that used at the University of Maastricht and reported in various sources, not least through the Educational Innovations in Economics and Business (EDINEB) conferences and publications (Gijselaers *et al.* 1995). Year three moved to the approach in 1997/8, year four in 1998/9 and, finally, year one in 1999/ 2000, by which time all four years of the programme were being taught in English using problem-based learning.

The academic year is divided into four ten-week quarters or 'blocks' which are designed to be structured around themes derived from the nationally agreed educational requirements for a particular occupational/ vocational area. In addition, all students study three foreign languages, with those from outside the Netherlands studying at least English and Dutch as well as having the opportunity to study one of French, German or Spanish at various levels. In line with a general movement within the Netherlands, IBS Breda has also identified 17 behavioural competencies that are developed through the programme and awarded credit. Students undertake a one-semester work placement and final semester graduation assignment for an external organization.

Initial evaluation of the programme

During the first three years of the programme, in which problem-based learning was introduced in 1996/7, a simple questionnaire was used requiring open responses from students to seven questions grouped under the headings 'learning', 'the role of the tutor', 'assessment' and 'what changes would you like to see made in the system of problem-based learning?' The questionnaire was administered in May each year, analysed and fed back to tutors prior to the beginning of the next academic year. Results of the earlier evaluations have been reported to a number of conferences and publications (Broersma and Macdonald, 1998; Brouwers and Macdonald 1996; Macdonald 1996, 1997, 1998). However, the 1999 responses to the questionnaire suggested all was not well with the programme, and that there was a need for a more intensive investigation of the student experience and immediate action to bring about change. While there were still very many positive comments and an appreciation of the value of the problem-based approach, a number of areas of concern, or suggestions for change, were made.

Students from some educational backgrounds felt that too little theory was covered and that the instructional lecture could have been used in a more didactic, transmission form rather than seeking to open up more questions and provide broad structure and signposts. There was a feeling that the differences between blocks were too great in terms of amount of work, depth of coverage and the experience of the tutors in certain specialist areas. The role of the tutor as a facilitator or coach was not always understood or appreciated (by some tutors as well as the students). Some tutors also had difficulty in aligning their assessments to a problem-based learning approach, with some examinations continuing to demand and reward a surface approach to learning. Not all students were experienced in group work, leading to complaints about the incidence of 'free riders', though some students also complained when they had the opportunity to do something about this through the use of a 'contribution' grade for participation in the tutor group sessions.

During the summer of 1999 a programme of evaluation, feedback and action for change was developed that, in addition to building on the positive points highlighted, sought to be much more responsive to student concerns. The study was funded by the Dean of the Business School and supported by managers and the quality department. As a consultant I had a long relationship with the programme as a business studies course leader arranging student exchanges with IBS Breda and I was asked to take a lead role as both researcher and educational developer.

Research approach

The study was focused on how to improve the students' learning experience in problem-based learning through changes in practices used by the programme tutors. Given that I had been invited to be both researcher and educational developer to support subsequent change and knew the tutors so well, the approach was modelled on a collegial form of consultancy (Boud and MacDonald 1981). However, it went further as I also worked closely with the management of IBS Breda to ensure that proposed changes were located within the policy framework of the Business School, thus giving them more power and credibility (Webb 1996). The study was thus strongly located within an action research approach using a series of spirals or cycles of planning, action, observing and reflecting. It also reflected the essential aims of all action research: to *improve* a practice, the understanding of a practice and the situation in which the practice takes place; and the *involvement* of all those involved in the practice – tutors, students, management and the researcher/educational developer (Carr and Kemmis 1986).

Research in practice

The first stage of the study was to administer a questionnaire to all second, third and final year students following the examination at the end of each 'quarter' (the academic year comprises four ten-week quarters or 'blocks'). The questionnaire (Macdonald 2001) comprises 30 questions requiring responses on a five-point Likert scale as well as two open questions. The questions cover aspects such as the tutor's role (six questions), the block content and instructions (five), assessment and feedback (five), training sessions and skill development (four), as well as other aspects of the block organization and experience and, finally, 'overall I was satisfied with the quality of the course'. The two open-ended questions are 'what were the best aspects of the block?' and 'what aspects of the block are most in need of improvement?' The questionnaire was piloted with a number of students and feedback was received from some of the tutors. However, in retrospect, two or three of the questions remained ambiguous or required inverse answers compared with others. When developing the research method it was thought to be particularly important to be able to analyse a mix of both quantitative and qualitative information. While the former has some basis for comparison between blocks, tutors and quarters and is favoured by management, the latter gives a better feel for the real learning experiences of students.

On completion, the questionnaires were collated according to tutor group. Students were promised anonymity and, because they were asked to complete them at the end of compulsory examinations, there was a 100 per cent return. Although this might be argued by some as being coercive, students did not have to complete the questionnaires. They did realize that giving feedback would enable staff to make immediate changes that would impact upon their experience. The quantitative data were compiled using *Excel* and the open responses were collated by the tutor group.

Within three weeks of completion of the questionnaires I conducted individual meetings with all tutors and with the Head of IBS Breda and provided written feedback to students on the actions to be taken and by whom. Some meetings with small groups of students also took place to provide greater insight into some of the responses. For example, it was not clear what students meant when they said they wanted 'more feedback' and the group sessions enabled this to be examined further. The students also gave valuable information on the timing and format for administering the questionnaires. The meetings with individual tutors enabled them to examine the scores from the quantitative questions along with the responses to the open questions and from the interviews. The open questions, by highlighting the best aspects of the block as well as those in need of improvement, provided a focus for a discussion about what needed to be addressed further and what strengths could be built upon. The meetings were mostly positive, though with some defensiveness at times, as might be expected, when negative comments had been made by students. Most tutors felt that they could learn from the feedback being given to them, particularly if there was support to bring about change. They also welcomed the opportunity to receive positive feedback and to look for opportunities to build on the aspects that students liked or valued. However, tutors who were more negative about problem-based learning and more student-centred approaches to teaching in general were more likely to be defensive about any criticism of their teaching – whether explicit or implicit. At the mid-point of each year a meeting was held with the heads of the quarterly blocks to discuss what action was being taken to address the students' concerns and to share good practice of ways of doing so.

At the end of the 1999/2000 academic year a meeting was held with all staff to examine the fourth quarter results and also to look at the issues raised throughout the year. In addition, three questions were addressed:

- What has been done?
- What needs to be done?
- What can blocks learn from each other?

By identifying the need for further developmental activity and drawing on the experiences of other blocks, it was hoped that staff would see that others might have already addressed any problems they were encountering. The intention was to develop a spirit of openness and sharing rather than blame and defensiveness. During 2002/3 further staff development days were spent examining the key issues which continually arose from the data as the basis for further developments, such as: the nature of problem-based learning; assessment and feedback; the role of the tutor; and the nature and quality of the tasks used. During 2002, more detailed semi-structured interviews were also held with groups of students from all four years. These allowed some of the ambiguous results from the quantitative data or comments from the open questions to be explored in more depth. Therefore, four times a year over a period of four years, the continual action research cycles led to continual changes to practice aimed at improving the student learning experience of problem-based learning.

Findings

The quantitative data up to the end of 2001 has been analysed in detail and reported elsewhere (Macdonald 2001). The qualitative data from the open questions on the questionnaires were collated by the tutor group and analysed by me in conjunction with the Head of IBS Breda. This was followed up by discussions with the block tutor as the basis for interpreting some of the quantitative results. The results were also presented to all tutors in a staff development session. Results were aggregated by block so as not to identify comments about individual tutors. General findings from the interviews, supported by extensive quotations, were provided for the tutors. This process of triangulation (Winter 1996) helped to provide a range of perspectives on the same phenomenon. Over a period of time, as the author, Head of IBS Breda and tutors all became more familiar with the data, patterns began to emerge as a number of aspects of the curriculum and processes were continually raised by students, including the way problem-based learning was implemented, tutor roles and assessment and feedback.

The way problem-based learning has been implemented

The way that students respond to problem-based learning can be influenced by a number of factors: their previous educational experiences, the way problem-based learning is introduced and the commitment and approach of the tutor. For many students the experience of problem-based learning, while challenging, has many benefits, including the need to develop understanding rather than just learn by rote, along with the development of skills within and for a real world context. For example, students commented:

> problem-based learning has nothing to do with a system in which you just sit down, listen to the teacher and take notes. Here you interact a lot more. You have to be careful of the way you are being perceived by others. Team working is a very demanding situation.

> At the end I really see a complex 'picture' about finance and organization and I do understand more about the surrounding world.

> I hated school. Here it's *fun*!

Students not only began to see the relevance of the theory as it was applied to the real world but also began to value the greater responsibility they were given for their own learning. Yet it was not just application and autonomy that became important; it was also the sense of freedom and creativity that many had not experienced in previous educational experiences. They explained:

> The centre of ideas and creativity is the student, not the teacher.

> I think we learnt less subjects, but each of them much deeper than with the normal teaching.

This latter comment reflects quite a sophisticated understanding of learning and represents one of the main motives for introducing problem-based learning. In the previous curriculum model used at IBS Breda there was a feeling that students experienced an overloaded curriculum and that they only studied in the few weeks prior to examinations. As a result, they were seen to adopt a surface approach to learning characterized by memorizing information and cue spotting for the likely questions. Problem-based learning is an approach to curriculum design and delivery which is thought to encourage a deep approach to learning (Biggs 2003), where students have to make greater sense of what they are learning and are motivated by the need to know something. This student's comment demonstrated that he recognized that there was something very different in this programme from the way he had been taught previously.

This did not mean, however, that everything was perceived as being positive and effective by all students, as some were convinced neither of the efficacy of problem-based learning nor of the way it was being implemented at IBS Breda. Students from some countries, notably France and Hungary, particularly felt that they were not learning unless they were being taught theory: 'Life itself is already problem-based solving so just give us that desperately needed theory!' These students were often frustrated by the different amounts and level of theory understood by students from other countries. However, they also recognized that some students, notably those from China, while they might have the theoretical background, lacked confidence in their English language abilities and so only spoke if they were asked directly. Furthermore, some students saw little link between the components of the curriculum – lectures, tutor groups and training sessions. They also felt that they were overworked, though this was often related to the educational system in which they had previously studied and the number of hours they had been expected to study there, both in class and independently. It was not clear whether this claim was related to the need to undertake paid work, a lack of motivation or a genuine feeling of being overworked. When specifically asked how many hours a week they spent studying it was only the Chinese students who admitted spending more than 30 hours or so. This was because they were finding it difficult to study in English, which meant they spent much longer over the tasks they were undertaking. Other students adopted a more strategic approach and merely divided tasks up among themselves, so ending up with only a partial understanding of a problem. As one student remarked: 'While writing reports we usually divide the tasks. It results in no overall insight in the given problem. We solve small issues instead of general problems.'

Students adopted a strategic approach as they seemed to be rewarded for using an atomistic rather than an holistic approach to learning, though some subsequently came unstuck when they sat the examinations because the questions they were asked were more holistic in nature. Although the way the problem-based learning programme operated in practice was an issue for many students, many concerns revolved around the perceived expertise of the tutor as either a subject expert or as a skilled facilitator.

The role of the tutor and the tutor group session

In general, students experienced tutors adopting a range of roles. The range was from the highly didactic, teacher-focused tutors who were not really committed to problem-based learning at one extreme, to the highly facilitative, student-focused tutors who were excited by problem-based learning at the other. A common positive comment was that:

> The best aspect was the help, support and understanding of my tutor. Our tutor helped us very much during the tutor group sessions with his behaviour. If he saw that the group, or better the students in the session, are not enough motivated, he was active to make us active. But generally, if the level of the tutor group session was good for the problem-based learning system, he was passive – he let us run the session.

Students recognized that the tutor was there to help them to learn, either by prompting and encouraging them or by letting them take responsibility for what and how they learned. As the study progressed students began to recognize that different tutors approached problem-based learning with different levels of expertise and enthusiasm:

> Good tutor so good tutor group.

> Lack of consistency between tutors; a difficult balance between keeping quiet and intervening.

What counted as being a good tutor tended to vary across the groups but most students recognized that it was a complex role and thus tutors' approaches tended to vary depending upon the tutors' perspective on learning and teaching and their view of their role as a problem-based learning tutor. There were also new tutors who, depending on the block team they belonged to, adopted a particular approach that was attuned with that of their colleagues. Subsequent staff development sessions were designed to introduce them to the principles underpinning problem-based learning so as to help them to challenge their more sceptical colleagues. Some tutors and the way tutor groups worked attracted more negative comments. Two main concerns emerged: first, the extent to which the tutors had an understanding of the topic area; and second, the skill of the tutor in facilitating learning rather than adopting a more didactic teaching approach. These were reflected in students' concerns and views about what they felt tutors should be doing but there was relatively little reflection on their own role in learning in the problem-based context, as demonstrated by these three students:

> Some of the tutors do not know anything about the subject we are dealing with.

> Tutors lean back too much and come in unprepared for the task.

> Not stimulating students to look at alternatives; a lack of freedom.

Over the years the differences between tutors have been discussed regularly with them as students continue to report these experiences. An interesting thought is whether some positive comments are coming from students who have their traditional expectations met in the classroom, and are not stretched in the way others feel appropriate by a tutor facilitating a more authentic problem-based learning experience. This is not unique to problem-based learning and there is certainly anecdotal, if not empirical, evidence of teachers seeking to maximize their scores in student satisfaction surveys. Some students reported having been given 'mini lectures' in tutor group sessions, thus satisfying their craving for more theory, and others acknowledged that tutors 'helped them solve their problems'.

Assessment and feedback

Unsurprisingly, students had a lot to say about how they were assessed and
the amount of feedback they received. As students came from many different educational systems they had very different expectations based on
their previous experiences. There were some positive comments, particularly in terms of how individual tutors gave feedback:

> We have a clear idea of how we are doing at the moment and this
> regular assessment makes us able to correct our mistakes.

> You are assessed during the whole quarter: presentation, participation/
> contribution, to the meeting, group reports, exams.

The clarity of feedback and the realization that students were being assessed
continuously was something that was valued because it was perceived to be a
helpful process by several students. Yet an American student made the
interesting observation that: 'Resits can take some pressure off exams
because there is the opportunity to get feedback and then retake'. Unlike in
many programmes elsewhere the resits at IBS Breda occur within ten days of
the original examination. This means that students can use failure and
feedback to improve their learning and this opportunity in many ways could
be argued to support the philosophy of learning through self-development
engendered by problem-based learning. There was, however, a considerable
amount of disquiet about what was being assessed, how it was assessed and
what students knew about their progress. Students recognized a misalignment between the intentions of problem-based learning, the pedagogic
methods used and the assessment approaches adopted:

> The exam does not fit with the concept of the block, i.e. not problem-
> based learning exams.

> You are assessed mainly with a final exam and only partially with con-
> tinuous assessment, which is the opposite of the idea of problem-based
> learning.

Many students believed that the system was still heavily examination
focused, based on 'looking for the answer the tutor wants', with questions
not being problem-based. There was also evidence of an approach to
assessment through tests, where students were expected to learn one
chapter from a textbook on which they would be asked short-answer
questions: 'The exam questions are not really practical and they stick
heavily to the book.'

Students had recognized the lack of alignment between the aims and
objectives of the programme, the use of problem-based learning as the
curriculum model and then examinations that, they argued, prompted only
a narrow recall of knowledge. This misalignment proved to be one of the
most intractable problems for me to resolve as an educational developer.

While there is a significant amount of continuous assessment as part of the problem-based learning process, the examinations provide a threatening and anxiety-provoking focus (Gibbs 1992) which seems to indicate to many students that it is still rote learning that, in the end, is rewarded most, further encouraging a surface approach to learning.

What were the real findings?

The comments made by students in the questionnaires and interviews cover only one dimension of their experience of problem-based learning: how they immediately experienced and articulated it. Ashworth (2003) examines the research assumptions regarding 'verbal material' and suggests that it may well be that what students mean by what they say is not what they think it means and that further interpretation is needed; or that what they say is only part of the story. For example, responses to open questions on the questionnaires suggested that students felt they were not getting enough feedback. Subsequent questioning in interviews indicated that they felt feedback was primarily about explaining or justifying a mark rather than feeding forward into future assessment. As in many responses, it was also difficult to isolate their current experiences from their previous ones and the expectations they brought from the educational system under which they had previously studied. With a different analysis of the data it may be that more general underlying themes would have emerged, reflecting more about the backgrounds of the students (educational, cultural and personal), their expectations and anticipations of problem-based learning and studying in the Netherlands, and the ways in which they have been prepared for the different learning experience. Similarly, the tutors bring many different backgrounds, experiences and personal and professional aspects to the programme. This impacts on the way they present problem-based learning to the students. There is also an issue around English being the medium of teaching, learning and assessment on the programme, with few, if any, students or tutors being native English speakers. Different student groups felt more or less confident about studying in English, often criticizing the tutors if they found it difficult to understand, which may or may not have been a legitimate complaint.

Discussion and reflections on being a researcher and educational developer

The work reported here is part of a longer-term process of development and evaluation and, as such, is very much a report of 'work in progress'. It has progressed through the action research cycle a number of times, with minor changes being introduced regularly and more substantial curriculum changes occurring every couple of years. The overall effect has been to allow for a rapid response to identified problems and a general feeling among tutors that they are receiving the sort of feedback that allows them to make changes in the organization and delivery of their blocks and the way they work with their colleagues. This ability to 'close the loop' has meant that students and tutors are more likely to engage in the process of review and evaluation and it also gives the management of the department confidence that issues are being addressed.

One issue that came to the fore particularly was the need for tutors to meet more regularly to communicate experiences and concerns. While there is a constant core of tutors, there have been, and will inevitably continue to be, changes to the team. This necessitates regular induction of new colleagues, discussion as to how groups and individuals are performing and consideration of any problems. My continual involvement allows staff to reflect on the evidence from the study while also enabling me to suggest, negotiate or support changes. Thus my role as an educational developer has provided an external element which has been more acceptable and less managerial to most tutors than if it had come from elsewhere within the Hogeschool Brabant. There is always the danger of students becoming over-familiar and even bored with a questionnaire. Different students move in and out of the programme, as many are on an exchange programme. By providing swift feedback to students about the results of the questionnaire and the actions to be taken as a result of their responses, it was hoped that they would see the value of taking the exercise seriously. Through the interviews and other more informal contacts over a period of time some students began to see me as an ally who could be trusted to bring about changes to improve their experiences or, if unable to do so, at least was able to provide good reasons for the lack of change.

A revised process has been introduced to evaluate improvements in the student experience. This involves more detailed interviews with students, as well as questionnaires being completed at the beginning of the following block rather than at the end of examinations. However, it is still not clear that all tutors have taken the feedback on board in order to implement problem-based learning more effectively, rather than just to obtain better scores. As there remains little knowledge about what happens in individual tutors' classrooms, other than by observation or using student comments, it may be that a more traditional form of teaching is being undertaken to provide students with the information they need to solve problems and pass the examinations. Yet many tutors have welcomed the feedback and acted on it more positively to improve the way they implement a problem-based learning curriculum.

Conclusions

The study has provided, and continues to provide, a useful basis for examining and improving the student experience of learning through a problem-based learning approach. Evaluation of practice, reflection on the basis of timely feedback from students and the opportunity to make changes that can have an immediate impact on the student experience are all notable characteristics of this study. This has proved uncomfortable for some tutors, while others have welcomed the opportunity to gain such specific feedback about their teaching and facilitation skills, both positive and negative. The process has allowed for ongoing developments to emerge from the feedback provided by students and is helping many tutors to become reflective about their practice. It is hoped, in due course, to build on this experience when introducing new staff to the team by developing mentoring and support systems, as well as ongoing peer support within and across block teams. The programme is by now quite mature but this has not prevented a number of the tutors from being prepared to adapt and develop on the basis of the evidence provided by the study. Providing continual educational development support to enable staff to reflect and learn from the study is leading to a culture among many tutors of continually looking for ways to improve the student experience.

Note

This chapter is based on papers presented at conferences in Linköping, Sweden (September 2000), Singapore (December 2000), Manchester, UK (January 2001) and Yeppoon, Australia (December 2001). The background information and some of the analysis remains largely unchanged, though the emphasis has shifted from the presentation and analysis of quantitative data to the qualitative responses and interviews.

Acknowledgements

This study would not have been possible without the support and encouragement of Jan Broersma, Head of the International Business School, Breda and Nicole Dupuy, lecturer in IBS Breda, Nadine Nesvabda and Melanie Lips who typed up the qualitative responses and Elvira Verschuren who prepared the quantitative data for analysis. My thanks to them all, though any mistakes remain my responsibility.

4

Investigating the Effectiveness of Teaching 'On-line Learning' in a Problem-based Learning On-line Environment

Roisin Donnelly

Introduction

This chapter reports on the evaluation and subsequent redesign of an e-learning module that utilized a problem-based pedagogy. The module was a component of a postgraduate diploma in third level learning and teaching for lecturers from a range of higher education institutions in the Republic of Ireland. The on-line delivery took the form of using a range of electronic resources and on-line asynchronous and synchronous discussion to solve a problem-based learning scenario. In designing the original module I had envisaged that the key to the module participants' success would be to collaborate on-line and share valuable information with colleagues from a variety of other disciplines. However, on undertaking an evaluation after three years I realized that a conflict existed between individuals' right to learn on-line, using the on-line learning environment (WebCT) in their own time and at their own pace, and the obvious benefits of interacting on-line with peers in a problem-based learning group. The actual learning situation entailed interpersonal complexities and subjective depths of meaning that challenged my assumptions about how problem-based learning would happen on-line. From an analysis and interpretation of the evaluations of this module I gained a better understanding of the problem-based learning group process in an on-line environment. The module was then redesigned using a blended learning approach in which weekly face-to-face problem-based learning sessions were complemented by the use of the WebCT on-line learning environment.

In this chapter I report on participants' experiences and the analysis of collected data, and present a structure for the development and design of a blended approach to problem-based learning, where the problem-based face-to-face learning in a classroom is integrated with an equivalent e-learning component.

Research methodology

The research context

The postgraduate diploma is voluntary and attracts lecturers who are keen to implement novel pedagogical approaches in their own subject disciplines. The aim of the particular module that I researched is to enable the participants to become aware of the practicalities of designing, delivering, supporting and evaluating an on-line module in their own subject discipline. Generally, there are between six and eight participants in the problem-based learning group. Over the three years of the module's existence, a wide variety of subject disciplines have been represented.

Research question

This research study was instigated to uncover which aspects of the on-line learning module on the postgraduate diploma in third level learning and teaching were problematic for the participants, and what changes could be made to the module to improve the learning experience for the participants.

Research design

I chose to adopt an interpretive, participative approach to the study. I felt that a participatory action research approach would assist in enhancing the understanding of the module context for both myself, as module tutor, and the participants. The phenomenological meaningfulness of lived experience, people's interpretations and sense making of their experiences in a given context, constitutes an appropriate and legitimate focus for social inquiry (Greene 1994). Understanding meaning as the goal of interpretive inquiry is not a matter of manipulation and control, particularly with respect to method; it is instead a question of openness and dialogue. Central to this study was the concept of learning and working with other people, and therefore it was important to concentrate on eliciting the reality of the participant experience on this module. When change is a desired outcome of the research, as it was in this study, some participative form of action research is often indicated. In this study, 'participative' is interpreted as a partnership between the teacher as researcher and the academic staff as participants.

Participatory action research was chosen ultimately as the methodology for this work, because the issues that had emerged from past evaluations of the module were very important to me, as the researcher and tutor on the module, and equally important for the academic staff that participated in the module. This form of action research is research *with* rather than *on* other people. I explained to the participants how I hoped to improve the educational situation for them in the module *here and now*. The intention was to create a structure for partnership between the group currently undertaking the module and myself. This would help to increase the honesty with which the group members reported information as it was to their benefit to have accurate information on which to make changes. The acquisition of specialized and detailed information from participants would provide a basis for analysis and elucidatory comment on the topic of enquiry. A process of concurrent analysis involved data transformation from the raw state to a form that allowed them to be used constructively to make changes as the module progressed and, ultimately, to redesign the module.

Data collection

Data were collected through questionnaires and focus groups. A qualitative questionnaire was presented to the participants in the final week of the module. The questionnaire consisted of a series of open questions under three main headings: the module structure, the role of the tutor and the content, including the problem-based scenarios. The questionnaire also addressed the participants' perceptions about the on-line delivery method as well as the educational implications of their patterns of usage of the on-line problem-based learning resources.

Semi-structured focus groups were held halfway through the ten-week module and one week after the module ended. Focus groups are a form of evaluation in which groups of people are assembled to discuss potential changes or shared impressions (Rubin and Rubin 1995). As a general rule, focus groups are an appropriate research vehicle when the goal of the investigation is to gain an understanding of the 'why' behind an attitude or behaviour (Greenbaum 2000). The focus group discussion was structured on three areas: the improvement of practice (through the design of the module), the improvement of understanding (individual and collaborative learning on the module) and the improvement of the situation in which the action takes place (the delivery of the module).

To complement the end-of-module questionnaire and the two focus groups, I kept an electronic reflective journal of my interpretation as tutor of how the module was progressing. I found that writing down thoughts about this module was a way of introducing me to the discipline of critical reflective thinking. I used the journal to store personal accounts of my 'observations, feelings, reactions, interpretations, reflections and explanations' (Elliott 1991) to help me to reconstruct the research position at any given time.

The selection, design and implementation of these research methods were based on practical need and situational responsiveness (Patton 1987) rather than on the consonance of a set of methods with any particular philosophical paradigm. However, in interpretive study, it is important to authenticate the interpretations as empirically based representations of programme experiences and meanings, rather than as biased inquirer opinion. As the issue of validity of evidence can be difficult and complex (Macintyre 2000), I considered it important to have a form of triangulation in place. Coupled with this was a belief (see Savin-Baden and Fisher 2002), that it was important to situate myself in relation to the participants in this study. I felt it was important to tell my own story as designer and tutor of this module and to ask myself questions that emanate from a desire to understand the participants' lived experiences of this module.

Questionnaire analysis and interpretation

In the analysis of the questionnaires, I adapted Kirkpatrick's (1975) model of evaluation, with each of the three successive evaluation levels being built on information provided by the lower level. In the context of this study, each successive level represented a more precise measure of the effectiveness of the module.

Level 1 was concerned with *reactions*. It is purely a measure of participant satisfaction and not a measure of the quality of the participant's experience. There was a wholly positive reaction here: the blended learning approach to the module was seen as challenging, yet entirely worthwhile. Level 2 was concerned with *what was learned*. Assessing at this level moves the evaluation beyond learner satisfaction and attempts to assess to what extent participants have acquired advances in knowledge, skills or attitudes about on-line learning. All participants indicated that they were armed with considerably more knowledge about on-line learning and had learnt from the experience of both being an individual student in the on-line environment and working in their problem-based learning group face-to-face. Level 3 was a check to see if the learning that took place in the module is actually used or has impacted on the participant's subsequent behaviour and, for this study, to see how they will facilitate on-line learning in their own subject disciplines in the future. All participants indicated that design and development of on-line learning materials would be taking place in their own subject disciplines in the next academic year.

It was confirming for me to see that the participants had a wholly positive reaction to the module. The blended learning approach had been designed to be supportive of their learning in every respect. A large range of resources about on-line learning was available to them both in the classroom and electronically. Another factor to take into consideration in explaining their positive reaction was to ascertain the impact of the opportunity to work in a small team with like-minded people. This issue was followed up in more depth in the second focus group.

Focus group analysis and interpretation

There were three steps in the process of analysing the focus group transcripts.

1. Data reduction. This involved careful reading of the recorded material to identify the main themes of the studied process and behaviour and categorization of the material.
2. Data organization. This involved assembling information around specific themes, categorizing information in more specific terms and presenting the results in the form of text and, in one of the themes, in the form of a matrix. I followed this by multiple readings of the data therein for regular episodes of events, situational factors, circumstances, strategies, interactions and phases relating to the problem-based learning group process in on-line learning. The recurring regularities became the themes into which subsequent items were sorted.
3. Interpretation. This involved making decisions and drawing conclusions related to the research question. There were a number of findings to this research, which are discussed below. They can be categorised as problem complexity, language and communication, group learning versus individual learning and the role of the tutor.

Findings

Problem complexity

In past evaluations, participants had expressed a wish for the module objectives to be clearer to them through the topics they were exploring, outlining that it was unclear what they were supposed to achieve:

> They were challenging but the work potential was not reached. Problems too complicated.

> The group could not understand what was required from the problems even up to the last week.

> I think that PBL requires us to teach each other, but that process never really happened from these problems.

The two problems that were presented for completion by the problem-based learning group on-line over the ten-week period of the module had been judged too complicated by the participants and the associated work-load too heavy for the timeframe. This was changed to a single, two-part problem. In the second focus group, the participants in the study indicated that they found that one problem, in two parts (part one being theoretical, part two being practical), was more in line with a reasonable workload for a ten-week duration, allowing them to move beyond surface learning of the relevant issues.

Language and communication

The participants highlighted that problem-based learning requires complex social interaction and attempting to do this fully on-line was difficult for participants lacking experience in on-line learning. Part of the group process problem was the fact that messages on-line were being read differently from what was intended by the person posting the message to the asynchronous discussion board, as highlighted by some comments from the module participants in the first focus group:

> PBL requires complex social interaction and on-line this is difficult to achieve.

> Language has to be used carefully as it can be read very differently from what was intended.

Group versus individual learning

The analysis indicated that, despite being aware of the problem-based nature of the module from the outset and willing to overcome initial reservations about working in a problem-based learning group on-line as opposed to individually, by the end of the module participants were still requesting individual learning technology support to enable them to learn in their own time and at their own pace. In addition, they wanted more organization and tutor input than was present in 'traditional'   problem-based facilitation.

Overall, it was felt that the on-line medium and activities required were acceptable, but the associated challenges of working with a problem-based group experiencing process problems needed to be addressed explicitly and early so that they could be overcome. Some comments from the most recent module participants reflect the pull and tug of the group process:

> I genuinely feel we are putting our shoulder to the wheel yet recognizing individual constraints.

> I learn from the others' contributions; the multidisciplinary nature of the group has huge benefits for me as an individual.

At times, I feel I contribute very little. This feeling stems from the fact that my colleagues are at (as I see it) a more advanced stage of development than me. Last week I did not feel on the periphery, but this week I feel as if I am back on the margins of the group. Some group members seem to be brilliant – steamrolling ahead in terms of their comprehension and contribution.

I actually feel we have gone beyond the group and are a real team.

The persistent pull between group goals and the tug of individuals' motives within small problem-based learning groups is represented by the matrix in Figure 4.1. The group pulls together to accomplish tasks and to produce work, but also tugs to maintain cohesiveness and an optimal level of morale. The four categories that emerged from the analysis of the data under this theme were task–group, task–individual, social-emotional–group and social-emotional–individual. The group can become more effective if its members are able to pursue more than one of these activity categories simultaneously.

	Task	**Social-emotional**
Group	Setting learning goals Problem-based learning tutorial discussions Group project	Discussion about group process Setting and reviewing ground rules Peer discussion and review
Individual	Fixed resource inputs Independent learning Individual paper	Supportiveness Reflection Mentoring

Figure 4.1 Matrix of individual and group activities.

The role of the tutor

A hugely important area in problem-based learning is the role of the tutor. The tutor's role of encouraging participation from the students, showing interest in their progression, responding positively to their enquiries, providing helpful feedback on module work and making the students feel that their contribution to module activities was valued was defined early in the module. Previous evaluations indicated problems with the tutor's role, namely that the on-line component needed a more authoritarian tutor. They acknowledged that this was against the grain of 'traditional' problem-based learning.

I feel the tutor's level of on-line participation was hindered due to the PBL approach. What was needed was a more authoritarian tutor which would have been against the 'PBL rules'.

For me, the key to on-line learning is the level of interaction and the factors that determine a student's level of interaction must be conspired, e.g. motivation through tutor interaction.

In the redesigned module I solicited feedback from the individual participants, listened throughout the entire process and was concerned about the participants' success. Every individual needed to be given the opportunity to improve until the learning experiences came to an end and reasonable accommodations for the participants' needs and desires were made. This appears to have been successful:

> The role of the tutor was significant. I cannot imagine what it would be like with a larger group. In our case the tutor was so supportive with encouragement but also guidance and feedback when needed. This was also done in a quiet gentle way which was refreshing.

Some further issues to be considered by the tutor included providing an effective induction, encouraging participation on-line, knowing when and how to make the resources available, how to make the problem-based on-line group process visible both to the tutor and to the external examiner and juggling the e-tutoring role with that of a face-to-face problem-based learning facilitator. For this last point problem-based learning typically requires intensive contact between tutor and students and this proved to be more difficult to implement on-line, particularly when problems of group dynamics arose. A major challenge for me as tutor was to help to ensure that each individual participant learned while also gaining the experience of working collaboratively. With regard to the problem-based learning group, I kept participants aware of where they stood with respect to the module assessment process on a regular basis. The tutor gave the participants timely and quality feedback on their contributions to group discussion, as part of the group process, along with their contribution to the end product.

Discussion on the design of a blended module using problem-based learning

The research surrounding this module was based on the belief that interaction between participants in the problem-based group was the key element to a successful on-line learning experience for all involved. As a result of the findings of this research, a number of changes were implemented to both the design and delivery of the module. Changes fell into two broad areas: module design and collaborative learning.

Module design

From the design perspective, it was decided to strip the module down to reflect the reality of the context in which it was being delivered. The participants were not in the position of having to present courses entirely on-line. A blended approach with appropriate face-to-face encounters was deemed much more relevant for both their needs and the needs of their students. As established, previously the on-line delivery took the form of using a range of electronic resources and on-line asynchronous and synchronous discussion to solve a problem-based learning scenario. Now, there are a small number of face-to-face sessions strategically placed at the start and middle of the module to facilitate cohesiveness, good dialogue, quality tutorial input and individualized support.

Figure 4.2 is a site map of the redesigned structure of the module. There are three elements to the module: supports, resources and tasks. In terms of support, the main features are the collaborative discussion features of discussion board, chat room and e-mail. The resources facility provided links to a wide range of learning material in the area. The tasks area is an information centre holding details on the weekly on-line tasks, the reflective journal and the problem.

Prior to starting the module participants are now asked to complete a Learning Style Inventory, based on the theories of David Kolb, and an access and technology comfort survey.

Learning styles

The redesign of the module followed Felder's (1996) view that teaching designed to address all dimensions of any learning styles model is likely to be effective. The participants on the OL/PBL module were familiar with Kolb's experiential learning model (Kolb 1984); therefore the dimensions of concrete experience, reflective observation, abstract conceptualization and active experimentation were now utilized both on-line and face-to-face. The changes made to the module design attempt to cover the range of Kolb's learning styles. Effective visuals have been added to appeal to the learner who tends more towards reflective observation, preferring to generate a wide range of ideas and to gather information from many sources. Reflective journaling and on-line chats that involve thought showering have also been included to aid the reflective observer. Incorporation of fieldwork and development work through the provision of authentic problems may assist the learner who is more likely to learn through concrete experience. A video-conferenced lecture session coupled with reflective writing is geared towards the abstract conceptualizor. Incorporation of a gradual move towards asynchronous conferencing, where the active experimenter is encouraged to view issues from different perspectives and interpret the

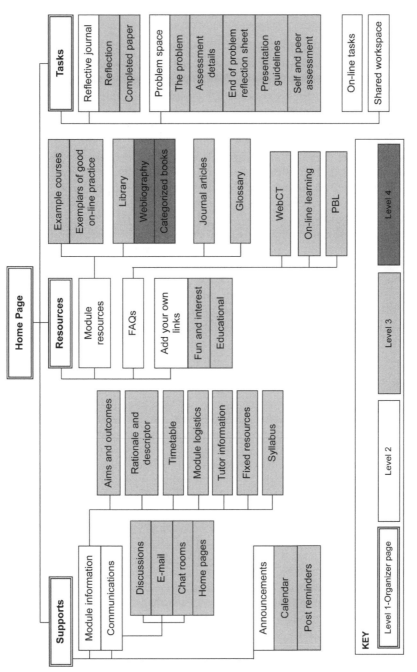

Figure 4.2 Site map of the redesigned module.

meaning of events, will support interaction and facilitate a sense of community among participants.

Technology comfort

Jonassen *et al.* (1999) believe that what computers can do best is liberate the student to explore, discover and create personal meaning from diverse sets of material in a proactive manner. They argue that technology should be used as an engager of thinking and knowledge construction rather than merely a transmitter of information. Other research (Mioduser and Nachmias 2001) has shown that individual on-line learners use the web for e-informing rather than e-learning. Many individuals undertaking a module with an on-line component find that these modules support processes such as rote learning or information retrieval, rather than promoting engagement in collaborative group learning. In the research literature, there are developments investigating whether an on-line tutorial can be used as a tool for learning, in addition to being a tool for delivery of information. Curtin (2002) examined whether on-line tutorials can be used to encourage participants to undertake prescribed readings, distinguish the evidence and arguments of these and relate the ideas to everyday experience through peer discussion on-line. One suggestion is that participants who use on-line materials individually may then search for more opportunities to interact with their peers.

Collaborative learning

The key to collaboration was found to be the ability to give the participants the opportunity to experience on-line learning as a student, first as an individual, then in pairs with one in a mentor role and finally in a series of on-line group and reflective activities. Therefore, the engagement now begins with content-centred academic interaction between individual participants and on-line resources. It then moves towards collaborative participant interaction, complemented by social interaction between the participants and the tutor, the latter taking the form of interpersonal encouragement and assistance (Jung *et al.* 2002). After individuals have gained experience with the flow of activities face-to-face in problem-based learning and are thinking deeply about the problem, their on-line collaborative work can begin. The group can meet on-line with the asynchronous feature of an on-line learning environment, which is designed to scaffold students as they organize their task and then synthesize, post and critique the results of their deliberations. Collaboration now takes the form of a member of a group working towards three common goals: learning collaboratively, problem-solving collaboratively and achieving individual curricular outcomes collaboratively.

From a constructivist viewpoint, studies on web-based learning environments have shown that there are three critical components to interaction. First, an academic (learner-to-content) component occurs when learners access on-line materials and receive task-oriented feedback from the facilitator or from a technology-driven feedback system. Second, a collaborative (learner-to-learner) component occurs when learners are engaged in discourse, authentic problem-solving and product-building using web-mediated communication and collaboration tools. This integration component helps learners to validate their learning experiences, and requires a level of reflective articulation that promotes collective knowledge-building and a deeper personal understanding of what is being studied. Finally, an interpersonal/social component occurs when learners receive feedback from the facilitator and/or peers in the form of personal encouragement and motivational assistance. Social interaction can contribute to learner satisfaction and frequency of interaction in an on-line learning environment. Without the opportunity to interact and exchange ideas with each other and the facilitator, learners' social as well as cognitive involvement in the learning environment is diminished (Grabinger and Dunlap 2000).

The problem

The problem scenario for this module now includes the steps of analysing the need for on-line learning in the context of any of the group's subject disciplines, finding and investigating useful information for producing a design of an on-line learning module in this subject discipline, finding and understanding appropriate theories and synthesizing a plan of action for the development of such a module. Each year a new problem will be presented to the group. The context and landscape of e-learning is constantly changing and the nature of the problem should reflect this.

Mentoring

The essence of the redesign concentrates on the collaborative learning aspect of the module, which had been somewhat in conflict with individual differences in the preferred learning styles of the various participants. Based on individual differences, adult learning emphasizes learner-centred instruction. Additionally, social constructivism contends that knowledge is constructed by social interaction and collaborative learning (McDonald and Gibson 1998). In an attempt to bridge these two perspectives within the module, a mentorship role was encouraged in the module redesign, so that experienced individuals can help inexperienced learners by cooperating together in their learning.

Currently, there is a lack of research describing the role of the on-line leader, particularly for academic programmes that also utilize mentors (Boyer 2003). Boyer's research identified three levels of leaders involved in a programme of international collaboration, networking and mentoring relationships, namely: student (participant) leaders, process leaders and instructor leaders who struggled to define identity roles within the virtual group. A clear need for purpose, identification and role clarity to scaffold the virtual experience and fortify the mentoring process surfaced from their research.

In essence, the blended approach used for this module redesign can be likened to the 'wrap around model' of on-line learning (Mason 1998). This model consists of tailor made materials (module handbook, activities and discussion) wrapped around existing materials (textbooks, web resources and face-to-face problem-based sessions). The tutor's role is also extensive because less of the course is predetermined and more is created through the discussions and activities each time the course is delivered. Real time on-line events feature in this model. The synchronous chat room feature of WebCT is used for problem-solving areas of the curriculum so that the tutor can help students on a one-to-one or one-to-small group basis. Participants interact with each other by posting e-mail and discussion board questions.

Recommendations

Having discussed how the findings of the research have influenced the redesign of the module in context for the future, I offer the following recommendations to anyone designing and implementing a blended on-line problem-based learning course in a third level context:

- Following the principles of constructivism and engagement is vital in creating collaborative and authentic learning for participants on blended learning courses.
- Participants benefit greatly from being given an opportunity to interact face-to-face first before collaborating on-line.
- The design of such courses benefits from scaffolded collaboration. Working on-line individually, then with a mentor and then in small problem-based groups, individuals will be prepared more adequately for collaborative work on-line. This preparation should be followed with collaborative activities conducive to reflective guidance of group inter-action.
- Completing an individual reflective journal provides participants with an all-important space in which to record, revise and synthesize their thinking. The journals can be evaluated by the tutor, who can give formative, individualized feedback.
- The tutor has a very specific role:
    (a) The tutor should aim to create a learning environment that utilizes

life, work and educational experiences as key elements in the learning process in order to make it meaningful.

(b) The tutor should present the curriculum in a manner that allows participants easily to translate theories into applications and provides participants with the proper tools to transcribe theory into practice.

(c) It is the tutor's responsibility to help the group to probe more deeply. This can be done in a number of ways, including by raising questions that need to be explored, pointing out conflicting evidence or asking questions that would extend the inquiry in key directions.

Conclusion

This study aimed to investigate the existing problems of an on-line learning module in a postgraduate diploma in third level learning and teaching, with a view to redesigning the module as a solution to these. While it is acknowledged that a certain amount of caution should be employed in drawing conclusions from this study, as it involved only a small sample, the findings nevertheless provide encouraging results. The findings indicate that working collaboratively on an authentic problem is enhanced by face-to-face working in addition to being supported on-line. This can help to eradicate communication problems among group members. Using problem-based scenarios with a theoretical foundation, illuminated by the opportunity to apply this theory to an authentic, interdisciplinary learning situation, works well in this approach.

Individual learners can benefit from scaffolded support, both face-to-face and on-line, before being required to collaborate in a problem-based group in an on-line learning environment. The self-directed learning focus of problem-based learning, combined with a blended approach to delivery, can produce learners who are motivated, know what they want to learn, set their own objectives, find resources and evaluate their learning progress to meet their goals. Although the participants have felt that there was an increased workload for them as individuals within problem-based learning, they did appreciate that the pursuit of the learning goals was their own domain, with the group performance being evaluated by peers. They also acknowledged that the self-directed learning trails that they followed within the problem-based learning group, both on-line and face-to-face, did lead to a greater awareness of individual interdisciplinary thinking.

The problem-based learning facilitator has a very distinctive role to play in a blended learning delivery. Many technologies can meet varied individual needs and each technology has its own particular instructional strengths. The redesign of this module needed appropriate selection and the choice of a blend of delivery methods to meet the learners' needs.

Thus the role of technology in this instance is the same as the facilitator's: to be a facilitator in on-line learning.

In line with the participative action research approach used for this study, another cycle of research will take place on the module with a new group of participants when it is repeated. The aim will be to continue to shed further light on the challenges of using a problem-based learning approach to deliver on-line learning.

Part 2

Facilitator Experiences

This part addresses that section of the problem-based learning debate pertaining to the role of facilitator of learning within problem-based seminars. Barrows (1986) expressed concern that inadequate tutoring of problem-based learning groups would affect the effectiveness of problem-based learning as a strategy; yet the role of the facilitator in problem-based learning is often regarded as non-central and taken for granted. Maudsley (1999) reported that tutors in problem-based learning are seen as being 'shadowy' figures, their legitimate role being undermined by the view that student-centredness equates with teacher inactivity. Miflin and Price (2001) suggested that many facilitators have only a hazy understanding of their actual role. The argument about facilitation in problem-based learning is almost as contentious as that about what constitutes problem-based learning. One set of proponents argues that facilitation in problem-based learning is simply 'good teaching' (Margetson 1994, 1997). This position conflicts with the view that new skills need to be learned, as facilitation skills are not commonly used in traditional education (Katz 1995; Wetzel 1996; Haith-Cooper 2000). Barrows and Tamblyn, as far back as 1980, claimed that the skills required were 'new' and needed developing.

The debate about whether facilitation in problem-based learning requires new or existing skills is much less straightforward than it may appear initially. The 'good teaching' argument assumes that teachers possess facilitation skills and that no further exploration of, training for or support in the role is required. This may be true for institutions that foster a student-centred culture, where teaching staff engage with students and the process of learning is viewed as being at least as important as the content to be learned. The 'taking for granted' that teaching staff already are equipped to facilitate learning in problem-based contexts, however, may be more a lack of recognition of the centrality of the role than a belief that teachers already possess the necessary expertise. In contrast, in institutions where the emphasis is on the content to be learned, teachers' abilities may lie in promoting the memorization and replication of material. Staff working in this context may indeed have to acquire new ways of assisting students to learn. Conversely, many experienced teachers already have a considerable bank of teaching techniques, such as questioning, probing, encouraging, critical reflection, suggesting and challenging, role modelling and scaffolding of learning, which can all be applied to the facilitation of problem-based groups. Neville (1999) pointed out the conflict in the literature surrounding the facilitator's role. In particular he highlighted the dichotomy between fostering the learning of content and assisting students to develop learning processes. Neville claimed that effective facilitation requires that both of these aspects be addressed. However, there is little guidance on how to achieve this. The literature reflects the set of assumptions, skills and strategies for facilitation pertaining to the institutions in which the research was undertaken, making it difficult for novice facilitators in other institutions to decide how to act. The literature about implementing problem-based learning ignores the need for a shift in beliefs about both teaching and student learning, and the effect that such a shift in teaching styles and beliefs will have on the individuals involved in accomplishing the change. The facilitative role is complex and varied. It is one in which there is challenge, not only for the student to learn, but also for the teacher to adopt a different set of actions and interventions.

The lack of emphasis on facilitators and facilitation is reflected in the dearth of research into what facilitators actually do within problem-based learning seminars. Such research that has been undertaken into the role of the facilitator in problem-based learning largely focuses on what facilitators 'ought to' do, rather than on what facilitators actually do, why they do it or what effect changing to problem-based learning has had on them. Barrows (1988) set out 13 general principles that he intended to be sufficiently detailed to guide facilitators. Although some of the general principles suggested by Barrows were specific and understandable – for example, 'The tutor should avoid giving information to students' – others are less well defined and open to misunderstanding. To 'modulate the challenge of learning between boredom and overload', for example, would require considerable expertise in a range of interpersonal and teaching skills. Des Marchais and Chaput (1993) produced eight tutor tasks that included managing the problem-based method, facilitating group functioning, guiding the study of specific contents, favouring autonomy, motivation, evaluation and collaborating with the administrators of the study programme. Wilkerson (1996) identified four categories of assistive behaviours: balancing student direction with assistance, contributing knowledge and experience, creating a pleasant learning environment and stimulating critical evaluation of ideas. De Grave *et al.* (1998, 1999) identified four dimensions of tutor behaviour: elaboration, directing the learning process, integration of knowledge and stimulating action and individual accountability. Coumeya (2001) identified the need for medical tutors to have training in modelling self-evaluation, as she discovered that facilitators had difficulties in discerning where there were shortcomings within group dynamics. Although these studies have identified what facilitators ought to do during problem-based learning seminars to promote effective learning, the actual implementation of guidelines and principles is rarely reported. Evidence on the effectiveness or otherwise of the specified interventions in action is also poorly addressed.

The shortage of studies into the actual processes and behaviours that take place within problem-based learning seminars was noted by Hak and Maguire (2000), who claimed that only qualitative studies of the process itself will help teachers to begin to understand how the desired effects of problem-based learning are achieved. The four authors in this part have taken up Hak and Maguire's challenge to provide more qualitative studies on facilitation. Each chapter examines the experiences of tutors who were engaging with the problem-based learning process for the first time. Qualitative data from each study are presented, with the researcher's interpretation. The studies were undertaken independently in higher education institutions in different political systems, in different disciplines and using different methodologies. Despite the contextual differences it is clear that changing to a problem-based learning approach presents personal challenges for teachers, even when they firmly believe in a student-centred pedagogy. Old habits die hard. Letting go of methods that have worked well for teachers in the past does not happen without considerable effort by the tutor.

The part begins with a study that explored the experiences of a single lecturer. Hocking presents the results of collaborative action research which evaluated the effects that a change from a traditional to a problem-based learning approach had on a colleague lecturing in business operations management. Her findings indicate the difficulties experienced in translating the conceptions and pedagogy of problem-based learning into teacher actions. Although changes in personal epistemology may take place, these need to be supported by assistance in developing the facilitative skills necessary to empower student learning. In Chapter 6 Wilkie offers findings from another study that explored a similar aspect. As a participant observer she examined the shifts made in the pedagogical beliefs of nursing lecturers implementing a problem-based diploma in a nursing programme. The lecturers in this study initially were similar to Hocking's colleague, in that, while their expressed beliefs about teaching and student learning reflected a problem-based learning philosophy, their actions within seminars were similar to actions used previously in subject-based teaching. However, over time and with ongoing staff development, the majority of the lecturers in the study developed facilitation skills that were congruent with problem-based learning. Wilkie makes the point that not all of the lecturers did develop these skills. Two continued to employ their existing skills, modifying their expressed beliefs about problem-based learning to fit with their actions within seminars. One lecturer exhibited behaviours that actively discouraged students from developing skills for self-directed learning or critical thinking. The findings raise issues related to the imposition of problem-based learning curricula and facilitator selection. Barrett is also interested in the perceptions of tutors about problem-based learning. In Chapter 7 she reports on the use of critical discourse analysis to find and interpret patterns of the ways in which teachers talk about key characteristics of problem-based learning. The participants in Barrett's study are lecturers from a range of disciplines who were using problem-based learning as part of their training for facilitating problem-based learning groups. The analysis of the discussion identifies the likelihood of conflict between new and existing skills and beliefs. There are similarities and differences between problem-based group processes and processes in other group meetings. This creates the potential for facilitators to adopt already familiar processes rather than engaging with the new problem-based learning process. The identification of participants with problems and the situating by individual group members within problems points to the need to address problem design in order to provide problems that not only have meaning for students, but also allow them to articulate how they identify with the problem.

While Hockings, Wilkie and Barrett examined the creation of and alterations in beliefs and behaviours related to problem-based learning, King provides insight into the emotional effects of changing to problem-based learning. In the final chapter of this part she presents findings from a participant observer exploration of the emotional dimensions for radiographers changing to problem-based learning. Very little emphasis is placed on the feelings or emotions evoked by change (Fineman 1993). King's study highlights the disruption that can be caused to the implementation process by emotions provoked by adopting problem-based learning. Few educational institutions have legitimate pathways for dealing with feelings and emotions. The provision of opportunities within the study to express and reflect on individual and collective emotions helped to create new understandings of the facilitator role.

Each of the studies in this part provides unique insights into problem-based learning facilitation. While the interpretations are individual examples of their respective methodologies, all reflect dissonance caused by adopting beliefs and behaviours required to support problem-based learning. The findings from these studies have implications for practice, particularly for those preparing to implement problem-based programmes. Adopting problem-based learning may be a difficult and disturbing process for teachers even when they are fully committed to student-centred learning. Altering existing teaching behaviours can be arduous and difficult to maintain. The shift of focus from self (teacher) to student will not happen overnight. It may take several months for teachers to develop enabling rather than directive actions and some may never become truly facilitative. Therefore staff development must address problem-based learning facilitation skills as well as its philosophies. It should be ongoing and supportive, recognizing that challenges may occur at emotional as well as at cognitive levels.

5

Practising what we Preach? Contradictions between Pedagogy and Practice in the Move to Problem-based Learning

Chris Hockings

Introduction

Until 2000 most of the quantitative-based modules within the University of Middlewich's School of Management (a pseudonym to protect the identity of the institution where the study took place), such as operations management, data analysis and quantitative methods for business, had been taught using a tutor-focused, content-led approach with the emphasis on the acquisition of theory and practice of techniques. However, for many years students had failed to perform well in these subjects. I found the arguments in the mathematics education literature convincing that the traditional approach to teaching mathematics – that is, as a set of rules that must be followed – has little relevance to students or indeed the real world and that many students simply switch off (Schoenfeld 1988: 145; Boaler 1996; Cock and Pickard 1996; Burton and Haines 1997: 290; Houston *et al.* 1997: 136). The fact that business students should be able to make sense of complex and uncertain situations and problems seemed more important to me than that they are able to perform a series of calculations accurately. Making sense of a situation requires much deeper thinking than simply selecting the 'right' mathematical technique. It requires mathematical thinking, a dynamic process involving specializing, generalizing, conjecturing and convincing (Mason *et al.* 1982) that leads to greater *understanding* and that may also lead to the search for alternative quantitative techniques, adaptation of existing techniques or the development of new ones. Therefore I came to believe that real world management problems, relevant to the students' experience, should be the point of departure for any lesson or course and that the students themselves should derive the mathematical techniques and principles from thinking through the problem mathematically.

I believe that a tutor's role in this process is to present problems or scenarios (or to help students to frame their own), facilitate students as they work through the problems, create a supportive and nurturing environment in which they can question and challenge each other constructively and stretch them to think beyond the immediate situation. This lies at the heart of problem-based learning and is consistent with the use of situated learning in mathematics education (Schoenfeld 1988; Seely Brown *et al.* 1989; Wenger 1998).

Lecturers within the School of Management regarded my view of mathematics teaching with great scepticism. Nevertheless, I managed to persuade two of them, Simon and Des (pseudonyms used to protect identities), to change two of their normal sessions to a problem-based approach. In the first problem-based session my colleagues began to see their students discussing and making sense of typical operations management problems using mathematical thinking skills (Mason *et al.* 1982). For example, Des was impressed that the problem-based activity had encouraged students to consider:

> both sides of the argument which they may not have done [otherwise]. They all see it [just-in-time management] as the best thing since sliced bread. They don't think of the negative aspects. So there was an opportunity for them to do that if they wanted to. (Des, Pilot evaluation meeting)

This had been the first time since the module began five weeks earlier that students had had the chance to discuss and apply what they had learnt. The fact that so few drew upon the theories presented in lectures was an indication to my colleagues that their traditional methods had been ineffective:

> What I wanted for the assignment was that they could relate just-in-time theoretically to operations management. And mostly they couldn't, could they? (Simon)

> In all honesty they couldn't for a variety of reasons ... They did not relate to layout, job design, quality or stuff like that ... The only constructive comments that one or two made were the ones that we prompted them to put up. (Des, pilot evaluation meeting)

This session highlighted for my colleagues the qualitative difference in learning between the problem-based approach and their traditional approach. For Simon this was a turning point. The problem-based sessions had caused him to question his practice as a teacher, examine his conceptions of teaching and learning and reflect on his ways of knowing mathematics. Having read about and seen the advantages of problem-based learning, Simon took the decision to redesign the whole of his operations management module using a mix of problem-based and enquiry-based approaches. For him, the redesign and subsequent implementation of the module proved to be challenging and rewarding, but also stressful and unsettling, since it disturbed his fundamental epistemological, conceptual and behavioural norms (Savin-Baden 2001: 16).

For me, Simon's attempt to change raised a number of questions. In this chapter I focus on one of these: how might the epistemology, conceptions and practices of the lecturer affect or be affected by a change to problem-based learning? I believe it is important to reflect on the connections between these because:

> the position [lecturers] take up guides the ways in which they design and implement curricula. Such frameworks impact on the pedagogical stances students may be able to adopt within the curriculum because of the forms of problem-based learning on offer.
>
> (Savin-Baden 2000a: 92)

In the next section I explain how I intended to address my question and why I chose a mix of action research and democratic and feminist research principles to guide my investigation.

Methodology and methods

Methodology

My beliefs, values and assumptions about teaching, learning and mathematics have influenced the way I practise as a teacher and as a researcher. As a teacher I reflect on and evaluate my practice to improve students' learning. As a researcher I seek not only to understand a situation, but also to improve it. It seemed to me that action research, with its focus on practitioner research and improvement, provided me with an appropriate methodology for understanding both the relationship between epistemology, conceptions and practice and the potential improvement in the learning experience of operations management students.

In classical action research it is normally the practitioner (the actor) who carries out research on their own practice 'and only secondarily on other people's practices' (Kemmis and McTaggart 1981: 22). However, in my case I wanted to study the changes in my colleague's practice. I needed to watch Simon teach and to listen to him describe his thoughts and feelings as he changed to a problem-based approach. I needed to observe and evaluate his classroom practice and to find out how (or if) it had influenced his epistemology and/or conceptions of teaching and learning.

To do this I wanted to build an open, honest and trusting relationship with Simon (Lincoln and Guba 1985: 303) so that he might share with me deeply personal views and beliefs. His vulnerability in this new situation

(Martin 1999: 136; Savin-Baden 2001) would require sensitivity, as would introducing and discussing with him the principles and methods of problem-based learning. My research methodology had to accommodate all these needs and so, in addition to action research, I also adopted strategies and methods from democratic research (Norris 1977: 6) and feminist research (Walker 1978: 214; Oakley 1981; Renzetti and Lee 1993: 178) since they seemed to me to keep the needs, concerns and rights of participants at the forefront of the research process. This combination of methodologies and strategies enabled Simon to become an equal and active partner in the project, from reviewing the data to writing up the findings.

Methods

To record changes in Simon's epistemology and conceptions of teaching, data collection took place at the start of the project and continued throughout the planning, redesign, implementation and evaluation of the module. This spanned some 18 months during which I anticipated significant epistemological and conceptual changes.

I used a number of methods for gathering evidence of Simon's epistemology and conceptions during these stages.

1. *Weekly module planning and development meetings.* These provided the opportunity to work collaboratively in the production of lesson plans and teaching and learning materials. We shared expertise, knowledge and workload and we began to trust and respect one another. Simon allowed me to tape record these meetings so that I could analyse their content for insights into his beliefs and assumptions about teaching and learning mathematics. After checking and editing the transcriptions we discussed them further thus clarifying meanings and interpretations.
2. *E-mails and module materials.* Simon and I worked some 18 miles apart and the distance between us meant that we had to work on the design and production of module materials individually in between our scheduled meetings. We used e-mail to maintain contact and communicate ideas, draft documents and materials. The messages Simon sent with these documents provided a virtual running commentary on how he was thinking about problem-based learning in mathematics.
3. *Weekly post session review meetings.* The new problem-based module ran two or three times a week in semester one and again in semester two. Simon agreed that I should take the role of participant observer/ teaching assistant in these sessions while a video technician recorded one three-hour session per week. The videotapes and sound track provided a rich and referentially adequate (Eisner 1975) source of material on the effects of problem-based learning on students' learning and on Simon's adaptation to it. We used these tapes as starting points for discussion at our weekly post-session review meetings that, again, I tape

recorded and transcribed for later analysis. From these taped meetings we were able to identify the conditions under which Simon moved towards or away from the problem-based approach.

4. *Classroom video recordings.* In order to understand how Simon's classroom practice affected or was affected by the change to a problem-based approach, I wanted to observe what teaching skills he adopted and how he responded to students whilst they were working on a problem. The problem-based approach requires facilitating and questioning skills, and skills that encourage student reflection and conjecture. The traditional approach relies heavily on telling through lecturing and demonstrating skills. Simon had been more accustomed to the latter, so I was particularly interested to see how often and how effectively he used problem-based teaching skills. The videotapes provided this information.

The data generated from the above activities provided most of the information I needed to assess how far Simon's introduction to problem-based learning had affected his ways of knowing mathematics, his conceptions of teaching mathematics and his classroom practice. In addition I could identify the factors that helped or hindered his transition to problem-based learning.

These methods produced a large amount of data (for example, over 40 hours of audio and video transcriptions). Therefore I chose NUD*IST (Non-numerical Unstructured Data Indexing, Searching and Data Analysis), a software package that classifies qualitative data, to help in this respect. Through NUD*IST I set up a coding system for analysing Simon's conceptions of teaching and learning based on the phenomenographically derived categories developed by Prosser *et al.* (1994). These categories for conceptions of teaching seemed to fit many of Simon's, and therefore it seemed appropriate to adapt this scheme as the basis for my analytical codes. I set up another set of codes for analysing Simon's classroom practice. I derived these codes from grounded methods, namely repeatedly watching the videos to identify Simon's range of skills and behaviours, then reducing these to a dozen or so codes. To analyse Simon's way of knowing mathematics, I adopted Burton's (1995) epistemology model. In the next section I discuss how Simon's epistemology, conceptions and pedagogy affected were affected by the implementation of problem-based learning.

Findings

Epistemology

From our discussions at the start of the project I had mistakenly gained the impression that Simon had come to view mathematical knowledge as a value-free, unbiased body of 'truths'. I had conjectured that an 'absolutist' epistemology had influenced his conception of teaching and learning mathematics and that it had led him to adopt a transmission approach to teaching. However, I discovered, through the process of 'member checking' (participants check the researcher's interpretation of the data; Guba and Lincoln 1981; Reason and Rowan 1981), that Simon's way of knowing mathematics was in fact closer to the social constructivist view; that is, as a product of people and societies, as intuitive, aesthetic, interconnective as well as error-prone (Thayer-Bacon 2000: 2; Burton 2001: 590).

Simon clarified his position:

> Simon: I'm saying that this is an epistemological matter. *That mathematics, like science, is* something that arises from human beings, is created by human beings to represent the world. I certainly DON'T think we *can assert truth in the sense that we* can always apply it accurately or precisely. *Furthermore we need to know where and when it can be applied.* We need different rules *(different mathematics)* for different situations. So you need to know when to apply *certain procedures* ... You can test an argument to see whether it's valid or not.
>
> CH: By using the rules of mathematics?
>
> Simon: Which are a human invention. *Which have developed from antiquity: Archimedes, Aristotle and whoever else ... Russell and Gödel, more recently,* and people like that. But as a '*true* sound body of knowledge' no. It's not that ... (Meeting to review my interpretations of Simon's epistemology, sections in italics are Simon's additional or edited comments)

This revelation surprised me because the social constructivist view of knowing in mathematics is inconsistent with a pedagogy of transmission, which, from my analysis of the classroom observation data, dominated Simon's practice in the first semester despite his attempts to adopt problem-based approaches (see Table 5.1). On further investigation Simon admitted to this apparent contradiction, saying:

> You've got to draw the distinction between what I do in class and what I am trying to say. What I do in class and what I do when I'm not in class, that is what I think. (Meeting to review my interpretations of Simon's epistemology)

This contradiction is not uncommon among mathematicians. It would appear that even those who have come to know mathematics as a product of people and societies nevertheless adopt a transmission pedagogy in which mathematics is considered fixed and non-negotiable (Burton 1995: 281; 1999: 135, 140; 2000: 2).

Some months later, on reviewing a draft report of my findings, Simon insisted that his epistemology had not influenced his classroom practice,

Table 5.1 Spread of conceptions during the first stage of the project

Categories of conceptions of teaching	No. of text units coded in each category during the first phase of the project
A Syllabus transmitter	82
B Knowledge transmitter	47
C Acquisition of syllabus helper	55
D Acquisition of teacher's knowledge helper	61
Total for traditional conceptions	245
E Development of conceptions helper	*31*
F Conceptions change helper	*28*
Total for alternative conceptions	*59*

Italics denote alternative conceptions.

arguing instead that it was the culture of the classroom and the more immediate institutional and political factors that had:

> however well one might enjoy and want to argue crucial epistemologically important aspects of the corrigible, tentative and partial nature of knowledge (i.e. to be critical), if students have little or no understanding of the key debates in one's subject then critical discussion is impoverished. It falls back to a naive rationalism, back to common sense, back to a primitive 'intuitionism'. (Simon's written comments)

However, this extract suggests that Simon's focus on traditional knowledge dominated his learning and teaching. He had a high regard for knowledge that had been subjected to public criticism and peer review but little regard for knowledge unreferenced or unvalidated by an established body of knowledge, created by students, such as that generated during problem-based activities. While his epistemological framework appeared to be more social constructivist than absolutist, his position on knowledge seemed to prevent him from fully relinquishing his transmission pedagogy despite his espoused desire to move to problem-based learning. In the next section I focus on Simon's conception of teaching and the relationship between it, his epistemology and his practice in the problem-based module.

Conceptions

Throughout the planning and redevelopment of the module, Simon's conception of teaching seemed to be consistent with the 'knowledge transmitter' (Prosser *et al.* 1994). Although he derived great pleasure himself from making connections within and between areas of knowledge, this constructivist aspect of his epistemology did not seem to have much effect on how he thought about teaching. Instead of seeing his role as a provider of problem scenarios within which students are empowered to make connections and develop what Savin-Baden (2000a: 100) calls 'complexity skills', Simon saw his role as providing explanations, disentangling complexities and making connections *for* students:

> *Simon:*   I don't know really, *because* when I teach it normally, when *I taught* it before, *I build* it up in a certain way and connect things across. As I said before, I very *early in the module* go into inventory management. So I talk about the opportunity cost of inventory and that leads into just in time, *and it* builds up on that. So *with* the EOQ [economic order quantity] *kind* of conceptual models of inventory, you can quite nicely go into just in time *with* an understanding of how the cost curves move. (*I am* talking as an economist again.)
>
> *CH:*   YOUR understanding.
>
> *Simon:*   Well AN understanding. And then going in with employee involvement and job design issues and quality issues, so you see how this whole complex constellation of things fit together and how they depend on one another and *so on.*
>
> *CH:*   But at the end of the day you are telling them a story. And it's SIMON'S story. What I'm saying is that if you just say, this is how things are and this is how I see things and this is how other people see things, then where does the student come in? Where is their opportunity to be critical and challenge and so on? We've got to get them to engage with that and I think that just telling them a story is not going to get them engaged. This is why we need ...
>
> *Simon:*   Well some do and some don't. (Review meeting. Italics show Simon's editing of the transcript.)

Simon's knowledge transmitter conception (influenced by an epistemology dominated by a respect for traditional, but contestable, knowledge) is consistent with a model of problem-based learning in which the facilitator guides the students 'to obtaining the solution and to understanding the correct propositional knowledge' (Savin-Baden 2000a: 126).

During the module redevelopment period Simon's conception of teaching appeared to be moving towards that of 'knowledge acquisition helper' (Prosser *et al.* 1994), a conception consistent with the model of problem-based learning in which the facilitator coordinates 'knowledge and skill acquisition across boundaries of both' (Savin-Baden 2000a: 127). By this stage of the project Simon had immersed himself in the teaching and learning and problem-based literature and had begun to draft a paper in which he outlined his new approach.

During and after the implementation of the module, Simon and I evaluated the effects of our changes on students' learning. We identified a number of positive effects, including an improvement in students' mathematical and critical thinking (Hockings 2003). I anticipated that this would have increased Simon's confidence in problem-based learning and triggered a shift towards the 'conceptions change helper' (Prosser *et al.* 1994) conception of teaching. This conception seemed more in line with Simon's epistemology, in that it focuses on helping students to change their conceptions of subject matter by arguing, challenging and scenario building. It complements the 'critical contestability' model of problem-based learning that sees knowledge as 'contingent, contextual and constructed' and the teacher as 'a commentator, a challenger and decoder of cultures, disciplines and traditions' (Savin-Baden 2000a: 127). At times during the review, Simon appeared to have adopted this conception:

> So for me it was particularly pleasing to get them talking about different ways of seeing work, i.e. from different ideological positions. That is something that is important to me theoretically about management as a subject ... and something I would hope students would see as important too. If that focuses the lens through which they carry out their subsequent studies, then that would be wonderful. (I hope it is clear that I am not saying that I want students to see things as I see them. I simply want them to be critical, and to engage with what other critical people say and have said in the subject.) (Post module review meeting, amended by Simon)

However, the evidence suggested that Simon's conceptions oscillated between the range of conceptions (see Table 5.1) largely in response to factors within the immediate teaching context, such as classroom culture, physical environment, institutional policies and procedures. These factors moderated his overall conceptual shift and hindered his effort to adopt a 'critical contestability' model of problem-based learning (for a discussion of these factors, see Hockings 2003).

Practice

So far I have discussed Simon's epistemology and conceptions of teaching and found no strong evidence that one influenced the other. In this section I focus on Simon's classroom practice and explore the relationship between his conception of teaching and the teaching methods and skills he used to implement the problem-based strategies.

After long hours reviewing the videos and re-reading my field notes I developed a set of codes to describe the types of teaching behaviour that seemed to promote mathematical thinking and deep learning. I called this category 'alternative' and included in it codes for 'facilitating', 'encouraging discussion', 'independent thinking' and 'reflection', 'the giving and receiving of feedback' and so forth. I had another set of codes to describe teaching behaviour that seemed, from my observations, to encourage students to adopt surface learning behaviour such as 'lecturing', 'telling', 'covering only what is in the set syllabus', 'setting drill and practice exercises'. I called this category 'traditional' behaviour.

During the first semester Simon experimented with facilitating problem-based learning sessions for the first time. This required him to use a range of teaching skills with which he was unfamiliar. He seemed to respond to this challenge in three ways: by adopting new skills and practices with ease and confidence, by supplementing alternative methods with traditional methods and by avoiding them and reverting to traditional methods. These strategies appear to be common among tutors unaccustomed to facilitating problem-based learning (Savin-Baden 2001a; Wilkie 2002). However, by the end of the year Simon appeared to be using more of the alternative teaching skills than in the first semester, although he was needing to supplement the problem-based learning with his own knowledge (see Table 5.2). I conjectured that his epistemological preference for traditional knowledge and his dominant conception of teaching as helping students to

Table 5.2 Comparison of the usage of teaching skills and behaviours between semesters 1 and 2

Teaching methods, skills and behaviour	No. of text units coded	
	Statistical process control session semester 1	Statistical process control session semester 2
Traditional		
Lecturing	112	115
Telling	0	7
Creating tutor dependency	0	65
Sticking rigidly to the syllabus	43	0
Drills	0	0
Total	155	187
Alternative		
Facilitating	0	48
Discussion	0	0
Encouraging reflection	2	48
Giving and receiving feedback	0	0
Encouraging independence from tutor	0	32
Encouraging activity	7	8
Flexing and adapting lesson to interests of the group	0	0
Total	9	136

acquire that knowledge had been influential in his behaviour to supplement or 'fill the gaps' (Savin-Baden 2001a: 16).

In my mentoring role, I realized too late that Simon not only needed, but also would have welcomed, some practical help with developing facilitating skills:

> I was not really sure exactly what I was doing or what my role was, particularly at the beginning. This is of course hindsight ... but we really should have found more time (that is to say it would have been an advantage) to discuss at length some of the wider, general details of what we were doing and translate that into some more practical help for me at the classroom level. (Simon's reflections on the process)

We had focused on change at the deeper levels of epistemology, conceptions and strategies. I had anticipated that this would be enough to bring about a change in pedagogy. However, I overlooked the support he needed to develop facilitating skills and I underestimated the level of stress that changing his approach to teaching under difficult conditions (for example, very large groups) created. These factors, together with his limited confidence in problem-based learning, may have been enough for him to revert to traditional practices.

Implications for practice

It is clear to me from our study that in order to help lecturers to change their conceptions and practice of teaching, they need support at both the conceptual and the skills levels. Martin *et al.* (2001), in their study exploring academics' understanding of subject matter and teaching, also concluded that:

> if we want to change and develop the ways in which teachers approach their teaching and help their students to learn we need to help them think differently about what it is they are teaching and how their students will come to know this. Staff development exercises which do no more than teaching strategies will have little effect on teachers who at a fundamental level see teaching and learning as a matter of giving and getting and subject matter as an entity which exists outside of individual knowing but is remembered by a student who receives it.
>
> (Martin *et al.* 2001: 336)

The kind of fundamental change that Martin *et al.* (2001) call for and that Simon and I began takes time, commitment and continuous support. The approach Simon took to help him to see and practise teaching differently included immersing himself in the teaching and learning literature, discussing what he had understood with me and trying it out in the classroom. The fact that Simon was prepared to devote so much time, energy and risk of 'exposure' is a sign of his commitment to self- as well as student-development. Even so, his conception of teaching shifted only slightly. But perhaps I was expecting too much, too soon, particularly under conditions that hindered rather than helped. Case *et al.* (1999) remind us:

this is a long and convoluted process which requires dedication and confidence on the part of the lecturer. Where there is no explicit concern for changing students' perceptions there is little chance of students coming to value new teaching approaches, and therefore little chance of the lecturer achieving her/his fundamental aim in adopting these new approaches.

(Case et al. 1999: 13)

Unfortunately there was and still is little management support and recognition for Simon's efforts. Without this, we cannot expect an expansion of problem-based learning across the curriculum. I argue, therefore, that senior managers should invest in staff development programmes that support and encourage all those who take up this challenge in future. In addition, I call for a review of and a commitment to change institutional structures, systems, policies and procedures mentioned in this and other studies (Weil 1999: 184; Hannan and Silver 2000: 115; Savin-Baden 2000a: 143; Hockings 2003) that currently frustrate the wider use of innovative teaching and learning strategies, such as problem-based learning.

6

Becoming Facilitative: Shifts in Lecturers' Approaches to Facilitating Problem-based Learning

Kay Wilkie

Introduction

This chapter presents some of the findings of a qualitative study that aimed to explore the espoused and actual conceptions of facilitation adopted by a group of nursing lecturers on an undergraduate nursing programme that utilized problem-based learning. There is very little qualitative research into what actually happens within problem-based learning seminars and research into facilitators' actions has tended to be quantitative in nature and linked to student perceptions and satisfaction.

The facilitator role

Several studies into teachers' attitudes and beliefs indicated that for a curricular change to be successful there had to be a corresponding change in teachers' beliefs (see, for example, Rando and Menges 1991; McFalls and Cobbs-Roberts 2001). Without this shift in pedagogical stance, attempted changes will not be completely successful. Implicit beliefs are individual and personal and often do not fully equate with formal educational theories. Maudsley (1999) reported that the facilitator's role is often overlooked, and perceived as being of little importance. The student-centred nature of problem-based learning may lead to the facilitator's role being interpreted as 'teacher does nothing', thus reinforcing the lack of value placed on the role. Through my research I wanted to get beyond idealized representations of what facilitators ought to do (see, for example, Barrows 1988; de Grave *et al.* 1998, 1999) in order to produce an account of problem-based learning facilitation in action that would increase understanding of facilitation.

The context of the study

The research followed a group of 18 nursing lecturers over a three-year period as they implemented problem-based learning within a three-year diploma of higher education in nursing programme. Knowles (1975), writing of his experience of moving from being a teacher to becoming a facilitator, described the 'fundamental and terribly difficult' change required in self-concept. All of the lecturers in the study had a teaching qualification and a minimum of ten years' experience as teachers. They had undertaken a three-day facilitator preparation course with an external consultant before the implementation of problem-based learning and received support during the implementation. Most of the lecturers in the study found that they needed to develop a different approach to group facilitation in order to achieve the benefits of problem-based learning.

Methodology

The research design was situated within a constructivist interpretivist paradigm. The constructivist approach is concerned with understanding and reconstructing rather than explaining or predicting. As researcher my role was to speak as a 'passionate participant', an interpreter who tried to elucidate meanings, clarify the actions and language of the participants and, through an interpretive account of the findings, make the problematic lived experience of the facilitators available for others.

I gathered the data for the interpretive account through both semi-structured and unstructured audio taping of problem-based learning seminars and field notes. Lecturers were interviewed three to four months after the implementation of problem-based learning and again when they had had experience of facilitating both first and third year students. Each facilitator audiotaped three 'sets' of three seminars[1] in each year of the programme. As the research progressed I became aware that, although my aim was to study the experience of lecturers, I could not ignore the views of the students. As part of obtaining consent to audio tape problem-based learning seminars, students had been given full details of the project. A number of students approached me spontaneously with comments that I believed added another dimension to the lecturers' experience. I therefore set up two focus groups with each of the four student intakes involved in the study. Student comments were triangulated with data from the taped problem-based learning seminars and the interviews with facilitators. The views of the students provided clarity and insight into the actions of the facilitators. Their comments also gave indications of which actions students found helpful (or otherwise).

Data analysis was undertaken by immersing myself in the data. Wolcott (1994) and Denzin and Lincoln (1994) each pointed out that, while there are some guidelines for interpretivist analysis, the researcher's analytical thought processes cannot be replicated and there are few straightforward tools that check the validity of qualitative data. Further, Alvesson and Sköldberg (2000: 248) stated that interpretation implies that there are no self-evident, simple or unambiguous rules or procedures. Patton (1987: 147) claimed that the person who has lived with and reflected on the data is in 'as good a position as anyone' to interpret the data. I began by building cases, starting with a brief biography of each participant. The tapes of interviews were transcribed, analysed and interpretive comments made, then the tapes and transcripts of the problem-based learning seminars were analysed. During this stage of the analysis I found that I was working more and more with the actual tapes, rather than with the transcripts as the intent of the dialogue was more apparent from the tapes. Voice tone, pauses, spacing and emphases could alter meanings and hence the progress of the seminar. I therefore began to include a rudimentary level of conversational analysis (Garfinkel 1967; Sacks 1984). I then attempted to match espoused theories with theories-in-action using the interview transcripts and interpretive comments. Finally, I compared the interpretive accounts to identify similarities and differences among facilitators.

Findings

Developing an approach to facilitation

This section presents the four approaches to facilitation identified from the data, namely:

- Liberating supporter: this approach was characterized by minimal facilitator intervention and promotion of self-directed learning, with the focus on content acquisition.
- Directive conventionalist: this group of facilitators retained control of both the material to be learned and the method by which students were expected to learn.
- Nurturing socializer: the approach was student-centred, nurturing and supportive with an emphasis on socializing students into 'good' standards (as defined by the facilitator) of nursing practice.
- Pragmatic enabler: this approach developed with experience as facilitators recognized that one style of facilitation did not meet the needs of all student teams and that the problem-based process was affected by factors such as student characteristics, the nature of the problem, frame factors (see Chapter 10) and the amount of dialogue. Facilitators adopted this approach in an attempt to match the student-centred, self-directed nature of problem-based learning with the demands of the competency-driven pre-registration nursing programme.

The approaches were neither fixed nor hierarchical but were time- and context-dependent in relation to factors associated with students, with the problem-based learning material or in response to changes in the facilitators themselves. One of the approaches, the pragmatic enabler, was not identifiable at all in the first research year. However, by the end of the study the pragmatic enabler was the approach most commonly used, occurring increasingly as facilitators became more experienced in the problem-based learning process. The convergence in approaches was confirmed by students at the end of the second year of the study, who reported fewer variations among the approaches of their facilitators than students had done at the end of the first year. Each of the approaches will be presented with data from participants in order to highlight the transition.

Initially, all 18 participants were enthusiastic about problem-based learning and appeared to have embraced the student-centred philosophy of the strategy. At the commencement of the study the lecturers expressed a desire to develop the 'right' way to facilitate problem-based learning. This mirrored the students' desire for reassurance that what they were doing was correct. Participants recognized that there would be differences in facilitation resulting from their own individual characteristics. There was a general feeling, however, that there was a new set of skills to be learned and that this set of skills would be common to all facilitators. In the first interview each of the participants expressed similar concepts about the role of a problem-based learning facilitator. All emphasized the 'student-centred' nature of problem-based learning and the facilitator's role in encouraging students to take responsibility for their own learning.

> [Problem-based learning]'s about getting them [students] to think for themselves. To look at the triggers and think 'What do I need to know about this, what do I know, what should I learn?' It's not about telling them, keeping quiet. (Lily, lecturer, child branch, interview, first year of the study)

This remark from Lily was typical of the views given. Despite this expressed belief initially, only two lecturers actually used the approach (liberating supporter) that matched the concept. All of the others instead used the directive conventionalist approach.

The liberating supporter approach

This approach was characterized by minimal intervention. Within the limits of the trigger, the students were free to decide on their own learning, in terms of both the content and learning method. Although there was some emphasis on encouraging students to acquire self-directed learning skills, the overall purpose of the session was seen as being content acquisition rather than learning processes in their own right:

My role as a facilitator is, well, it's really prompting the group to *look* at the trigger. To try to get them to clarify what was in the trigger that they needed to look at. I tended to turn it back on the group ... trying to get them to look at things in a different way. (James, lecturer, adult branch, first year of the study)

At the start of the study most facilitators had expressed the belief that the student-centred nature of problem-based learning equated with a lack of intervention by the teacher. Although the liberating supporter was the approach adopted least often, it was the one that best matched the lecturers' expressed beliefs and was the one to which most facilitators aspired, at least in their initial experience of problem-based learning. The two colleagues who employed the liberating supporter approach as their theory-in-use continued to use this approach during the whole study. While there was some refinement of the approach with respect to student characteristics and trigger material, the overall approach remained constant. Unlike the other participants they did not demonstrate a shift in their approach.

The directive conventionalist approach

The directive conventionalist approach was typified by the content-focused nature of learning that remained under the direction of the facilitator. The approach was associated predominantly with novice facilitators who may have selected it for reasons of familiarity and feeling in control. Students were encouraged to seek out and learn facts. Aspects of problem-based learning, such as learning skills or the promotion of critical thinking, were of less importance than factual content. The most characteristic feature of the directive conventionalist approach was the use of convergent, directive questions to elicit content. Control of the group process remained with the facilitator, who told the students how they should learn the material and the format the presentation should take. This approach had the advantage of being similar to lecturers' previous experience of small group work and thus was tried, tested and familiar. Lecturers reported that, despite having a belief in the ability of students to be self-directed in their learning, in practice as facilitators they had found it very difficult to hand over control to the students. Over time, with increased experience and understanding of the problem-based learning process, most facilitators became dissatisfied with the directive conventionalist approach and developed a different theory-in-use. The directive conventionalist approach was exemplified by the experiences of Karen and Gordon.

In her initial attempts to facilitate learning for a problem-based learning group, Karen expressed anxiety about ensuring that the group learned everything that 'they ought to know' from the problem-based scenario. Thus she gave the group clues as to the topics she wanted them to choose, as exemplified below:

> This trigger is about an elderly lady, frail, mobility problems, hard of hearing, elimination problems, fussy about her food and anxious about being in hospital. What issues should the nursing staff be addressing? (Karen, lecturer, adult branch, first year of the study)

If she thought that the group members were missing a topic that she considered to be important she had no hesitation in telling them. If the group did not bring 'sufficient material' to the feedback sessions she would provide a short lecture on what had been missed.

Similarly, in the first year Gordon took control of the problem-based sessions. He gave out the problem-based scenarios, but often withheld some of the supporting material. By withholding material, Gordon made it difficult for the team to make informed decisions about potential interventions. It also allowed him to identify the topics that he thought the students should cover rather than allowing students to make their own decisions about what they needed to learn. Controlling the material in this manner allowed Gordon to provide further information at a point in the discussion where *he* felt that it was relevant. Student-identified topics potentially might be areas in which Gordon had little expertise and thus could be threatening:

> My biggest concern, I think, was, I just, I felt that I wasn't free to just facilitate, that I really felt that it was far too active and far too directive, for my own comfort. They were asking lots of questions, and I was just throwing them some back. Instead of saying, 'yeah, you probably should be looking at this', or 'maybe you should be varying things', or whatever, you know. I just said, 'whatever you think's appropriate.' I tried to take a back seat, right from the beginning. (Gordon, lecturer, mental health branch, interview, first year of the study)

Gordon's dilemma was evident from the conflicting thoughts he expressed. From one perspective he felt that he was constrained by being too active and directive and that this had made him feel uncomfortable with the facilitation process. The amount of direction he had given the students did not match with his concept of facilitation in problem-based learning. Conversely, he went on to state that he had not given the students enough direction in the early stages of problem-based learning. Gordon thought that he had returned too many questions back to the students when, with hindsight, he should have given more answers, more direction. He had taken a 'back seat' from the beginning, but the students had not responded as he thought they should have done.

On reflection, both Karen and Gordon recognized that they found it very difficult to hand over control to the students:

> How much do you influence? ... because it's not small group work. Where you can manipulate in a small group and say, 'right you do this, this and this or you haven't done enough or you must em, em' ... This [PBL] is something much looser where the student has to take charge.

So sometimes one does wonder, maybe I do influence too much. (Karen, interview, second year of the study)

I didn't think that it would be so hard. I've had a lot of experience with small groups in clinical and education settings. But problem-based learning is different. The students have control, even down to when we have coffee. (Gordon, interview, second year of study)

Handing over control to the problem-based learning group was not as easy as they had thought it would be. Other participants took longer to realize that they were controlling the students' learning, despite their expressed beliefs.

Shifts in facilitator approaches

Although the behaviour of a small number of facilitators remained unchanged, as the study progressed into its second year I began to notice changes in the actions of several facilitators. Having adopted the problem-based learning philosophy, lecturers had to find ways of turning the concepts of student-centredness and self-directed learning into reality; to support students without controlling them. The difficulty for facilitators arose in trying to select, from existing skills, those that fitted comfortably with the newly formed concepts. Instead of matching beliefs with actions, most of the lecturers in the study were trying make actions fit with beliefs. Participants frequently stated that their interaction with the students did not 'feel right' or that they were 'not comfortable' with facilitation, particularly in the early stages of the study, indicating that they had feelings similar to those labelled 'cognitive dissonance' by Festinger (1957):

Sometimes it feels as if I've got it right ... sometimes it doesn't. It just doesn't feel comfortable. I think that ultimately, you've got to be flexible ... to go with the students. Let them go if they can, help them to get there if they can't. I don't think one size fits all. (Meg, lecturer, adult branch, interview, second year of the study)

According to Festinger's theory, cognitive dissonance is a feeling of psychological discomfort experienced when an individual encounters new knowledge that does not fit with previously acquired understanding of the topic. The discomfort will motivate the individual to seek ways of eliminating or reducing the feeling. The resulting dissonance causes examination of the teachers' own existing beliefs, promoting acquisition of further knowledge and personal growth. Argyris and Schön (1974: 23) make reference to a similar mechanism, alleging that where an adequate espoused theory is matched with an inadequate theory-in-use, the incongruence will stimulate a change in the theory-in-use. Lecturers who adopted a liberating supporter approach as their theory-in-use from the start continued to use this approach as it was congruent with their espoused beliefs about problem-based learning. Two facilitators adjusted their concepts of problem-based learning to fit with the directive conventionalist approach. The remaining participants' search for a facilitative approach that fitted with their espoused beliefs about problem-based learning resulted in the development of two more approaches: nurturing socializer and pragmatic enabler.

The nurturing socializer approach

The nurturing socializer approach was student-centred, nurturing and supportive. Facilitators and students made extensive use of narrative. The approach was supportive, with facilitators believing that students had to feel valued in order to be able to value and care for patients. Although the nurturing supporter approach valued students, facilitators tried to influence students' values and beliefs in an attempt to begin the process of socialization into nursing in the school setting. Attempting socialization in theoretical sessions was intended to promote good practice, the implication being that in the practice area students were all too easily socialized into poor practice:

> It's not so much about teaching them the hip bone's connected to the thigh bone stuff, but more about the essence of nursing, about being with people. This caring, nurturing, empathy that makes people feel valued. That's what we need to get across. (Karen, interview, third year of the study)

Valuing students was related to engagement with them. Facilitators who engaged with students were less likely to be directive and more likely to allow students to follow their own interests. Several students summed up the concept of engagement as 'teachers who enjoy teaching'. The supportive factor also encompassed elements of safety and comfort within the group, with confidentiality and mutual respect being integral components. For discussion to be free and relaxed, students needed to feel that they could speak out within the problem-based learning seminar without being ridiculed. This was done by giving narratives from the facilitator's experience in practice and encouraging students to do the same. Comfort in problem-based learning had strong links with critical challenge. For problem-based learning to be effective in promoting learning, students need to challenge each other and to develop the skills to defend their argument against challenge. However, if the climate within the group was too comfortable – for example, with all material being accepted unquestioningly – the cognitive skills prerequisite to critical thinking were not developed. Students could present material that was, for example, taken straight from an Internet site with no critical evaluation or any attempt to link it to the problem under discussion. If there was a high degree of comfort within the group no attempt would be made by either the facilitator or group members to question the source, seek explanation of the relevance or ask questions about the material, giving the message that simply bringing material to the group was the aim, rather than attempting to understand and synthesize the material with that contributed by other members.

The pragmatic enabler approach

The pragmatic enabler approach developed over time with increased exposure of facilitators to problem-based learning. The approach emphasized learning processes rather than content acquisition. It had similarities with the concept of scaffolding student learning (Hogan and Pressley 1997) and with modelling (Schön 1987). Facilitators related to the requirement to produce qualified practitioners, recognizing that for many applicants, nursing was just another job rather than a chosen career. To enable students to achieve their maximum potential, facilitators required a flexible approach, which was time- and context-dependent and responsive to the needs of a diverse range of students.

Gordon's shift in approach demonstrates the recognition by facilitators of the need to allow students freedom to develop. The thoughts expressed by Gordon reflect his transition, as his existing beliefs about problem-based learning and student learning and his previous experience of teaching came into conflict with the experience of facilitating a team of students in identifying their own learning needs and supporting them in the associated learning. The feeling of 'not being free to facilitate' was uncomfortable, but being directive was also uncomfortable. This led Gordon to develop an approach that was less directive but still provided sufficient support to encourage students to identify and fulfil their own learning needs.

By the end of the study Gordon was no longer controlling the problem-based material. His introduction to seminars was factual, without suggestions as to the topics to be studied. Students began to clarify terminology and develop shared understanding of the trigger before beginning to identify learning issues. Gordon allowed this to happen without interrupting or taking over the discussion. Comments made by Gordon during an interview in the third year supported his shift away from a directive, teacher-centred approach towards a more student-orientated, facilitative approach:

> The group are perfectly capable of dealing with the issues without me having to prompt them at all. I don't know if it is because I started out better, or if it is the personalities that are in it. (Gordon, interview, third year of the study.)

Although Gordon recognized that the team were 'perfectly capable' of identifying their own learning issues and developing them for themselves, he was unwilling to attribute all of the improved performance to changes in his facilitation style. Some of the changes, he claimed, were due to the different 'personalities' within the team. Recognition that the students within the group had an effect on the required facilitation indicated a transition away from a fixed approach, and applied to all problem-based learning teams regardless of the make-up of the team.

Discussion

The study highlighted that promoting dialogue, recognizing when students need assistance, timing interventions and adjusting interventions to student level are vital elements of facilitation. Teachers began to alter their actions as they became more aware of the importance of dialogue, not only between facilitators and individual students but also among the students themselves. Thomas *et al.* (1998) pointed out that any new learning strategy would alter the ways in which learners and teachers talk together. They contended that the key to success in influencing the nature of the transition is to understand the interactions that take place between the learner and the teacher. Understanding of the nature of the interactions has to be examined *in situ.* It cannot be assumed from the teacher's espoused theory. The study highlighted the dialogic nature of problem-based learning as a strategy. The concept of dialogue in teaching is not new (see, for example, Mezirow 1981). The findings of my study suggest that problem-based learning has a degree of congruence with the theories put forward by Vygotsky (1962, 1978) and more recently Habermas (1984, 1996) and Shotter (1993), which reflect the importance of dialogue and communication in internalizing knowledge and developing understanding. The connection of reason with communication is central to problem-based learning. As facilitators developed understanding of the communication within problem-based learning they intervened less, asked fewer directive questions and became more willing to let students develop their own ideas.

Toxic facilitation

All of the above approaches, including the directive conventionalist, demonstrate a positive perspective on problem-based learning. The participants in the study were drawn from the first group of teaching staff to implement the problem-based programme. It could be assumed that these were lecturers who already subscribed to a student-centred pedagogy. However, one of the participants developed an atypical approach that was 'toxic' in that it turned students against problem-based learning. This facilitator's expressed belief about problem-based learning was that it took 'too much time', time that could be used 'more productively' in lectures. Students did not require all of the time allocated to problem-based learning just to 'consider a few issues'. She communicated her view of problem-based learning to the students in her group. They too began to perceive problem-based learning as a waste of time. Her seminars were run 'back-to-back' (feedback from one scenario followed by the introduction to the next one). Other facilitators had found that running seminars back-to-back reduced the amount of discussion and exploration. It gave students the message that problem-based learning was something that could be rushed through and was of little importance. Initially students approved of the back-to-back seminars as it gave them more free time. However, when these students progressed into the later years of the programme with another facilitator they were less enthusiastic about the practice:

> I thought it was great at the time. We had days off when the other poor buggers had to come in for problem-based learning. But now, well, I feel a bit done. I like it [PBL] now, get a lot out of it, but I just wonder what I should have got before. (John, third year student, focus group)

Difficulties caused by toxic facilitation, such as poor attendance and lack of input, could last for the whole programme and affect other students. By opting not to espouse the problem-based learning philosophy and spending as little time and effort on it as possible, facilitators encourage student groups to do the same. In implementing problem-based programmes it cannot be assumed that all staff will react favourably to the change.

Conclusion

The interpretive analysis of the data from the first year of problem-based learning sessions indicated that initially facilitators maintained a degree of control over the content, running and feedback style of the problem-based learning session, in a manner that was similar to previous behaviours in small group work. Directive questions were used to elicit factual content from the students. The pattern of dialogue in the session was facilitator-centred, in that all discussion took place through the facilitators. Open discussion between students was not encouraged. Between year one and year three 11 facilitators demonstrated a shift in approach. Questions were more open and asked less often. Students' comments were accepted, allowing students to develop discussion around the scenario and to identify issues for themselves. Lecturers became less likely to intervene or to suggest issues to students. Silences were better tolerated and were usually broken by students, rather than by facilitators. Student experience was more valued, in that students were allowed to report on their practical experiences, particularly where the issues from the scenario could be linked to practice.

Over the three years of the study 13 of the 18 participants developed their approach to fit with the concept that students could acquire the skills necessary for lifelong learning. Of the remaining five, four retained their original approach throughout the study. Two of the four had adopted a non-interventionist flexible approach as their theory-in-use from the start. Their beliefs about student learning were similar to the pedagogy of problem-based learning and therefore they adopted an enabling approach from the first. Through individual experiment and the sharing of experiences, the majority of facilitators developed an approach that shifted from reliance on directive, content-orientated questions to process-orientated comments; from information-giving by facilitators to increased student contribution; from static presentation of material to dynamic debate; and from a position of teacher and expert to that of honorary group member.

Problem-based learning requires a different set of pedagogical beliefs from other teaching methods. Dissonance between existing teaching behaviours and beliefs about problem-based learning may act as the driver for change. The shift in approach appears to lie less in the acceptance of the new belief system and more in exploring how the espoused concepts apply in practice. The findings of this study indicate that for a specific approach to problem-based learning facilitation to be maintained, teachers' behaviour must be congruent with their beliefs about the nature of learning and teaching. The chosen approach to facilitation could only be maintained if the theory-in-use matched the espoused theory. For the majority, however, the effort of applying previous teacher-centred actions to a strategy that focused on the needs of the students brought about a lasting change in espoused concepts from the traditional reproductive pedagogies of nurse education to an approach that helped students to develop skills for critical thinking.

Note

1 A 'set' of seminars consisted of three sessions. The trigger was presented in the first session. From this the students identified their learning outcomes. The second session took the form of a review, when the learning outcomes were revised as necessary, material was shared and the presentation format was discussed. The final session consisted of the sharing and integration of new learning. Thus for each participant there were nine audiotaped sessions in each year.

7

Researching the Dialogue of Problem-based Learning Tutorials: A Critical Discourse Analysis Approach

Terry Barrett

Introduction

Although the problem-based learning tutorial is the central and key learning encounter in problem-based learning curricula, little research has been done on what actually happens in problem-based learning tutorials. This chapter demonstrates that a critical discourse analysis approach is an effective methodology for analysing the dialogue of problem-based learning tutorials. It presents the findings of a study that explored the dialogue of lecturers undertaking a problem-based learning module as part of a diploma in learning and teaching. Each of the problem-based learning tutorials for the two teams undertaking this module was video or audio recorded. The lived experience of these lecturers as problem-based learning students was documented through analysis of discourse of these problem-based learning tutorials for all phases of the problem-based learning module. The findings of the research have implications for problem design, staff induction and the importance of review sessions in the problem-based learning process.

Hak and Maguire (2000: 769) identify the need for more studies on what actually happens in problem-based learning tutorials. It is a vital yet under-researched area of problem-based learning. They stress that: 'research to date has largely neglected the issue of the *actual* activities and learning processes that mediate and moderate the relationships between these programs and their cognitive outcomes' (Hak and Maguire 2000: 769).

There are a number of studies of problem-based learning tutorials (Evensen and Hmelo 2000a, b) but none that uses a critical discourse analysis approach. The scarcity of studies in the area of problem-based learning staff development is stressed by Murray and Savin-Baden (2000). This chapter analyses the dialogue of one of the two tutorial teams of eight students (who were lecturers) and a tutor who met once weekly for 14 weeks. They worked on two problems about problem-based learning. This research is based on the transcripts of the tutorials for this team.

These lecturers were problem-based learners for this module, as problem-based learning was the learning process. Thus in this dialogue both the process and the content were problem-based learning.

Four of the key characteristics of problem-based learning are the problem (Margetson 1997), the problem-based learning tutorial (Barrows 1988), the problem-based learning process (Engel 1997) and learning (Barrows and Tamblyn 1980). This study focuses on one of the key characteristics of problem-based learning: the problem-based learning tutorial. The research question initially was 'How are participants talking about the problem-based learning tutorial in the dialogue of the tutorials of a problem-based learning staff development module?' This research is part of a wider study that is investigating how the two teams talk about these four key characteristics of problem-based learning. This study examined the process the participants went through by analysing their perspectives from their language in use.

Methodology

In terms of major paradigms this research is situated in a critical theory paradigm (Lincoln and Guba 2000) and my philosophical and epistemological stances are Freirian (Barrett 2001). The methodology used in this study is a thematic analysis, informed by a critical discourse analysis approach to analysing dialogue. The problem-based learning tutorials of one of the teams were video or audio recorded for the module. The themes were derived from the data by analysing how problem-based learning students were talking about the problem-based learning tutorial, in the course of working through two problems about problem-based learning. A thematic approach involves naming and analysing the themes in the dialogue, in relation to the problem-based learning tutorial. It involves quoting extracts from the data under each theme in order to form the basis of arguments (Holliday 2002).

Critical discourse analysis makes use of systemic linguistics, continental pragmatics and cross-disciplinary trends 'but attempts to go beyond them in providing a synthesis of necessary theoretical concepts and analytical frameworks for doing critical analysis' (Fairclough 2001: 11). The analysis involves finding patterns and proposing interpretations of the patterns together with accounts of the meanings and ideological significance of these patterns (Cameron 2001). Fairclough provides a detailed checklist of questions to use when doing critical analysis (Fairclough 2003). The wider study focuses on one of his key ideas that language in use figures in three main ways in social practice:

1. Genres (ways of acting).
2. Discourse (ways of representing).
3. Styles (ways of being).

Thus the data are examined in terms of how participants talk about the problem-based learning tutorial through genre analysis, which highlights issues of acting and interacting in tutorials. The problem-based learning tutorial is the pivotal site for acting and interacting in a problem-based learning curriculum.

Jørgensen and Phillips (2002) advise researchers whose research questions are informed by disciplines other than linguistics (in this case education) to 'translate' their research questions into language compatible with discourse analysis. Fairclough goes further in asserting that critical discourse analysis can best be viewed as a method for working on research questions that have not been defined by linguistics but have been defined by disciplines other than linguistics (Fairclough 1992). My research question was 'translated' and became 'How are participants acting and interacting with one another in the problem-based learning tutorials?'

The value of using critical discourse analysis for this research was the potential to investigate the critical, dialogical, social and political dimensions of problem-based learning tutorials. As a non-linguist it provided me with some questions and tools for analysing the language of the dialogue of the tutorials. It is a model of discourse analysis that can investigate the extra discursive elements outside the dialogue that are in dialectic relations with the social dimensions of discourse. Furthermore, it is an approach to discourse analysis that has the potential to deconstruct the ideological operations of discourse. Critical discourse analysis is an approach through which it is possible to explore both the restrictive and empowering potential of problem-based learning tutorials as language is seen in a dialectical relationship of constituting and being constituted by social practice. This critical discourse analysis approach, unlike some other approaches to discourse analysis, can capture the notions of ideology and power in the language in use. Jørgensen and Philips (2002) determine that critical discourse analysis is situated in the centre of the spectrum of discourse analysis methods, lying midway between the point where discourse is constitutive and the point where it is constituted.

Data analysis

Four levels of analysis have been established in this study. The descriptive level is an extract from the dialogue of the problem-based learning tutorial where participants are discussing the problem-based learning tutorial. The analytical level looks at how participants are talking about the tutorials. The interpretive level looks at what this means. The decisional level involves making recommendations for consolidating and improving this module in particular and problem-based learning curricula generally.

I have been informed by three sets of ideas in deciding to use these four levels. First, Kirkwood and Kirkwood (1990) use four levels for decoding experiences: descriptive, affective (feelings), reflective and decisional (what you would do the next time). Second, Holliday (2002) argues for clearly separating three levels of analysis: the data, discursive commentary and argument. He stresses that this approach indicates that 'during the process of data collection and analysis itself, the researcher has exercised a degree of discipline within her own mind, as she has tried to manage her own perception of the difference between (a) noting physically what can be seen and heard and (b) noting what this means and why it is significant' (Holliday 2002: 119). Third, Alvesson and Sköldberg (2000) consider that talk that occurs spontaneously, such as the talk in problem-based learning tutorials, can be interpreted on three levels:

1. *The discursive level*, at which language use and expressive mode do not stand for, or are not interpreted as, something else (for example, reflecting external conditions or the minds of the language users), but are themselves the object of study.
2. *The ideation level*, where the researcher discusses meaning based on the interpretation of the talk, which in this case was the talk of the dialogue that occurred in the natural setting of problem-based learning tutorials.
3. *The level of action and social conditions*, where the researcher interprets what can be said about social relations, social patterns and structures 'out there', which cannot be regarded as language but can be interpreted in this case from the data of the talk of the dialogue of the tutorials (Alvesson and Sköldberg 2000).

Findings

The participants were asked to give informed consent. In order to maintain confidentiality they have been given pseudonyms and their teaching areas have been described broadly, rather than naming their specialisms, to ensure confidentiality.

- Mary is a lecturer in visual communication.
- Sue and Julie are lecturers in hospitality management.
- Kate is a lecturer in business.
- Noel is a lecturer in music.
- Ruth is a lecturer in nursing.
- Bob is a lecturer in culinary arts.
- Frank is a lecturer in engineering.
- Ann was the tutor for this team.
- I (Terry) was the module and course coordinator as well as the researcher.

For the first problem Frank was the chairperson and Kate was the recorder. Normally in critical discourse analysis work I would quote the complete dialogue that I am working with, but I have used shorter illustrative quotations here in order to meet the limitations of this book.

Problem-based learning tutorials: traditional committee meeting versus problem-based learning process

This theme addresses the question: 'how are participants talking about the problem-based learning tutorial?' The problem-based learning tutorial is the main site of interaction in a problem-based learning curriculum. The analysis begins at the descriptive level in describing the two genres of formal committee meeting and problem-based learning process, with transcripts of dialogue from the team. The analytical level looks at how some of the participants talk about this genre hybridity. The decisional level examines ways of improving the module based on this analysis and general recommendations for problem-based learning curricula.

Description

Discussion of this theme begins at the descriptive level, with an extract from the opening minutes of an early tutorial of the module which shows a formal committee meeting genre in the language in use. However, it also shows some language that is not part of the traditional committee genre but part of the language of the problem-based learning process. Frank was the chairperson for the first problem. Mary was the chairperson for the second problem. Frank:

> I am very aware of, I think, I am very task orientated. I would be very aware of the time scale we have; we have three or four weeks to get the job done. Normally groups perform and storm and norm and all these things normally take about eight weeks as they say, according to the books ... my role is to encourage, facilitate and to clarify, that kind of thing. So if you don't mind I will stay quiet as best I can and if I do say something or interject or whatever I would just ask you to take what I say at face value, trust my judgement as best you can. Because again some of you don't know me at all but you are going to just have to trust me as chairman to make the right decisions and if I do call it one way or the other, you know, if you don't agree with it fair enough, talk to me later about it, we can always try these things the next problem try them differently. But we don't really have too much time to debate about how we are going to do it. We have to try and shape how we do things, you need say your piece, etc., but once we kind of, are going along a certain way, we just have to trust each other and as I say if it doesn't work or it's not the way you would do it, that is fair enough, but you have to try shape it and then we need to go on and progress ... free expression, collective responsibility that touches on what I said before. Once we make a decision or once we are heading in a direction let's stick with it unless you know, we are going off the cliff, you know

and hopefully I would be able to spot that kind of thing. And if someone has a problem with the way we are going just say it to me maybe after a meeting or some other time, if you think there is something radically wrong ... we need to produce a product, we need to agree what the product is, etc. We won't fail, we will do a good job and that is what we are going to do here. What I would like to see at the end of the day is a good product produced. I would like to see good ideas from the group. The presentation, can we do something different with the presentation? What I am saying is I am not a great ideas man, I can get a process moving, etc., but if someone had ideas about how we can do the presentation with a bit of style or a bit different, say it and kick it to the group and we will try. Something with a bit of fun or whatever, you know ... An example will be today we need to choose a module today to work on and if somebody has an idea of a module to concentrate on for the whole thing sell it to us. And all we can do then is choose and trust your good judgement and don't worry if it doesn't turn out to what you hope it to be. It's getting there and making the best of it we can. And we learn so much from this particular group project, we have another one directly after it and we can learn from all the mistakes we made and all the things we did right and we can try and do it slightly different the next time ...

Analysis

The analytical level looks at how participants are talking about tutorials. Fairclough (2003: 65) defines genres as follows: 'genres are the specifically discoursal aspect of ways of acting and interacting in the course of social events: we might say that (inter)acting is never just discourse but mainly discourse.' This particular extract is not 'in' the traditional committee meeting genre. There is a chairman's address, discussion about an 'agenda' and 'minutes' being read. However, there is genre mixing. We can see the hybridity in the text where there is both the talk of the traditional committee meeting and the talk of the problem-based learning process in this same short extract (see Table 7.1).

Interpretation

The interpretive level examines what dialogue means. In the extract we see the participants interpreting the difference between these two genres in terms of ways of interacting with one another and issues of power and control. We see them link the traditional committee meeting genre with their social practices of being on academic committees in the wider social structure. Their language of traditional committee meetings – for example, 'agenda' and 'minutes' – was transformed through the tutorials into a

Table 7.1   Traditional committee meeting versus problem-based learning process

Traditional committee meeting	Problem-based learning process
'You are just going to have to trust me as chairman to make the right decisions'	'we just have to trust each other'
'trust my judgement'	'And all that we can do then is to choose and trust your judgement'
'and if someone has a problem with the way we are going just say it to me maybe after a meeting or some other time, if you think there is something radically wrong'	'free expression, collective responsibility'
'we need to produce a product, we need to agree what the product is, etc.'	'and don't worry if it doesn't turn out what you hope it to be. It's getting there and making the best of it we can'
'what I would like to see at the end of the day is a good product'	'learn so much from this group project, we have another one directly after it and we can learn from all the mistakes we made and all the things we did right and we can try and do it slightly different the next time'

language of the problem-based learning process such as 'action plan' and 'whiteboard'. The traditional committee meeting can be seen as emphasizing 'product', whereas the problem-based learning process was seen as giving importance to 'process' and 'product'. There was a genre chain that began with a traditional committee meeting genre, moved to a hybrid genre that included some elements of the problem-based learning process and then moved to a problem-based learning process genre. Moreover, the language of the traditional committee meeting was more individual and hierarchical compared with the language of the problem-based learning process, which was more group-orientated and democratic. In interviews the participants are aware of the underlying power issues in both genres and in the mix of genres. They explained:

> *Terry:*   But what would you see as the major differences between your two types of processes, the business style meeting and the problem-based learning tutorial?
> *Julie:*   One is very structured, that is the big mess really. But it's all the thought process that go into the big mess that actually comes maybe, there is a learning process at the end. It's not really messy.
> *Frank:*   People are very clear on most meetings that I have ever been at, and I said that when I volunteered to be chairman

for the first team, I am used to chairing meetings, as such. But it's all in the end product, it's very clear and that is what you are driving towards. Whereas what the realization in the problem-based learning is, it's not about the product, it's about the process and about learning something along the way certainly. But that is the very big difference for me. The one thing I haven't let go in my critical incident was that my concern was that our presentation would be poor if I couldn't get all these people thinking the way I thought they should think. But I kind of had to say to myself, well it's not only people here, is that important, or the meetings we are in now, the tutorials I was sitting in at the moment, that is the important thing. That is the realization that problem-based learning brings to you.

Terry: Any of the rest of you see anything in the difference between the two processes?

Sue: One of the different things that I found about it was the problem-based learning process was group, and there were group decisions and the group action plan. And with the agenda it was maybe one person's agenda and what was going to happen and some of the items on it may have become unimportant overnight and didn't need to be discussed, but we were very much saying in the group we must follow this agenda and then eventually the realization came in, instead of the agenda lets follow last week's action plan and take up from there and use that as a starting point to the following week. So again it was just bringing the group in rather than one person being the hierarchy and leading it and everybody sharing together.

Social relations vary in two dimensions, 'power' and 'solidarity' (Brown and Gilman 1960) or 'social hierarchy' and 'distance' (Fairclough 2003). This team can be seen as moving from hierarchical and distant social relations to less hierarchical, more democratic social relations with less distance and greater solidarity among participants, through changing their genre from a traditional committee meeting to a problem-based learning process.

What is striking is that these issues of social hierarchy and distance emerge not only at the micro level of the problem-based learning tutorial but also at the macro level of institutions. Problem-based learning tutorials are more democratic than traditional committee meetings. The importance of these issues is highlighted by Fairclough (2003: 75):

An issue of particular interest is the relationship between what a social analysis of networks of practices, institutions etc might suggest about social hierarchy and distance and how social hierarchy and distance are construed in genres.

Decisional level

The decisional level examines recommendations for action in terms of consolidating and/or improving this module in particular and problem-based learning curricula generally. The problem-based learning process is both similar and dissimilar to another common way of acting and inter-acting that the participants were most familiar with, namely the traditional committee meeting genre of academic committee meetings. Induction for new problem-based learning students for this module should address the question of how the problem-based learning process is similar and different to other group or team genres that they have already experienced. Generally student induction to problem-based learning should address the language in use involved in interacting in a problem-based learning tutorial generally and in the functioning of specific roles: chairperson, scribe, reader and any others in particular. Education in general and problem-based learning in particular are not apolitical. Freire (1985), for example, analyses the politics of education. Tutors need to be aware that they are engaged in a political process. Student induction and review sessions should facilitate participants' analysis of emerging power issues.

Recommendations

This research points to some of the implications for student induction, and the importance of review sessions in problem-based learning tutorials and the design of staff development initiatives. Particular strategies that are useful for staff development include the use of video clips.

Use of video clips of tutorial interaction

Participants reviewing a short video clip of their interaction may be a way for them to become more aware of the way they are interacting in problem-based learning tutorials. The tutor has a key role in facilitating participants moving from a descriptive level to more analytical, interpretive and deci-sional levels, in terms of both their understanding of the content of the problem and the process of the problem-based learning tutorial. The ways they can do this include the use of probing questions and designated times for reviews and presentations of the team processes of tutorials.

Review of video clips of tutorials

In terms of staff development, new and experienced tutors could be given opportunities to review video tapes of tutorials to analyse the different ways participants are acting and interacting with one another. This would trigger them to discuss the role of the tutor in becoming more aware herself of the genre analysis of tutorials and of facilitating the development of this awareness in students. Tutors and students need to understand the democratic nature of the teamwork and ideally want to work democratically. If tutors and participants are experiencing democratic social relations in tutorials, then they may be prompted to advocate greater levels of democracy in the wider structures of the programme, including course committees of staff and students, staff meetings and institutional committee meetings where they experience contradictions between tutorial and other levels in terms of levels of democracy. Course leaders and heads of school should be aware of this when planning and implementing problem-based learning curricula. Democracy is a fundamental educational, social and political value in problem-based learning. Staff and student induction should stress the democratic nature of the teamwork in problem-based learning and the wider implications of this value of democracy.

Conclusions

From a methodological point of view a thematic analysis informed by a critical discourse analysis is an effective way of analysing the dialogue of problem-based learning tutorials. This approach explored how lecturers, as problem-based learners, were acting and interacting with one another in problem-based learning tutorials. As the dialogue of problem-based learning tutorials has the pivotal role in problem-based learning curricula, it is vital that we find effective ways of analysing this dialogue. The dialogue of the problem-based learning tutorials of this module can be seen as an antithetical pattern, namely problem-based learning tutorial: traditional committee meeting versus problem-based learning process.

The four levels of analysis used in this research are paralleled with four levels of analysis (descriptive, analytical, interpretive and decisional) that we want our students to move through, in terms of both their understanding of the content of the problems and the processes of the problem-based learning tutorials. This research points up some of the implications for student induction, the importance of review sessions in problem-based learning tutorials and the design of staff development initiatives. Further research will analyse how participants from this team are talking about three other key characteristics of problem-based learning and how another team is talking about four of the key characteristics of problem-based learning. This study is challenging research into problem-based learning, as it is one of the first studies to use a critical discourse analysis approach to investigate the dialogue of problem-based learning tutorials.

8

The Emotional Dimension of Collaborative Change to Problem-based Learning: The Staff Experience

Sharron King

Introduction

Developing and implementing problem-based learning curricula affects educators at multiple levels of their personal and professional lives as it represents a significant conceptual shift from the conventions of traditional teaching and learning in most higher education institutions (Little 1990; Major *et al.* 1999). Much of the literature associated with problem-based learning describes the process of developing and implementing curricula and provides examples of how to structure the curriculum, to develop the learning packages and to learn facilitation skills. However, little is written on the collegial or emotional dimensions of the change process for educators themselves.

This chapter presents the findings of a participatory action research study that explored the emotional dimension of developing and implementing a fully integrated problem-based learning curriculum for the School of Medical Radiation curriculum development team at the University of South Australia. The research was undertaken over a three-year period and incorporated elements of Fullan's (1992) three phases of educational change; initiation, implementation and institutionalization. This reform project was significant in that a whole-curriculum model of problem-based learning was implemented, together with major changes in the organizational and management structure of the school.

Context

The School of Medical Radiation's change to a problem-based learning curriculum began in the early 1990s with the move to a more student-centred curriculum. Various aspects of problem-based learning techniques were piloted in individual subjects and the success of this learning approach acted as a catalyst for all staff to consider further development along these lines. A curriculum development team was established and the services of an external consultant were engaged to provide the team with training in problem-based learning and curriculum development processes (King and Cottrell 1997). The team took a collaborative and inclusive approach to the reform project, and all stakeholders likely to be affected by the proposed changes in curriculum were invited to attend a series of experiential workshops. Due to the complexity of the curriculum, which covered the three streams of medical radiation – diagnostic radiography, nuclear medicine and radiation therapy – a two-year curriculum development phase and a two-year implementation phase were planned.

Research approach

The collaborative team approach that was developed and maintained throughout this reform project was based on the principles of participatory action research (Grundy 1982; Carr and Kemmis 1986; Kemmis and McTaggart 1988) that aim to encourage active participation and ownership of the process. Responsibility for decision-making and action was devolved to the curriculum development team, with both the head of school and external consultant taking advisory roles rather than direct leadership or coordination roles. Team membership was voluntary and included all members of the undergraduate teaching team, all of whom took active roles in the curriculum design and development process. Of the ten staff members in the curriculum development team, five team members worked full-time and five worked part-time. Eight of the team members were female and the largest professional stream representation was diagnostic radiography, with six members of the team being former radiographers. The ages of team members ranged from 24 to 56 years at the commencement of the project, with the two youngest staff members having less than two years' teaching experience within the tertiary sector. Table 8.1 presents the participant profiles. The data are presented in ranges in order to preserve the anonymity of individual participants.

Over a number of years the medical radiation programme had been upgraded from diploma to degree status and changed its focus towards student-centred teaching practices. As a result, the longer-term team members had considerable experience in curriculum reform processes. However, few of us had any experience in using problem-based teaching

Table 8.1   Participant profiles

Gender		Work status	
Male	2	Full-time	5
Female	8	Part-time	5
Age range (years)		Years of tertiary teaching experience	
<25	1	<2	2
25–35	2	2–5	2
36–45	5	6–10	3
>45	2	10–20	2
		>20	1
Professional stream affiliation			
Diagnostic radiology	6		
Nuclear medicine	2		
Radiation therapy	1		
Unaffiliated	1		

and learning methodologies and so, in relation to the context of this project of developing and implementing an integrated problem-based learning curriculum, we were all relative novices.

Research method

My role within this project was twofold: first, as participant, I chaired the curriculum development team; second, as researcher, I observed and analysed our progress and shared this information back with the collaborative team. Team members actively contributed to the research process with reflective discussion of the preliminary analyses in team meetings.

As this project was conducted in my own workplace and with colleagues as co-participants, it was important to reduce the separation of researcher from the researched and understanding from application (Gitlin *et al.* 1989). As such, collaborative inquiry as a mode of action research was incorporated into the research design, which enabled us to identify and confront the unseen constraints of assumptions, habits, precedence, coercion and ideology that lay beneath our practice (Carr and Kemmis 1986). Every effort was made to ensure that the confidentiality of data and the anonymity and privacy of my co-participants was maintained. However, as this research was conducted in the workplace, maintaining the anonymity of the organization has not been possible. As Altheide and Johnson (1994) emphasized, valid interpretation of data needs to be contextualized and, hence, in the interests of providing a description of the specific characteristics of this particular change initiative, it has been necessary to disclose the research setting.

Data sources

The data sources were interviews and 'informal conversations' with members of the curriculum development team, documents pertaining to the curriculum development and implementation process and my research journal which contained both field notes and personal reflections.

Three interview rounds were undertaken that corresponded to Fullan's (1992) three phases of educational change: the curriculum development phase, early implementation phase and late implementation/early institutionalization phase of the project. As interviewer, I initiated topics for discussion but also replied to questions posed by interviewees, a style that could be defined by Patton's (1990: 288) 'informal conversational style' or Minichiello *et al.*'s 'in-depth, semi-structured' form of interviewing (Minichiello *et al.* 1995: 62). The interview style chosen reflected my belief that in this context of collaborative workplace research it was important to enter into reflective discussion with co-participants in order to incorporate their understandings and interpretations of critical issues and events as they unfolded.

The issues raised in individual interviews were coded and thematically organized and presented to team members in a summarized format for discussion in subsequent team meetings. This enabled us to review critically our ongoing curriculum development progress and implement strategies to deal effectively with underlying issues and problems.

Data analysis

From the review of literature I developed an analytical framework to categorize the significant domains of change that the educators undertook when developing and implementing problem-based learning. This framework named the six domains of change, identified changes in course structure and resource distribution, management and organizational structure, teaching materials, teaching role, teaching beliefs and collegial relationships. A large volume of data was generated in this project and as a consequence computer assisted analysis was undertaken. Data were entered into the data management tool NUD*IST and subsequently coded under the six domains of change framework.

One interesting aspect of the data set that was produced was the degree and intensity of emotional reference made by participants in each of these domains. This was an unanticipated element of the data and initiated a subsequent review of the literature to see if this was a common experience for others undertaking major educational reform. This review revealed that the emotional dimension was gaining some precedence in the work and organizational learning literature (Hochschild 1983; Aune 1995; Goleman 1998; Tran 1998). However, much of this acknowledgement was in relation to how emotions could be utilized as variables for managerial control (Fineman 1993). As Putnam and Mumby (1993) proposed, emotions were often presented as 'weak' or 'disruptive' to the instrumental goal orientation that drives most Western organizations, which prefer to submit to the 'myth of rationality'.

The literature on educational change also demonstrated some recognition of the affective dimension of change (Jeffrey and Woods 1996; Fullan 1997; Hargreaves 1998) and the emotional work of teaching (Nias 1996). However, as Hargreaves, one of the major proponents of educational change, argued, this discourse still tends to exclude the more intense emotions from the discussion of ownership, collaboration and management of change, and treats emotion as an accompaniment to rational thinking and planning rather than as an integral element (Hargreaves 1997: 14–15). Fineman (1993: 9) also noted that within work organizations people are presented in 'emotionally anorexic' ways and where people's emotions are acknowledged they are portrayed as 'satisfactions' or 'dissatisfactions' rather than the more passionate emotions of worry, hate, anger, joy and excitement. Fineman (1993: 10) continues by reflecting that little recognition is given to the way 'feelings are produced, reproduced, camouflaged, communicated and acted upon in organizations'. Boler (1999) concurs with this premise and argues for more research into the roles that emotions play in shaping our perceptions, our cognitions and our values in our work and educational environments.

Given this review of the literature it was decided that the frequent and vivid portrayal of emotion within this project warranted further analysis. Therefore, a second layer of analysis was undertaken. Excerpts from interviews and journal entries that disclosed feelings and emotional terms such as 'frustrated', 'worried', 'angry', 'excited' or 'happy', and metaphors such as 'I felt like a fish out of water', were selected. Each emotional reference was related to the six domains of change and to the three time phases of the project so that a picture emerged portraying changes in participants' feelings in, for example, their teaching role, or their working relationships with colleagues. The computer-assisted analysis allowed for data to be intensively scrutinized across multiple fields and time frames.

Findings

The emergent findings demonstrated that each of the six domains of change evoked varied emotional responses for participants, and that these emotions fluctuated over time. For example, in the curriculum development phase there was intense frustration and confusion with constructing the complex integrated curriculum; in the early implementation phase there was worry, anxiety and a sense of dislocation with implementation of the new facilitation roles; and in the late implementation phase there was a developing sense of confidence and excitement with the improved student learning outcomes. However, throughout all phases of this project the domain that seemed to evoke the most intense emotional responses in all team members was the change in collegial relationships.

Prior to commencing this reform project our school had a collegial culture that, like many other academic environments, could be equated to Hargreaves's (1992) description of 'individualistic' or 'Balkanized' cultures. As a group of academics we individually taught and assessed in our discipline or professional stream areas. What little team teaching there was tended to be limited to interactions within our professional streams or with colleagues who had similar beliefs and values in teaching as ourselves. Occasionally we exchanged ideas and moral support in our informal teaching discussions but generally we maintained the privacy and isolation of our teaching practice.

Trowler and Knight (2002) propose that each university department or school has its own distinct culture or 'community of practice' (Wenger 1998) that is developed over time and encompasses context-specific workplace norms of behaviour, rules of engagement, recurrent practices, tacit assumptions and shared discursive repertoires. This workplace culture is influenced by both institutional and personal factors, but in particular, it is the social relationships between individual members of the group that construct, create and sustain the culture (Nias *et al.* 1989). The social interactions between colleagues are integral and pervasive to all aspects of daily work practice, yet the taken-for-granted assumptions and shared meanings underlying their foundations are often so deeply embedded that they rarely come into explicit focus (Wenger 1998).

We found that developing and implementing a problem-based learning curriculum raised these hidden elements of our practice and brought them into sharp focus as we confronted both our individual and our collective tacit assumptions, habits and recurrent work practices.

Curriculum development phase: deconstructing and reconceptualizing

Conway and Little (2000a) posit that developing a fully integrated model of problem-based learning is a process of deconstructing old curricula structures and practices of teaching and reconceptualizing them from a practice framework. As a collaborative team engaged in this process we found ourselves not only deconstructing our curriculum structures and teaching practices but also deconstructing our deeply internalized values, beliefs and attitudes. For many of us this was the first time we had clearly identified and articulated these beliefs and practices in a group setting, and disclosing much of what we had accepted as 'the way of doing things here' was both revealing and personally challenging. We felt vulnerable as we exposed our work to colleagues and as Jude, one of the participants, noted, there was notable tension among team members as we attempted to address our different understandings and beliefs of good practice:

> The tension is just sort of bubbling under the surface. Every now and again a little bubble bursts through and somebody will say something and you think, 'Oh where did that come from?' I'm just waiting for a huge explosion to take place because I don't think people are addressing issues properly. Instead of trying to work though issues people are only tending to see their own point of view and are feeling challenged if someone else doesn't agree with them. They are being protective of how they work and are sort of digging their heels in a bit.

Jude had been teaching in the school for approximately four years after many years of clinical practice. She was committed to the problem-based learning programme from its initiation and had been active in all stages of the curriculum development process. Of all team members, she was perhaps the most perceptive of the challenges to the team dynamics that were instigated by this reform process and commented frequently on this aspect of collegiality in her interviews:

> Working as a team has been a very interesting experience because what I thought was a very consolidated little team group, with the added pressure of the new programme, has shown some chinks in the armour. ... we always thought that we were a good school, team wise, but we all worked fairly singularly. And now we really are having to pull together as a team and it's brought a bit of tension and aggression to the surface, which I never, ever would have imagined was there before, but now it is.

As Jude observed, working as a collaborative team on the problem-based curriculum challenged many of our former tacit assumptions of collegiality. Other team members also noted this. Pat, as one of the more senior and experienced staff members, reflected that this new way of interacting was personally challenging for team members because it contrasted so sharply with our previous patterns of engagement with colleagues:

> In the past we've been able to operate independently of each other, you just had a topic to go by and you make up your own plan as to how you did it, whereas now our teaching is open for scrutiny and it makes us all that bit more vulnerable. I mean on a personal level it's difficult because we're not used to it, we've not been trained to do that.

As Pat suggests, the norms of our previous interactions as teaching colleagues had not involved the depth of scrutiny of practice that was entailed in developing this integrated curriculum.

We found it challenging to distance ourselves from our discipline or professional stream allegiances when reviewing our old curriculum. Creating a balanced problem-based learning curriculum meant that we had to discard some of our previous content, which at times meant favouring inclusion of a colleague's specialist material over our own. This evoked varied emotional conflicts for participants, such as irritation with others' preferences, a sense of loss and even anger when previous materials or practices were discarded, anxiety as to where our specialist input would fit in the new curriculum and fear that students would not have a sufficient grounding in the basic skills and knowledge of our discipline. The entire deconstruction process required much emotional work from all participants to achieve the task yet maintain harmony within the team.

The next stage of reconceptualizing the curriculum from a practice framework involved a process of collaboratively building new shared understandings, new values and new practices; in essence building what Trowler and Cooper (2002) refer to as a new 'teaching and learning regime'. This also required the development of a shared language with which to describe these concepts. Our first encounters with problem-based learning terminology were difficult, as we had no conceptual understanding of many of the terms that we were engaging with. Giving this new terminology meaning in our work context took time and much discussion and was often overwhelming for participants, particularly for those like Mel, who had only recently joined the teaching team:

> I found it quite difficult because I had just started working at uni and we started having all those problem-based learning workshops and all the terminology and I thought, 'I'm never going to understand all this … never in a million years.'

Mel found that trying to become acquainted with both the university environment and the constructs of problem-based learning methodology was quite overwhelming:

> I'm still trying to work out all of the academic terminology and the structure of the Uni and that sort of thing. Sometimes I feel really stupid in meetings, not confident or comfortable.

For the newer staff members in the team this dual integration into the university culture and problem-based methodology presented an additional challenge that compounded their feelings of vulnerability and dislocation.

All participants found that building a contextual understanding of problem-based learning was a complex task. It was not simply a matter of learning and using the terms in our everyday language, although that was certainly part of the process of engagement. It was more a matter of building a shared repertoire that included the new terminology, as well as developing a collective understanding of the genres, tools and actions that underpinned these new teaching and learning concepts (Trowler and Cooper 2002). Until this new repertoire and new forms of engagement were consolidated in practice there was a period of turmoil and disruption for participants.

Lou was one of the team members who initially was quite resistant to implementing problem-based learning, as he was worried that we were replacing an already successful programme with something for which there was no guarantee of success. In the curriculum development phase Lou described his concerns as follows:

> I suppose, first of all, we've had a very good course running for a long time now. It's been recognized throughout Australia. We've had, I think, a perfect type of course here. The students have been very happy with it ... we've been happy as lecturers ... the profession has been very pleased and involved with it ... It has been going along smoothly for years and everyone's happy. And then problem-based learning comes in. I discussed with Sam, 'why change if something's working, why change it?' I was a little bit down to start with and you probably picked that up. In early days I was very critical of it because I wanted to make sure that we were replacing the existing course with something that's better ... so that was my main concern. I suppose I was also concerned ... as a lecturer teaching the students with this method, that we were all used to the lecture type of format and we are well prepared for that format. It's going to be a new experience for me and it's going to be a new experience for the students. I haven't, even to this date, had enough evidence, personal evidence, that this whole process is going to work ... people have been saying that they're using it around Australia and the world and saying, 'Yes, it's great.' But, personally, I haven't seen any evidence as yet.

Like other academics (Sadlo *et al.* 1994), Lou had a powerful identification with previous teaching methods and his sense of competence and professional identity was founded in this experience. At the time he did not recognize the need for change and hence was critical of the reform process and wanted more evidence to be convinced that the change in curriculum would produce better student learning outcomes. For Lou, this confrontation with his beliefs and values as an educator added to the confusion of the curriculum development process so that he felt quite fragmented and critical of our direction at this time:

> I feel a little bit lost with the whole process because we're just going along ... we've basically got some building blocks and an old course and we're just remodelling it. We're not quite sure if what we produce is going to be the best model.

Like other participants, Lou found the process of sharing these concerns in the interviews enabling, as it meant that his underlying worries were given recognition as important issues. The subsequent collation and discussion of the issues raised in each of the individual interviews meant that as a team we developed a more comprehensive understanding of each other's concerns and the issues impeding our progress. From these discussions we were able to implement a number of strategies to overcome some of the more pressing issues and, just as importantly, this sharing increased our tolerance for each other's perspectives and enhanced our collegial relationships.

The early implementation phase: rhetoric and realities

Implementing the curriculum was a process of enacting the organizational structures and teaching roles and materials that we had theoretically constructed in the two-year curriculum development phase. As for the curriculum development phase, we did not appreciate just how conflictual this process would be for us personally, professionally and collegially. We found that all aspects of our teaching practice were new and nothing seemed familiar. There were new skills to be learnt as facilitators, new competencies to be developed in managing the tutorial group dynamics, new knowledge to be gained as we moved out of our speciality areas and new responsibilities to be undertaken in coordination roles. As numerous team members noted:

> It's a totally different style of teaching that we've never had to cope with before. (Robin)

> The first month was an absolute nightmare ... I was absolutely consumed by problem-based learning, I couldn't fit anything else into my day. (Gerry)

No single aspect of our previous practice seemed to be the same as before, nothing could be relegated to automatic processing or habit. Everything seemed to require our full attention and the continual conscious processing of all this new learning and new practice was exhausting and overwhelming. Adding to these pressures was the increased workload of finalizing the third year curriculum learning packages due to be implemented the following year. We were experiencing what Fullan (1992) refers to as the 'implementation dip', where the costs of implementing the reform far outweigh the rewards.

For participants the major collegial issue in this time period was the lack of clarity in the new coordination roles and responsibilities. This was particularly significant in this reform project as new organizational structures and new cross-disciplinary coordination roles had been created to support the problem-based learning philosophy and our integrated curriculum model. In the curriculum development phase we had theoretically constructed the responsibilities and duties of these new roles but when we came to implement them we realized that there was no common understanding of the nuances and specificities of the roles. The coordination of the subjects within the new curriculum structure was far more intricate than in our previous curriculum. Pat, who had taken on one of the new coordination roles, elaborated on the challenges of the new role:

> Coordinating has been a bit of a challenge because of the large increase in time and numbers of people with whom I have needed to liaise ... There's still some, conflict you'd have to call it I think,

within this realm within the school as to who is responsible for what
... It is a bone of contention. (Pat)

Other team members also found the more complex collegial interactions
difficult to conceptualize and for participants like Jude the lack of certainty
of who was in control made them feel confused and apprehensive:

At the moment I'm just confused. Who is in charge? I think a lot of
time we're just drifting along, everybody's still doing their own bit, and
we are not really sure who's in charge of this and who's going to control
this and who's going to look after this bit of the curriculum.

Evans (1996) argues that this is one of the most contentious aspects of
major reform as participants feel anxious and insecure when they no longer
have a clear understanding of what their duties are or who has the authority
to make decisions. These concerns were not specific to the problem-based
learning programme *per se*, as many such issues also exist in conventional
programmes and departments; it was the reform process itself that made
them transparent in this context.

The head of school also acknowledged that managing the new teaching
and coordinating roles was one of the most difficult aspects of the transition
process for team members:

I guess, looking back, we didn't work on this aspect in the two years of
planning because I don't think we ever perceived that it would be a
problem. But I think the management of the coordination and new
roles has turned into a major issue. It's interesting because I think the
staff are going to take longer than the students to come to grips with
working as a group. It's totally different to what's happened before.

To manage this, and other dilemmas, we had to confront some difficult
issues. This, as noted in my reflective journal at the time, was something
that went against our preferred ways of interacting as a group:

We are very good at rubbing along quite nicely together but we don't
confront the deep stuff underneath, so we continually accommodate
these issues and then wonder why at the end of the year we're all
absolutely exhausted. Maybe if we'd confronted the issue when it
happened it would have been dealt with by now.

Confronting difficult issues had not been part of our previous form of
engagement with colleagues, since in common with other collegial groups
(Nias *et al.* 1989; Weiss *et al.* 1992) we tended to avoid conflict and disagreement in a desire to maintain harmony and good working relationships. Fullan and Hargreaves (1991) note that conflict is more common in
collaborative cultures as educators' values and purposes are openly discussed and challenged. Initially, we found that the emotional dislocation
engendered in this conflict disrupted our collegial relationships and hence
hindered our progress. In order to work effectively as a team we had to

confront and resolve these critical issues. Overall, this early implementation phase was a time of intense emotionality as we transitioned from our former understandings of ourselves as academics in a traditional teaching environment to become collaborative colleagues in a problem-based teaching team.

The late implementation phase: personal and pedagogical integration

By the end of the first year of implementation there was a significant improvement in morale among the team members. Much of this was related to some resolution of former disruptions or fragmentations of personal or professional identities. As new understandings and new conceptions of roles, beliefs and purpose were established, participants moved from frustration and anxiety to satisfaction, confidence and enthusiasm.

Participants were excited by the students' integration of learning across the former academic–clinical divide and their use of problem-solving methods in practical assessment activities. Participants also felt more relaxed and comfortable in the new facilitation role as their skills consolidated with greater experience. Most team members acknowledged that they greatly preferred this form of teaching in comparison to the old mode of lecturing. Even Lou, who initially had been quite resistant to the notion of problem-based learning, found this form of interacting with the students much more enjoyable and rewarding:

> I think it is, for me so far, being involved in teaching for six years, the most enjoyable way of teaching. After experiencing the whole process [of facilitation] I find that I enjoy the actual teaching side of it. I enjoy working with the tutorial group … I like to bring the best out of the students, guiding them without giving them the answers … it's been good.

Similarly, there were positive outcomes for the team as a collegial group. This change in curriculum had led each of us to have a more integrated understanding of the medical radiation programme as a whole. As Lesley, one of the team members who facilitated in the first year of the programme, noted, the new programme facilitated our understanding of the three professional streams: 'I have a lot more knowledge of the other areas [professional streams], a much better understanding of my colleagues' areas than I've had in the past.' Facilitating the tutorial groups through the learning packages in each professional stream helped us to broaden our knowledge base and conceptual understanding of the overall curriculum. This also led to a concomitant improvement in collegial relationships. Gerry, one of the staff members from the smaller professional streams within the school, noted that the problem-based learning curriculum had significantly improved her sense of inclusion within the school:

> I've really enjoyed these last few years at work because of the challenge of problem-based learning. Because it was something different and because it was, I suppose, working in the team I didn't really feel so isolated. I think that was the biggest advantage, you don't feel so isolated now as you were before, where you came into work, did your own thing and nobody cared. Now I know people are very interested in what I'm doing.

The integrated curriculum had helped to break down many of the 'walls of privatism' and isolation (Fullan 1982) that had previously limited our interaction as colleagues.

Conclusion

Developing and implementing major educational reform such as problem-based learning significantly impacts upon the collegial relationships of the teaching team. As educators undertake the process of deconstructing and reconceptualizing the curriculum they also deconstruct and reconceptualize their deeply internalized attitudes, values and beliefs and the tacit assumptions, habits and recurrent practices embedded in their teaching practice. This process challenges not only participants' personal and professional identities but also their collegial identities. A more complex and profound form of collaborative practice needs to be established wherein the shared meanings and values underlying the common purpose are collectively developed and communicated.

It is not surprising that this profound degree of change in collegial practice will evoke intense and varied emotional responses in participants. Professional development for staff undertaking this process should not be limited to providing instruction in redesigning the curriculum, developing learning packages and learning facilitation skills. It should also provide a means for developing effective collaborative interrelationships and provide an avenue for participants to express and reflect upon how their emotional transitions help to shape and redefine their personal, professional and collegial identities in this new context.

Part 3

Student Experiences

This part focuses on the student perspective in problem-based learning, exploring issues related to how students may perceive problem-based learning and what students learn from problem-based learning in addition to the material stimulated by the presented problems. Problem-based learning is often credited with the potential to 'add value' to learning through the acquisition of less tangible skills such as team management, interviewing, lifelong learning, coping mechanisms and critical thinking (for example, Norman and Schmidt 1992; Boud and Feletti 1997). The authors in this section examined different aspects of this incidental learning. Palmer and Major's study looks at the development of leadership skills within master's level modules. Jacobsen explores factors that influence the ways in which students approach the problem-based material; this is approached from a different angle by Silén, who examines the potential of problem-based learning for encouraging students to look at the wider picture of what needs to be learned to meet the needs of professional practice, rather than simply to pass the course assignments. Each study highlights a different aspect of the learning that occurs in problem-based learning over and above the learning expected by the curriculum designers.

Intrinsically, students have always been of great research interest in studies on problem-based learning. Much of the focus, however, has been on student performance, as demonstrated by assignment results, in an attempt to discover if and why problem-based learning is a superior pedagogy (see, for example, Dolmans 1994; Vernon 1995; de Grave *et al.* 1998). Other studies involving students have concentrated on their opinions of the nature and quality of facilitation (Schmidt 1993; Dahlgren *et al.* 1998; de Grave *et al.* 1998, 1999). While there are a few studies, such as those undertaken by Wilkerson *et al.* (1991), Tipping *et al.* (1995) and Koschmann *et al.* (1997), that centre on students within problem-based learning tutorials, these tend to focus on behaviours, such as group interactions, rather than the types of learning that take place. Williams *et al.* (2003) report on the use of journals to assist students in identifying additional learning. Their results report increased awareness by students of group dynamics, learning processes and giving and receiving feedback.

This part of the book includes research that seeks to discover not only the experience of students engaged with problem-based learning, but also their understanding of problem-based learning and the uses they make of it in setting their own learning objectives.

In Chapter 9 Palmer and Major report on a qualitative study that examined the role of student leadership within problem-based learning groups. Barrows (1986, 1988) and Moust and Schmidt (1994) relate that one of the roles to be adopted by members of the problem-based group is that of group leader. Leadership skills at several levels are a requirement for many vocational disciplines, but the application of the theories is difficult to teach (Bridges and Hallinger 1997). Palmer and Major suggest that the nature of problem-based learning, with its requirements for team working and outcomes to be achieved as well as diverse interruptions, can provide an environment in which leadership skills can be fostered and developed. Their study reports on the leadership experiences of four groups of master's students undertaking a problem-based module. The findings suggest that groups that possessed a clear leader tended to perform better in terms of completing the task. Palmer and Major also found that, in the absence of a natural or so-called charismatic leader, leadership within groups would pass from member to member until sufficient work was done to meet the learning objectives. Students who had not personally taken on the role of leader were still able to identify learning about leadership, which could be applied to their professional lives.

In Chapter 10 Jacobsen presents the findings from an examination of communication with problem-based learning teams from a different perspective. He argued that the understandings held by both facilitators and students of the problem-based process influence the ways in which the problem-based scenarios are tackled. Problem-based learning makes use of problem-scenarios or 'triggers' based on challenges that students will have to face in working life. Working with medical students and their problem-based learning facilitators, Jacobsen employed reception analysis to examine the communication within problem-based learning tutorials. Jacobsen argues that, although the scenarios for problem-based learning are derived from practice settings, students, and indeed faculty staff, see them simply as paper cases. His results suggest that when students fail to treat the scenarios as being 'real', they do not fully explore the issues associated with the problem, but instead seek issues that it may be strategic to raise. This lack of appreciation of the issues as relevant to future practice was also noted in some facilitators, whose input reinforced the students' perception of the scenario. Thus the context and frame of reference within which problem-based learning is implemented will affect the nature of the problem-based learning process. Jacobsen identifies five frame factors from his study that impact on the construction of problem-based learning. The reception of students and facilitators to the frame factors will influence whether or not students will adopt a surface approach to learning or will engage fully in problem-based learning as a self-directed strategy.

The following chapter provides a contrast to Jacobsen's work. In Chapter 11 Silén explores the possibility that problem-based learning will encourage students to move beyond the content to be learned and direct their thoughts to the meaning of their learning context. In the role of an external observer, Silén followed a cohort of nursing students during the theoretical and practice element of a problem-based undergraduate nursing programme. Her qualitative analysis of the data resulted in three student narratives focused on the interpretation and implantation of the planned curriculum, their characterization of the goal of becoming nurses and, lastly, the processes of dealing with questions which students have about their own learning. Her findings also indicate that students learn not only about content but also about processes of learning and decision-making.

Chapters 10 and 11, although centred on students, provide insights into the influence on the problem-based learning process not only of individual facilitators, but also of institutional culture and the structure of the educational framework. Silén identifies that the relationship between students' independence and responsibility is complex. Students in Silén's study attempt to discern what is important to learn by comparing their conceptions with those of peers, facilitators, lecturers and role models from practice. Like leadership, clinical decision-making is a skill integral to the provision of high quality patient care. Like leadership, it is difficult to teach from a theoretical perspective to undergraduate students who may have little exposure to and even less personal experience of decision-making in practice. Encouraging students to consider and reflect on their experiences in problem-based learning and thus to identify learning of skills adds value to the content learned. From this they decide what learning is relevant from a professional perspective.

In contrast, the medical students in Jacobsen's study appear to decide what learning is strategic by following previously successful strategies. The variance may be due to differences in course structure, where nursing students are traditionally exposed to the realities of clinical practice earlier than medical students. The need for relevance, therefore, may be more imperative for nursing students. It could be argued that the strategies employed are similar, but that the nursing students had a wider range of sources on which to test their conceptions of relevancy.

This issue of what students decide to learn through problem-based learning, whether product- or process-orientated, and how they make that decision will be the subject of continuing debate and exploration. Findings such as those presented in this section support the claims made for the 'value added' aspects of problem-based learning. Not only did the students studied learn the material required for success in their chosen programme, but also they began to acquire some of the less tangible skills needed for professional life.

9

Learning Leadership through Collaboration: The Intersection of Leadership and Group Dynamics in Problem-based Learning

Betsy Palmer and Claire H. Major

Introduction

Leadership is an emerging issue in higher education and is receiving attention in a variety of arenas. Private foundations, for example, are making great efforts to help students to develop leadership skills; the Ford Foundation's International Fellows Program stands as a prime example of such support. In addition, through formal curricula and programme requirements, institutions are embedding leadership skill development into a variety of disciplinary areas. Students are also being provided with increasing opportunities for leadership, in particular through student activities, student life and organizations. Furthermore, student leadership conferences and academies targeted at various subgroups are being held throughout the United States of America. Educators seem to have a new interest in developing student leadership skills.

Unfortunately, traditional educational programmes and methods of instruction are not proving effective in helping students to develop leadership skills and abilities. Existing leadership programmes and methods impart knowledge but do little to link this knowledge to actual practice (Bridges and Hallinger 1995). In these traditional programmes 'students learn about leadership primarily through reading and discussing theories of leadership, rather than experiencing what it feels like to be a leader' (Bridges and Hallinger 1997: 131). This chapter presents a qualitative examination of how students enact leadership in democratically organized problem-based learning groups. After reviewing the literature on problem-based learning and leadership development, we present the findings of an investigation of student leadership from two problem-based courses at two universities in the United States of America.

Problem-based learning and leadership development

Some scholars suggest that problem-based learning has the potential to help students to learn about leadership (Bridges 1992; Bridges and Hallinger 1995, 1996, 1997, 1998). In this method, problems are intentionally characteristic of the challenges that leaders face in professional lives (Bridges 1992). The problems come first, as in life, and act as the stimulus for the learning that will occur. Students serve as project leaders and facilitators and, as supporters of the team project, realize the implicit dependency that is a part of the managerial role. Unlike the calm environment of traditional classroom instruction, problem-based learning provides the interruptions and necessity of working with people when occupying a leadership role. Participants are guided by the problem scenario and a list of expected outcomes, resources and questions that narrow the participants' thinking to target important concepts and applications of the knowledge base (Charlin *et al.* 1998). This educational approach provides students with the opportunity to try out leadership skills in safe, low-threat environments in which they can be encouraged and guided by other students and facilitators.

For promotion of leadership, problem-based learning goals are often the development of administrative and problem-solving skills, and the acquisition of the knowledge base that underlies administrative practice (Bridges 1992: 6). Problem-based learning helps participants to develop a knowledge base. It teaches time management, collaboration, resourcefulness, research skills, interdependence, identification and capitalization of individual skills, communication, problem-solving, team-building and a knowledge base about leadership and practice (Bridges and Hallinger 1995, 1997; Stinson and Milter 1996; Blumberg 2000; Duek 2000; Evensen and Hmelo 2000a, b; Kelson and Distlehorst 2000; Schmidt and Moust 2000b). Problem-based learning seems particularly appropriate for preparing leaders because of its goals to promote lifelong learning and collaborative leadership (Norman and Schmidt 1992; Tanner *et al.* 1997; Blumberg 2000; Kelson and Distlehorst 2000). Problem-based learning also provides a basis for networking, individual empowerment, self-discovery, self-directed learning, fearless problem-solving, replication of organizational behaviour and the use of higher order intellectual skills (Tanner *et al.* 1997; Evensen and Hmelo 2000a, b; Kelson and Distlehorst 2000).

In one study that illustrates an interesting dimension of problem-based learning's potential for developing leadership, Cockrell *et al.* (2000) examined students' perspectives on their learning in an educational administration course. The researchers, using qualitative methods, were primarily interested in the collaborative processes. They documented how, through problem-based learning groups, students developed a sense of ownership of their knowledge. As an offshoot of their research they found that leadership within the groups moved from student to student as situations arose and were resolved. This finding is particularly interesting because it indicates a collaborative conception of leadership. However, the understanding of leadership development in their study is limited because the instructors used trained facilitators within the problem-based learning groups to guide student activity. Our study furthers the research begun by Cockrell *et al.* and asks specifically: how and why does leadership manifest within democratically organized collaborative groups?

A cultural approach to studying leadership teams

As a theoretical framework for this study, we relied upon Bensimon and Neumann's (1993) work on academic leadership teams. These authors suggested a leadership model that focuses on the interactive and collaborative skills of all members of leadership teams, rather than on the personality characteristics of an individual leader. Bensimon and Neumann suggest that leaders are most effective as representatives of a team of administrators and that team members contribute to or hinder administrative leadership functions. These researchers also advocate a cultural approach to studying leadership in teams. They suggest that the combination of individuals and the context they create together has a distinct impact upon how leadership is enacted in a particular situation. In their study of 15 leadership teams, they found that each team possessed a unique culture and that aspects of these cultures hindered or helped the effectiveness of the leadership activities. Following this reconceptualization of leadership as a collaborative activity within a particular cultural context, we examined how individuals operating within a cooperative and interdependent team environment in the problem-based learning classroom perceive and enact leadership.

Methodology

Our research project sought to answer two basic questions:

- How and why does leadership happen in democratically organized problem-based learning groups?
- How do students in problem-based learning teams view leadership and does their perception change after participating in a problem-based learning team?

Thus the focus of our research is on the intersection of teamwork and leadership skills within problem-based learning cooperative groups.

The research used a qualitative case study method and took place in two courses offered at two different research universities in two consecutive years. The courses covered the same content area and Betsy taught both courses. The first course was the second of two required courses in an MA degree programme at a research university. Betsy assigned the ten students enrolled in the first class to one of two problem-solving teams. Four students were African American, one bi-racial and five white American. Two students were male, the rest female. All the participants had taken the autumn semester course and knew each other fairly well at the start of the semester. The second class was a required course for an MA programme at a different research university. The nine students participating in this course were assigned to two gender and race-balanced problem-based learning groups. Three students were male and six female. Seven students were white American, one African American, and one Asian American. In both courses, the groups worked together for the duration of the semester to solve a problem concerning higher education administration. Betsy, as the course instructor, had an insider perspective that allowed her to understand the nuances of the data, while Claire was affiliated with neither the courses nor the programmes at the time of the research. This gave her an outsider perspective that allowed for a level of objectivity during data analysis.

This chapter uses interpretative methods to portray how students experience leadership in the context of graduate level courses in education. To answer our research questions, we conducted in depth whole-population case studies of all four problem-based learning teams on the two different courses. We used multiple points of data for the study, including group observations, beginning and end of term student self and peer evaluations, student reflective journals, focus groups, interviews with student participants and researcher field notes. We reviewed evaluations that asked students to rate themselves and each other on collaborative leadership abilities. We analysed the data by reading and re-reading evaluations, reflective journals, focus groups, interview transcriptions and field notes identifying themes in the data and generating hypotheses based on the themes. In the tradition of Bensimon and Neumann, we focused our analysis on the cultural aspects of each group. While working on this project, we began to adopt 'insider' names for the groups. These names are from television shows and after we had adopted them we realized that in many ways they aptly described the group cultures. We are not suggesting through the TV show analogies that the groups perfectly match their TV namesakes; instead, we use the specific TV theme to highlight particularly salient aspects of a group's experiences.

Findings

The Brady Bunch: a family model

One of the groups of our study functioned together much in the way that you see idealized television families work together. One prime example comes in the North American television comedy show *The Brady Bunch*, where characters in the show had unique personalities and experiences as members of a hypothetical family. An important aspect of this TV family was that it was a coming together of two partial family units (the father and three sons combining with the mother and three daughters) to create a single cohesive unit. Another important aspect of this sitcom was the fact that the family was completely idealized: perfect daughters, perfect sons, perfect parents, living their perfect suburban lives facing occasional minor conflicts that formed the bases of the plots. We dubbed our first group 'the Bradys'.

Our 'Bradys' were similar to their namesake television series in many ways. They also came metaphorically from two families. The students in this group were from either African American or white American backgrounds yet created a cohesive unit across race. Our 'family unit' raged in age, maturity and experience. Yet, despite coming from different backgrounds and perspectives, all members of this group were seen as important contributors to the work of the family. They got along well and they supported each other. They all agreed that one person was the leader of the group and they frequently described their leader in 'motherly' terms. This leader was seen as nurturing and supportive. The leader maintained open communication in this group. She also stepped aside to let 'others step up and lead' when it was appropriate. This group encountered some small conflicts throughout the semester, but they resolved their disputes easily within group meeting times. One team member commented: 'I think group leadership is working together no matter what till we get the end result. You have disagreements just like a family but you learn to work together.' The members of this group celebrated each other's successes. A group member illustrates this with this story:

> We all evaluated each other, figured out what each other's weak points were and we tried to help each other build up those weak points, to make us better people, to make us function better. I just remembered that the most profound thing happened to Jan. She was the quiet person from the first semester, who barely talked. By the end of this semester Jan discovered that she had a voice, she could be heard and she wasn't going to take junk off of anybody. She was just going to say what she had to say and that was the end of it. And I remembered we all clapped and were like, 'yeah Jan, what happened? We are so proud of you.'

This group worked together across differences to create a 'happy ending' to their problem-based learning semester. Much like an episode of the TV sitcom, all disagreements were resolved in the end. They functioned at a very high level and created an outstanding final product. This happy ending had one slight hint of trouble. In the final week of the project, the stress of creating a presentation started to crack the otherwise cheerful image of the 'Bradys'. We were left wondering if this 'happy family' would have stayed cheerful if they had continued to work together over a longer period of time.

Survivors: a competitive, political model

A more recent television show captures some of the culture of the second problem-based learning group. The reality television show *Survivors* places a diverse group of strangers in a remote location to face precarious physical challenges and asks them to work together to 'survive'. The show has a built-in paradox, however, in that each team slowly eliminates member after member until only the top person is left. Members temporarily unite in coalitions that are continually built and dissolved but the overarching theme is competition for scarce resources and ultimate survival. As our second group functioned in much the same way we dubbed them the 'Survivors'.

Our 'Survivor' group mimicked some (but not all) of these unusual group dynamics. Even though the problem-based learning 'Survivor' group members were not strangers and had known each other for at least one semester, when they came together as a group they approached each other warily as if they had just met. The 'Survivor' group had a competitive edginess from the very beginning. Individuals in this group seemed to compete with each other, yet simultaneously tried to function as a team. Individual actions were frequently interpreted through a competitive lens: 'I think we all got our feelings hurt at some point when someone else's ideas replaced our own'.

The conflict among members in this group arose early and was palpable in many group sessions. One group member actively took on a leadership role, generating ideas, suggesting a direction and providing an abundance of resources for other group members. Her leadership, however, was hotly contested throughout the semester. One group member continued to be cheerful and enthusiastic throughout the semester but other group members described the process as discouraging and debilitating. One group member appeared to withdraw from the process entirely after battling for control over several weeks. At one point the course instructor intervened to help the group to establish goals and direction. At mid-semester, a relatively quiet group member became a 'co-leader', helping to ease tensions. Another group member described himself as trying to take on a mediator role.

The early leader of this group described her leadership problems in this way: 'I was so focused on things we needed to do and how we were going to get there, I didn't realize at first there were other people. I had to learn to relax and go with the flow.' To relate to our television metaphor, this leader focused more on survival tasks than on building supportive relationships among team members. Other group members described her leadership behaviours as not listening, not compromising and not being willing to accept other group members' ideas.

When reading transcriptions of interviews and focus groups, different group members described their experiences in our 'Survivor' group in completely different ways. At times, it was difficult to imagine that these group members were in the same group or even in the same class, and it is extremely difficult to sort out the various roles and responsibilities of the different group members. One member found the experience so difficult that she refused to comment on issues of teamwork or leadership because they were 'too painful'. In contrast, two of the group members, while acknowledging tensions in the group, evaluated the group as 'functioning well together'. Others described a process that started poorly and improved over time. Much like the individuals selected for the *Survivor* TV show, the individuals in the group seemed to be caught between actions to promote team productivity and actions that would help them to survive as individuals. They seemed to have little agreement on how to interpret their group experience.

Gilligan's Island: anarchy

We called our third group 'Gilligan' or 'The Islanders'. This short-lived sitcom of surprisingly enduring fame is a tale of a fateful trip aboard a cruise ship, in which a tropical storm strands the crew and passengers on an uncharted desert island. This good-natured group, while consisting of individuals with a variety of talents, seems to function in a system of anarchy, as no clear leader emerges despite many trials, tribulations and failed attempts to get off the island. The group does eventually manage to get off the island, but it does not happen because of their group effort (they are rescued) and it happens after a considerable time lapse. Our third group shared some characteristics with their TV antecedents. Indeed, this group, by traditional academic measures such as GPA or test scores, should have been the most successful group. However, the group tended to function in complete disarray. The group often focused on the appearance rather than the substance of work behaviours and the lack of a single leader aligned this group well with its TV show analogy.

In our problem-based Gilligan group, all of the group members resisted taking a leadership role. For several weeks this group seemed to float along rudderless. At one point a student stepped up to take a leadership role out of pure frustration. She described her leadership experience as:

> I think in the beginning with me I thought if I'm going to step up and take this leadership role I felt like I had to prepare for every class like I was going to run a meeting and it was just stupid.

We note here the appearance of leading – creating an agenda for a meeting, for example – without the underlying substance of leadership. As the semester progressed, one or two other team members in this group took on some leadership responsibilities over brief periods of time or for a particular narrowly defined aspect of the project. All group members seemed to focus on bureaucratic details of the work rather than facilitating a group vision. The Gilligan group focused their attention on finishing their 'to do' lists rather than seeing their actions as steps towards a conceptually integrated solution. In the end, much like most sitcom episodes, the Gilligan group did manage to pull together an excellent solution to their problem scenario, but it came with trials and tribulations.

Having avoided all conflicts or triumphs, the members of this group had little to say about each other in the focus groups, interviews or peer evaluations. Consequently, they left us few quotes to illustrate the culture of this group. Only in the instructor notes did we find a story that might help to paint a picture of this group's culture. Much like the character Gilligan, one of the students in this group consistently could not be counted on to do his job. Our problem-based Gilligan, extremely bright with great potential (perhaps a variation from the original), was frequently late in contributing material to the group solution. The other members became frustrated, but were unwilling to take drastic actions that might pull Gilligan into line. Other group members covered for him throughout the semester and then, in the end, Gilligan wrote an outstanding introduction for the group presentation and all his previous disappointments were forgiven.

The Partridge Family: a situational model

We called upon another TV family as the metaphor for our final problem-based learning group. Unlike the Brady Bunch, the Partridge Family is a cohesive 'homogeneous' family unit of mother and five children. The members of this TV family have quite diverse personalities and the problem-based learning 'Partridge Family' follows this example. The TV family's saving grace is its ability to come together across individual differences to make great music. Our 'Partridge Family', while homogeneous in surface ways, contained a diverse group of personalities. This diversity seemed to strengthen rather than hinder the 'harmonies' of this group, which functioned smoothly throughout the semester and completed an exemplary project. The two more experienced students took on leadership roles early in the project, although both seemed to be rather hesitant to do so. One of these two leaders excelled at the organizational aspects of the project and kept the group focused. The other early leader was a team-builder and 'cheer leader'. She continually expressed enthusiasm for her team and the project.

This group discussed their experiences of leadership at length in the focus groups, exploring nuances of the ways various group members experienced leadership. Here Keith and Danny discuss different ways to interpret leadership in their group:

> *Danny:* I think Keith and I think Laurie were like the main leaders and it was good because it gave us a little bit of structure you know because we hit the ground and like, 'just tell us what to do and we'll go get it', you know. So and then we were able to put in a little more input as far as decisions and the next moves, but earlier on we needed somebody to step up and I think that they both kind of stepped up and they both kind of had their own ways of participating.
>
> *Keith:* Um, I would second that. I also think, I remember in the beginning you said that you wanted to step back and have us say, 'go do this', but you're a leader even when you don't know that you are. So I think that you were a leader as well. And I think that Tracy was quiet in the beginning but really stepped up too and I think that by the second half of the project we were all more equal in doing some leadership stuff. But I think that in the beginning we were like directing it a little.

When a twist was introduced to the project mid-semester, Danny stepped up to take on a leadership role. He actively engaged the group in discussions on the second phase of the project. The early leaders, Keith and Laurie, continued to support the team and did not sabotage his active role. Finally, towards the end of the project, the fourth team member, Tracy, who had played a very quiet role through most of the project, stepped up to a leadership role in preparing the final presentation of the groups' problem solution. This team enacted the same type of situational leadership that Cockrell *et al.* (2000) described in their research on problem-based collaborative groups. Much like the TV Partridge Family, this group seemed to create a musical harmony from thin air. Their work flowed together throughout the semester and resulted in an excellent final solution to their problem.

Learning leadership in context

Several themes emerged from our analysis of these case studies. The most salient theme was that students learned about leadership whether or not their group functioned well or had clear leaders emerge. Instructors who use problem-based learning as an instructional method are frequently less concerned that all students master a fixed body of knowledge or develop skills in a set, predetermined way. They structure courses so that students may encounter a range of content and apply a range of skills. The leadership skills developed in these four groups follows this philosophy; different groups may have learned different lessons given their particular context. Students in groups that experienced conflict were less satisfied with their problem-based learning experience, but they were quite eloquent regarding the lessons they had learned about leadership. In the following themes, we explore how groups garnered leadership lessons from their problem-based learning experiences.

Conceptions of leadership

An eventual group consensus over a definition or conception of leadership was crucial for effective group functioning. The 'Partridge Family' and the 'Brady Bunch' developed collaborative conceptions of leadership similar to the one identified by both Bensimon and Neumann (1993) and Cockrell *et al.* (2000). This conception of leadership seemed to align well with the course goals and with the problem-based learning methodology, which emphasizes collaboration over competition. In the 'Survivor' and 'Gilligan' groups, a shared conception of leadership did not emerge. These two groups seemed to struggle throughout the semester, although several members of the 'Survivor' group indicated that conditions in the group improved once co-leaders stepped forward. The emergence of one or more leaders who assumed a role in accordance with the group's conception of leadership seemed essential to group satisfaction with their leaders and other group members, their experiences of the course and the functioning of the groups. We mean to suggest not that the collaborative model of leadership is the only conception of leadership that will work in problem-based groups, but that the group must have some underlying consensus about the leadership style appropriate for the group culture.

Heroic versus collaborative leadership

Early literature on leadership focused on the personality, characteristics and behaviours of singular individuals (Bolman and Deal 1997). This 'heroic' model of leadership has been replaced recently with models of collaborative, facilitative and situational leadership, focusing on how leaders help others to produce change. However, our data suggest that the heroic model of leadership still lives on. Several students described this model as their early conception of leadership and, as evidenced primarily by the 'Survivor' group, at least one student attempted to enact this model. Many of the students describe a deep level of conceptual change in their working model of leadership over the course of their problem-based learning experience. For example, this student describes how her view of leadership changed over the semester:

> I used to think as an undergraduate ... when I would look at a group, I would see who was the one ... doing everything, making the decision. And I did change my view because when I like think about how we interacted, there was definitely, like quiet leadership, you know, there was organization, there was like content. People all had different things at different times. And I think that true leadership really has to be about kind of keeping the group together and the relationships going and I think that we all contributed to that and I think that is what leadership is.

Team versus collection of individuals

One of the concepts that emerged in this research is that our highly functioning groups viewed themselves as a cohesive whole: a team or 'family'. The 'Bradys' and the 'Partridges' worked well together. They realized that they were interdependent and that they must support and promote each other. In contrast, our lower functioning teams viewed themselves as a collection of individuals who happened to be trapped together in a particular space for a period of time. The 'Survivors' and the 'Gilligans' each vied for leadership (as opposed to sharing) and ultimately were competitive with each other to varying degrees.

Valuing member contributions

One of the most important outcomes for the students on both problem-based learning courses was an increased awareness of the value of hearing different perspectives from a group of individuals. At least one member of each of the four groups highlighted the value of learning from the differing perspectives of peers. The leadership experiences of the different groups either enhanced or limited this particular outcome. All members of both the 'Brady Bunch' and 'Partridge Family' commented favourably on this aspect of learning in their problem-based learning experience. This was less true of the 'Gilligan' group. In the 'Survivor' group, students learned how an authoritarian leadership stance had the ability to squash diversity of opinions. This finding converges with Bensimon and Neumann's (1993) work on leadership teams. These authors suggest that the most important function of leadership teams is the cognitive function of developing and critiquing diverse perspectives on any given situation.

Leadership applications to real world context

The conflict-ridden groups were more likely to discuss how they might diagnose group process problems in the future and also what they would do differently in future group situations. One student commented in the focus groups: 'the [learning about] group dynamic is good because I know for sure in this profession we're going to work in groups and that's not going to be easy.' Students in groups without conflicts were more likely to discuss ways to refine and recreate their experiences of collaborative leadership in future group situations. They seemed to understand that in future situations, collaborative group culture might not arise so easily and they might have to work at producing a similar collaborative, democratic culture.

Problem-based learning as a context for learning leadership

Professional preparation programmes are in many ways a perfect practice field for prospective practitioners, yet they are also fraught with their own complexities. The students on both courses described their problem-based learning experiences as giving them a window on 'real world' expectations in their workplaces. One student commented on the classroom as a 'safe place' to rehearse leadership skills that she had studied, but as yet had been unable to put into practice:

> I never thought of myself as a leader and then when we got into this group, it was kind of like you had the opportunity you know when we were all kind of figuring out who was kind of going to do some of the leading and I felt like I was in a safe enough group that I knew my classmates well enough that I could say, 'OK, let's try this', or 'let's do this'.

Unlike work situations where responsibilities are defined and leadership roles often assigned, the equality of the student peer relationship posed a somewhat hazardous terrain for negotiating leadership. In the 'Gilligan' group, this context at first posed a barrier to any student assuming a leadership role. As one student put it:

> I think that like in a programme like this with such a small class you're going to find that most people in a group are talented in some way or another or else they wouldn't be at this level of education, you know, so I think that that might have caused a little tension here and there but overall I think that it balanced out.

When students were able to develop collaborative rather than heroic conceptions of leadership, they were better able to negotiate the idea of leading among equals.

An across-group comparison

The tendency of students to observe not only their own group activities but also those of the other group was an interesting phenomenon that arose in the focus groups and interviews. Students from both smoothly functioning groups ('Brady Bunch' and 'Partridge Family') and groups with complicated group dynamics ('Gilligan' and 'Survivor') compared themselves to their colleagues. They were keenly aware of how the other problem-based learning group did or did not function and also seemed to be able to analyse why that might be the case. For example, one member of the Brady Bunch noted 'We had Alice, they didn't.' So while students learned about leadership from their own collaborative group experience, they also learned by observing other groups. The opportunity to discuss leadership and group functioning at the end of the problem-based learning experience probably helped to solidify this learning into something that could be taken into practice in future situations.

Conclusion

Problem-based learning holds great promise as a pedagogical method that can not only introduce students to content knowledge, but also provide a safe environment for developing and practising leadership skills. Specifically, problem-based learning provides an excellent avenue for promoting the collaborative team-building and problem-solving leadership skills that are necessary for successful administrative teams. This educational approach provides democratically organized groups with the opportunity to let leadership emerge within an authentic context. They have the opportunity to begin to see leadership as emerging from a group, which can help or hinder a leader. They also have the opportunity to see how leadership changes based on the context, the situation and the composition of the members of the group. This study provides an initial understanding of how this important educational process happens.

10

The Influence of Participants' Reception of Problem-based Learning on Problem-based Learning Tutorials

Dan Yngve Jacobsen

Introduction

Ideological statements about problem-based learning, such as those found in university policy documents, may indeed differ from learning practices in real life. This was the case in my study of medical students engaged in small group tutorials. This chapter gives some examples from the study (Jacobsen 1997). A typical finding was that, despite an institution advocating and expressing a self-directed problem-based learning ideology, students often engaged in cue seeking and also focused on the surface structure of the proffered case descriptions. The case descriptions were often read as didactic texts rather than as representations of real life phenomena. This meant that the problems at hand were rarely discussed or indeed solved. Instead they triggered discussions as to what issues it might be strategic to raise. In the study there were examples of students trying to include learning issues not particularly relevant to the written cases. I even met tutors who, despite an explicit ideology advocating student-directed learning, piloted the students into certain focuses or into certain results. In this chapter I illustrate some of these patterns. Reception theory (see Holub 1984) and discourse analysis (Potter and Wetherell 1987) will be applied as appropriate to give a theoretical account for these phenomena. The phenomena in question could also be related to the frame factors of the setting and to frame factor theory (Dahllöf 1967, 1971, 1991; Lundgren 1972, 1996).

Methodology

My study of problem-based learning small group tutorials was conducted in the autumns of 1993 and 1996. The students initially were in their first year in medical school and I revisited the same students during their fourth year. At the time problem-based learning was a fairly new concept in Norway. The medical school at the Norwegian University of Science and Technology (NTNU) in Trondheim chose problem-based learning as its curricular approach when it started full-scale medical training in 1993. Keeping up with the students' strides in every aspect of the curriculum would, of course, be an impossible research mission. Since, however, the small group tutorials are a key feature of the curriculum they were chosen for more in-depth studies. During the first and eighth semesters quite a number of group sessions involving several students and their tutors were observed and tape recorded. During the fieldwork the main strategy behind the selection of tutorials was to obtain examples comprising as much variation as possible (Patton 1990). In order to pursue this intention, more traditional criteria for the selection of samples had to be set aside. The examples given in this chapter are chosen from one session during the first semester. At the meeting seven students out of eight were present. Their tutor, a senior staff member, was also present.

Obtaining sufficient technical quality of the recordings was an important issue during the fieldwork. At the time it seemed like a good idea to use audio recordings over video recordings. This was partly because a better sound recording system could be implemented. On the other hand, missing the picture meant that more thorough field notes had to be taken as to who was speaking and so on. A main benefit from this choice, apart from sound quality, had to do with the data analysis. Even though transcripts of the chosen sessions were written, it was still necessary to listen to the tapes several times to understand the deeper meaning of the discussions. Meanings could be discerned in the tone of voice, in irony, in laughter or even in the mode of laughter. Using audiotapes these non-verbal characteristics were still there during analysis. Essential parts of the conversation could be easily rewound and played several times. It could be argued that the same procedure is also possible using video recording. An obvious disadvantage would be the amount of technical equipment necessary during the writing process. Another apparent loss is body language and kinetics, proxemics and artefactual expressions. As it all adds up, though, the unit for analysis was the tape recordings as they were recorded during the group sessions I observed. Transcripts were mostly used as a means to manoeuvre through the recordings themselves and to make illustrations for publishing.

My approach to 'reading' the examples was qualitative and an accurate description of the analysing process would be reading 'meaningful units'. The units and their context are both important. The Marton group advocates a similar holistic view of learning, trying to study learning experiences in their natural setting (Entwistle and Marton 1984). In many respects the reading process is dependent on what we already know, but cannot express. 'To analyse data is to create meaning. To do this we have to bring with us both our explicit and implicit understanding' (Hoel 1995: 420, my translation). Considering these beliefs it is also fair to say that the data were analysed through a subjective understanding of the phenomena in question. A 'true' reading of the recordings, to my mind, is not an option. However, illustrations from the sessions make it possible for readers to make up their own mind.

My overall approach is *reception analysis*; that is, an attempt at analysing how the participants understand the case descriptions, the problem-based learning curriculum itself and the learning context based on semiotic properties of the setting. A more elaborate description of the concept is offered below. In the next section I also explore the nature of the communication within problem-based tutorial groups.

A short visit

On 25 November 1993 seven of the students in the brand new medical curriculum at NTNU came together in their problem-based learning tutorial group. This particular morning they concentrated on a situation related to the topic 'Health, sickness and genetics'. The proffered case was described as follows:

Heidi has earlier given birth to three healthy children.

She is 41 years old at the time of this birth.

Status of child just after birth:

Normal birth:

Weight 3900 grams, length 50 cm.

The child seems listless.

There is epicanthus, neck-fold, short back head, short fifth fingers, narrow thorax, large distance between 1st and 2nd toe and general muscular hypotonia.

After some days there is a systolic extra sound over the precordial zone. Cardiological assessment concludes AV communis and atrial septal defect.

About three to four months after birth the patient develops heart-failure symptoms with considerable shunting of blood from the left to the right side of the heart. Weight and growth development is poor.

After asking their tutor questions about some of the expressions, the group starts to identify which issues to focus on. This is how the conversation continues after the clarification of some key terminology and other small talk:

Kari:	Shall I write now?
Magne:	Down's syndrome, the signs are ... short back head ...
Hans:	Down's syndrome?
Anne:	Mongoloid [the term is used to explain the syndrome to other students].
Magne:	Heart problems are usual too ...
Tutor:	Good doctor ...
Anne:	I wonder, why isn't Down's syndrome mentioned in the text?
Kari:	Maybe, we're supposed to find out for ourselves ...
Magne:	Are we putting 'Down's syndrome' as a headline here?
Tutor:	Magne has decided that the issue is Down's syndrome. Do you all agree?
Magne:	Well ... I don't know ... it might be too hasty ....
Tutor:	I think you should keep it that way.
Kari:	We go for that one ... is it written this way? (Writes on the blackboard)
Magne:	Yes!

As Kari is ready to take down the suggestions from the others on the board, Magne immediately suggests Down's syndrome as the day's headline. He also starts to list findings associated with this particular condition. This behaviour is supported by at least two other group members. Even though there is no particular diagnosis mentioned in the text these students show little hesitance in identifying 'Down's syndrome' as the main topic. In fact, this understanding is so taken for granted that possible hesitance from two other students is interpreted as their not knowing and the term is therefore explained to them. To the non-medical reader it should be mentioned that several of the symptoms described in the case are in fact related to Down's syndrome. The malformation of the heart (AV communis and defect atrial septum)[1] occurs in 20 per cent of patients with Down's syndrome. The epicanthus,[2] neck-fold and so on are distinct signs of this condition. The diagnosis thus appears to be more or less handed to the students on a silver platter. The group's behaviour on observation may be described as *cue recognition*. The students recognized linguistic elements from the case description and based their further work on what they inferred from these, rather than from the whole content of the text. Marton and Säljö (1984) described similar patterns as a surface approach to learning. In the end the other group members seemed to agree with Magne and the tutor also confirmed his assumption. Even if these students were in their first semester, they were well aware of the signs of Down's syndrome and were able to use this knowledge to identify on which topic they were supposed to focus on this particular morning. It is also interesting to note that after about 12 weeks in the programme the students have established a broad consensus as to how to deal with the case.

What these students met, however, was not a mother giving birth to a child with Down's syndrome. To be more precise it is a written text representing this situation. The students are supposed to elaborate on this text in their group and this elaboration (see, for instance, Schmidt 1993) is expected to improve student learning. The process of elaboration and communication is one of the very reasons for group learning. Through mutual challenging, exploratory speech (Barnes 1976) and elaboration in a social context the students should use each other to construct their own socially viable explanations and solutions to medical problems. There is also a different layer of communication present in this situation. Not only do the students communicate with each other. The case descriptions and other artefacts present in the learning environment can be seen as instruments of communication in their own right. They carry messages about important learning issues or how to act in the problem-based curriculum.

The semiotic frame of reference

Fiske (1982) describes two main approaches to communication theory. One of these is referred to as the *process school*. The process school sees information as elements of a transparent process. Messages are transmitted via a channel and the recipient receives and stores the message more or less with its original meaning. Messages are presumed to have a direct effect on the state of mind or the behaviour of the recipient. Incorrect readings are due to unclear messages, transmission problems or simply misunderstandings. These assumptions about communication are present in problem-based learning research on 'problem effectiveness' (see, for instance, Dolmans 1994), where the objective is to produce as transparent messages as possible; that is, problems where the predefined learning objectives are more or less obvious to the students.

A different view of conceptualizing communication is the *semiotic approach* (Fiske 1982). In this school the message has no meaning in itself. It also has no direct effect on the recipient's state of mind or behaviour. The message is encoded in a symbolic form and has to be decoded before it can have any meaning. Obviously, the semiotic view empowers the students in a problem-based curriculum to define the meaning of case descriptions, thus promoting self-directed learning. However, as it is concerned with how people interact with encoded messages to produce meaning, this frame of reference also provides insight into complicated processes.

Hall's (1980) encoding–decoding model is a product of the semiotic viewpoint. A basic assumption is that phenomena or events cannot be passed on in their 'raw form'. Rather they have to be encoded and signified in some kind of symbolic form. This symbolic mode is the necessary form of appearance of the phenomena in the exchange between message producer and receiver. The transpositions in and out of the symbolic form are thus important processes to identify and understand in communication theory. It is also important to remember that these processes of encoding and decoding will take place within more or less dissimilar meaning structures.

The processes by which case descriptions are encoded are framed within discursive aspects in the context. Professional ideologies, historically defined professional skills and institutionalized knowledge, as well as assumptions about the student and the wider sociocultural setting, all scaffold the production. Embedded in the description of 'giving birth at 41' are a number of assumptions, including the amount of information necessary, what clinical topics to address and the students' general interests. In turn these messages will have to be decoded and it is these decoded messages that have a potential 'effect' on, influence, persuade or instruct the student. The meaning put into the case is related to the student's choice of learning objectives. I have suggested elsewhere (Jacobsen 2002) that this relation can be both ways. In particular, experienced students will try to negotiate with the case description in order to make it fit their already preferred learning objectives. Nevertheless, in decoding the cases the students will use a second meaning structure, consisting of their own frames of reference, pre-knowledge, prior experiences, expectations and priorities. Reading the case as a description of Down's syndrome means having prior knowledge about this condition. Students focusing on the genetic aspects of the case obviously have a different set of interests from those focusing on the psychological aspects. A similar shift in focus could also be related to a context where psychological aspects are less valued than biological science. Thus the meaning put into the case depends on the text, the context and the students' frame of reference, as well as how the students, as a group, negotiate these variables. In semiotic theory the idea of a polysemic message is central. A message has many meanings and the interpretation is coloured by the frames of reference used by the reader. Obviously, the case has a preferred meaning encoded by the author, but it can be decoded either in compliance with or in opposition to this meaning. As I have already mentioned, negotiated decodings are not unusual among experienced students.

The cue-seeking pattern identified at the beginning of this chapter, however, indicates a group of students looking for the dominant reading of the case; that is, 'What does the faculty really want us to study?' In a study of expert versus non-expert tutors, Davies *et al.* (1992) found that expert tutors would give directions that increased their influence in the group and that the students as a consequence were less likely to introduce their own issues during the tutorials. However, the students in these groups rated their problem-based experience higher than other students in terms of time well spent, being enjoyable and as an effective instructional method. This finding seems concurrent with our students aiming at a disclosure of the dominant reading of the proffered case description; in both cases the students want the institution or the teachers to take over the responsibility for their learning process.

Reception analysis

Reception analysis is a well established tradition in cultural studies. A key concept is that of decoding, which originates in the work of Hall (1980). In educational analysis, however, the concepts of decoding and reception analysis are newcomers. The term reception analysis derives from the German word *Rezeptionsästhetik* (aesthetics of reception), a term used by the literary scholar Hans Robert Jauss in the late 1960s. In his view literature should be seen as a dialectical process of production and reception. With regard to the content of the text the reader's effort to define its meaning was emphasized.[3] In reception analysis the notion of 'horizon of expectation' (*Erwartungshorizont*) is also central. This term refers to a *socially constructed frame of reference* that individuals might bring to the text. The concept thus comprises collective properties drawn from a shared cultural canvas. These socially embedded frames of reference are essential for the meaning given to a text by the reader.

In understanding and implementing problem-based learning practice our students draw on a wider cultural canvas, namely that of education and of educational discourses. Potter and Wetherell (1987) point out that 'discourse', in the more open sense, can be taken to mean all forms of spoken interaction, formal and informal, and written texts of all kinds. A major point in their book is that social texts do not reflect directly or mirror objects pre-existing in the natural world. Instead they actively *construct* a version of those objects. The way in which a phenomenon is signified in language also does something to the phenomenon (see also Taylor 1993). Discourse about education, then, does something to the expectations of education and educational practices. A term like 'transmission of knowledge' kicks off different associations from, for instance, 'construction'; 'syllabus' is different from 'self-directed learning'. Discourse constructs a frame of reference in which students' expectations are embedded when they come into the classroom. Together with their own previous educational experiences, these frames of reference shape how the students decode the case descriptions and, in fact, problem-based learning as an educational activity. In the early stages of the curriculum the case descriptions are read as school assignments to which there are correct answers. This is in line with their own learning history and socially constructed frames of reference. It is important to remember that these students have been very successful in the past using similar strategies. Like any other form of message the problem-based curriculum or artefacts conveying local ideologies have to be decoded before they can have any effect on the students.

Frame factors

Contributing to this frame of reference are also the frame factors. Implementing problem-based learning and designing a curriculum are political decisions at the institutional level. Such decisions provide certain structures in the learning environment. As much as these structures constrain activities, they also provide possibilities (see Giddens 1984). Frame factor theoretical thinking (Dahllöf 1967, 1971, 1991; Lundgren 1972, 1996) focuses on the relationship between structural variables and the process variables within. This relationship is not deterministic. Instead, the frame factors build up a field in which some patterns are possible whereas others are not. However, the patterns that are actually created depend on how the actors read the text;[4] that is, understand the social context based on shared frames of reference. This also addresses the relative importance of different properties of the learning environment as they are negotiated and defined by the actors.

The students' and tutors' reception of the frame factors obviously has an impact on how problem-based learning is constructed in the setting. My study defined five frame factors: the case descriptions, definitions of tutor role, the format of exams, available time on different tasks and the concept of problem-based learning itself. To explain this further I will illustrate the latter. Using problem-based learning sessions as a variation for a few weeks in an otherwise tightly scheduled curriculum may communicate to the students that 'what we do here is not really important but we do think you need a break'. In a number of Norwegian university colleges (for instance, nursing schools) problem-based sessions are currently used as a means of methodological variation. In some cases this could be a way to express a certain profile regarding the requirements in the Norwegian Quality Reform (MER 2002), which among other things emphasizes new methods in learning and assessment. But, as Margetson (1993) points out, problem-based learning amounts to more than this. To my mind, using problem-based learning as an instrument in a traditional curriculum also sends out a signal about what learning methods or epistemological views are really valid in the setting. It is well documented in international literature that the format of examinations has a similar effect in communicating to the students what learning strategies to employ (see, for instance, Entwistle and Marton 1984; Ramsden 1984, 1992; Boud 1995; Andersson 1997; Gynnild 2001). Frame factors are important features of a learning environment, facilitating certain processes while also inhibiting others. The participants' reception of these factors is decisive for their actual choices in problem-based sessions.

Piloting

Let us go back and visit the group. As we enter the setting the students are about to start their 'brainstorming:'

Tutor.	I don't think that the mother was too old . . . well, OK, too old to give birth maybe . . .
Magne.	Number of chromosomes . . . (silence, while waiting for Kari to write) . . . what chromosome, or one too many (?) . . . or how is that?
Anne.	What chromosome is there too many of?
Magne.	There is one extra . . . it has a special number . . . 21 or 23 (?)
Anne.	Well . . . I think it is number 21 or 23, but I'm not sure . . . There is one too many of one of them . . .
Magne.	What properties are precisely for that chromosome . . .
Tutor.	Well, you'll immediately find out that it is number 21. You just have to look it up in the book . . . and you will find out. So I might as well tell you that it is number 21.
Magne.	Then just write 21!
Anne.	What's number 23?
Tutor.	23 is a little bit problematic, isn't it? We just have 22 plus two gender chromosomes . . .
Kari.	Is it number 23?
Tutor.	There is no 23.

The passage starts with a comment from the tutor addressing the age of the mother. His statement that he does not think that the mother is too old has to do with the informal life of the group. Most likely, this is an attempt at reducing the significance of his own age (about 50) in relation to the students. Still, he is afraid that this informal remark may be misunderstood. This is why he adds a comment about the relation between the mother's age and giving birth. After giving this informal comment about his own age he is afraid he might distract the students from their task in finding suitable learning issues related to the case.

The students go on to ponder the number of chromosomes and which one is too prevalent. Their pre-knowledge of Down's syndrome is again evident; people with Down's syndrome have one extra chromosome. Magne and Anne agree that this occurs on either pair 21 or 23. Magne also wants to know the properties of this specific pair of chromosomes. Then the tutor interrupts the pondering. As he sees it, he may just as well reveal to the students that the problem is on pair 21, since there is no pair 23. The information is easily available anyway, and besides the students will not have to waste good time going down a blind alley. Shortly after he once again underlines that there are only 22 pairs plus the gender chromosomes.

Here the tutor is helping the students to focus. In his mind they should not be distracted by his comment about the mother's age related to human age in general (and to his own in particular), nor should they be distracted trying to clarify a minor detail regarding the number of chromosomes. His notion about problem-based learning tells him that he should not really do this, and so he justifies his actions by referring to the fact that it could easily be found in a book. However, his interruption then initiates a new, in this case short, dialogue between him and the students about the issue he comments on. This is a pattern that I have demonstrated elsewhere (Jacobsen 1997, 2002), in particular in relation to expert tutors. Small interventions from the tutor initiate more direct student–tutor interactions.

In the previous excerpt from the group we could also see the tutor being active when the students decided on the general issue. He reinforced Magne's ideas on several occasions, and when Magne hesitated about Down's syndrome as the headline he simply stated that they should keep it that way, since he saw no need for the students to go 'off course'. What is witnessed here is in fact an example of *piloting*. In the original study (Jacobsen 1997) there are several examples of this tutor activity. Piloting is a well documented phenomenon in educational literature. Lundgren (1977) describes piloting as occurring when students solve problems in interaction with the teacher. They were not able to solve the problem on their own. However, they have developed strategies *where attentiveness to how the teacher uses language* is the key to the answer.[5] In this case the tutor perhaps sees himself as an 'agent' for the faculty in a position to 'open the door'. The effect of these patterns is that the tutor (perhaps unwillingly) strengthens the significance of the text as a learning assignment rather than as a problem in the medical world. Even though this problem, in its proper context, is what the students should learn to understand, the above examples show us that students are attentive to both the tutor and cues in the text. The students focus on these details in order to discern the learning objectives on which they should concentrate.

Concluding remarks

Both cue recognition and piloting are non-intended patterns in the problem-based learning environment. None the less, we can easily see them during our visits to the first year tutorial. Through a mutual process the students and their tutor engage in a surface approach to the proffered case description, to discover the intended learning issues. This is not in line with problem-based learning ideology advocating student-directed learning. The difference was accounted for through reception analysis, a tool fairly new to educational science, but well suited to let us understand how participants' own frames of reference, and also the context including the frame factors, will influence the meaning of the proffered case as the participants initially consider it.

This constitutes a democratic paradox. Whereas the faculty constructs a problem-based curriculum where student-directed learning is part of the expressed ideology, the students use this freedom to maintain a more 'traditional' hierarchical learning model. The curriculum is one of the frame factors making true problem-based learning possible. Obviously, self-directed problem-based learning does not happen due to curricular decisions. Problem-based learning also needs to be constructed by devoted participants.

Notes

1. AV communis (atrioventricular communication) and defect atrial septum means that the dividing walls in the heart are partly missing.

2. Epicanthus: skin-fold near the eye.

3. A similar focal shift is also presented and amply advocated in modern semiotic theory (see, for instance, Eco 1984).

4. The term 'text' is here to be understood in a broad sense as all the properties of a social context.

5. The term piloting is my translation of the Swedish term 'lotsning'. The term was also used by Johansson (1975) in a study of children learning arithmetic.

11

Does Problem-based Learning Make Students 'Go Meta'?[1]

Charlotte Silén

A meta level of discernment in learning

When students are offered and accept the challenge to be responsible and independent in the learning process, they find it both frustrating and stimulating (Silén 2001). They struggle to understand what they need to learn and how to handle their learning process. A nursing student in a problem-based programme made the following statement:

> I am afraid that when I start to work after three years ... perhaps I didn't get the required knowledge [to be a nurse] ... that I will feel that as a nurse ... but on the other hand I think I ought to have that feeling already now when I am in the ward. I experience a lot. I can watch the way others do their work. I also get more and more responsibility in the ward the further I get in my studies. But there is always a kind of fear, of not managing ... But still, up to now I feel all right. I can test my knowledge while I am in the ward and somehow I have to rely on that. (Lilian)

The main message in this chapter is that the struggles that the students experience in their learning process creates a dimension of learning not previously described in relation to problem-based learning. When the students are invited to consider and take an active part in their own learning, they try not only to learn the content, but also to direct their thoughts to the meaning of their learning context and the professional domain. I describe this intention as a learning process including discernment (see Marton and Booth 1997) on a meta level. I would argue that this might lead to the students reaching a metacognitive level of understanding concerning their future practice. The way problem-based learning is understood and implemented is crucial in these processes.

The ideas presented above are part of my research that focused on the learner's responsibility and independence in learning (Silén 2000).

My reasoning about a meta level of discernment in learning deals with how students form conceptions about the relevance of learning objectives and how they go about learning a knowledge base in order to reach their objective of becoming nurses. The study also deals with two other areas:

• A dialectic driving force in learning, experiences of chaos and cosmos. A driving force emerging from the experiences of being challenged to take responsibility (Silén 2001).
• The students' attempts to handle their learning process in relation to the actual framework of the educational programme. Self-directed learning as a learning process related to interaction with learning resources, other people, the learning context and the framework of the educational programme (Silén 2003).

All these areas are connected and constitute a whole in my study. I will comment on their relationship when it is appropriate. The focus in this chapter is discernment on a meta level.

Research context

This research was undertaken in the nursing programme at the Faculty of Health Sciences (FHS), Linköping, Sweden. Today, the FHS is responsible for eight educational programmes in health care and social welfare. Problem-based learning has been the basic pedagogical approach in all programmes since the faculty's foundation in 1986. Problem-based learning is implemented in full in all the programmes, meaning that the whole curriculum in each programme is built on assumptions underpinning problem-based learning. Originally, problem-based learning was described and implemented in the faculty primarily on the basis of Knowles's (1975) theories about androgogy and self-directed learning and the ideas for application of problem-based learning provided by Barrows and Tamblyn (1980). Today, a broader theoretical base concerning student-centred learning forms the foundation for the interpretation and development of problem-based learning in the faculty. The assumptions underpinning problem-based learning are now based on pragmatism (Dewey 1911, 1916; Blumer 1986), androgogy (for example, Knowles 1970; Candy 1991; Garrison 1997), meaningful learning (Marton *et al.* 1984; Marton and Booth 1997), cognitive psychology (Norman and Schmidt 1992; Gijselaers 1996) and social constructivism (Boud 1988; Säljö 2000).

All students begin their studies by attending a common course where problem-based learning is introduced as the principal pedagogical philosophy and method. The students work with reality-based situations in small groups (six to nine students and a facilitator) called base groups. An inquiring approach (processing problems) in learning is emphasized in the base group (see Margetson 1996, 1998). Demands on the students' own responsibility and independence in their learning process is another characteristic of the interpretation of problem-based learning in the faculty. Other strategies and forums for learning, such as lectures, skills training, practice within the professional domain and studies concerning different resources (resource persons, books, journals, the web), are looked upon as parts of the problem-based learning approach. The unifying idea behind strategies for organizing different kinds of forums for learning and the use of these resources is to provide opportunities for, and to stimulate students in developing, an inquiring approach and responsibility. The students are encouraged to bring this attitude into their clinical practice. In some pro-grammes, clinical base groups are used and the facilitators challenge the students to integrate theory and practice. The main goals of a problem-based curriculum in the faculty are that the students learn to:

- explain, understand, relate to and handle situations they will meet in their future community of practice (Wenger 1998);
- understand, handle and assess their ongoing learning process (and the need for learning);
- work in teams related to an informed awareness of the possibilities and hurdles of group dynamics.

The nursing programme comprises three years of study at university level, leading to qualification as a Registered Nurse with a Bachelor of Science in Nursing. With the exception of the first term, which basically consists of theoretical studies, the terms comprise theoretical studies and practice in the field of nursing.

Methodology

The overall aim of my research was to understand the culture and meaning of student-centred learning from the learner's perspective. My interest was especially directed towards the students' interpretations of the meaning of responsibility and independence. I took as my starting point the discourse surrounding self-directed learning and assumptions underpinning the ideas of problem-based learning. The concept of self-directed learning is regar-ded as a core concept in relation to problem-based learning and, in a broader sense, the idea of responsibility and independence in student-centred learning.

The learner's perspective

I found that the literature does not provide much research based on the learner's own experiences of the meaning of self-directed learning. The dominant methods used in empirical studies involving students are differ-ent kinds of questionnaires that are already based on assumptions made about self-directed learning. This kind of approach also tends to measure self-directed learning as a general skill. In research on adult education today, there is a very high level of agreement about self-directedness being related to context. In order to broaden the research perspective of self-directed and student-centred learning, I chose a discovery approach, ethnography. This part of my research constitutes the empirical study. Further analyses, described below, were performed using theoretical frameworks from different perspectives.

The empirical study

Conclusive arguments for the choice of the field of study were the problem-based learning approach, the length of time it has been practised and my own background in nursing education. Problem-based learning is designed to implement student-centred learning, stressing the importance of the student's responsibility and independence in learning. My background was considered an advantage as regards access to the field, knowledge of problem-based learning, acquaintance with the context and the ability to understand the content the students studied. As regards the relationship to the students, I was an external observer. Even so, my familiarity with the context was recognized as a problem. There was a large risk that events and statements would be taken for granted, not even observed or problemized. I tried to handle these problems by adopting a reflective attitude throughout the thesis (Hammersley and Atkinson 1995; Denzin 1997). During the field study, while analysing data and when I produced written structures and interpretations, I continuously reflected on my pre-understanding and scrutinized interpretations using the students, the supervisor, other doctoral students and external help (people who did not know the context at all) to do so.

Observations and dialogues were the main methods used to collect data while in the field. I attended scheduled activities such as lectures, seminars, tutorial sessions and information meetings. I spent time with the students during their breaks, while working in the library and during their clinical practice period. During the term, I attended problem-based sessions in different groups, taking field notes and taping the conversations. Interviews were carried out with the students in their groups and with their facilitators. Documents, formal and otherwise, produced by the students were collected. Data were analysed continuously during the field study and the information thus obtained made it possible to pose more questions and collect additional data. It also made it possible to delimit my collection of data to situations I estimated to be informative.

Assumptions from ethnography, grounded theory and hermeneutics were used to analyse and interpret the empirical data (see, for example, Gadamer 1960; Glaser and Strauss 1967; Ricoeur 1986). The qualitative analysis resulted in different types of significant categories and patterns, constituting a coherent whole of three narratives. Based on Ricoeur's

(1986) reasoning concerning narrative, I regard them as the students' narratives. The meaning of the students' thoughts and actions related to learning were given shape in the narratives. In order to provide 'thick descriptions' (Geertz 1973), the narratives were based on the interpretations of different kinds of data. The narratives were kept together by my words, underpinned by the students' 'voices' as quotations, extracts from diaries and written evaluations.

In the first narrative, the students tell their story of the interpretation and implementation of the planned curricula. In the second narrative, the students' characterization of their goal of becoming nurses is highlighted. The students pose and try to deal with questions about their learning. These processes of dealing with questions are described in the third narrative. A significant aspect of the students' narratives about learning was that they considered questions concerning their own learning. They seemed to see themselves as agents in the learning situation, considering both their own learning of a special content and the framework of the educational programme.

A theoretical analysis

Two dimensions appeared in the students' narratives. One dimension concerned how the students form conceptions about the relevance of learning objectives and how they go about learning a knowledge base in order to reach their objective of becoming nurses. The other dimension concerned the students' attempts to handle their learning process in relation to the actual framework of the educational programme. In order to understand the empirical results on a general level, further analysis of these dimensions was implemented, using theoretical frameworks from different perspectives. Central concepts derived from the theories were applied and interpreted in the analysis. This part of the analysis was an application of a theoretical 'reflective distance' compared with the interpretations resulting in the narratives (see Ricoeur 1986). The aims were to reflect on and try to distance the results from the specific context in order to find out whether they contained issues on a more general level concerning the problem area.

Summary of the results

The analysis and the results concerning the dimension of internal processes of learning form the basis of the discussion in this chapter. But before this I summarize the results of the other analysis – the students' attempts to handle their learning process in relation to the actual framework of the educational programme – as an awareness of these other findings is essential for understanding the discussion.

A main theme throughout the students' stories is that they consider and try to engage with questions concerning their own learning. I found that a significant source and driving force that makes the students consider these questions is a dialectic relationship between chaos and cosmos (Silén 2001). The characteristics of the questions in which students involve themselves are the teachers' traditional didactic (pedagogical) questions: what is to be learned, how it should be learned, why the students should learn certain things and what the objectives of the learning process are. The experiences of chaos and cosmos relate to the student's conceptions and experiences of being confronted with demands to be responsible and in charge of the learning situation. On the one hand, it causes frustration; on the other, it is stimulating. I believe the students' involvement in pedagogical questions is a basis for the students' responsibility and independence in learning. The students are learners but they also assume a role similar to that of a teacher in their learning process.

In my study (Silén 2000), the students' narratives were analysed from a didactic perspective (see Dahlgren 1990; Jank and Meyer 1997; Uljens 1997). One main question was: 'Who is in control of the educational setting forming the basis of the learning process – the teacher or the learner?' The students' narratives and the didactic theoretical analysis indicated a complicated relationship concerning the students' responsibility and independence and the structure of the educational framework. The students' conduct as regards their own responsibility and independence, *vis-à-vis* dependence, is related to the tension between the prerequisites provided by the educational framework and the students' interpretation and ability to use them. I consider this relationship to be important when trying to support the students in becoming responsible and independent (Silén 2003).

Responsibility, independence and learning of a content

The dimension of how the students form conceptions about the relevance of learning objectives and how they go about learning a knowledge base in order to reach their objective of becoming nurses was analysed on the basis of the learning theory described in *Learning and Awareness* by Marton and Booth (1997).

Learning and awareness: a theoretical perspective

According to Marton and Booth (1997), one dimension of learning is the aspects of *what* and *how*. The *what* aspect represents the object the individual learns, the direct object of learning. A direct object might be the ability to console a patient facing a severe loss. The *how* aspect represents the way the individual learns. Marton and Booth argue that the *how* dimension consists of acts and indirect objects of learning. Students do things in order to learn and the way they carry out the actions is connected to their intentions regarding what kind of capability in learning they want to achieve. The indirect objects are the objects at which the actions are aimed. In the above example of consoling a patient, an indirect object might be to imitate an experienced nurse. The actions employed to achieve this could be to observe a nurse in practice. Another indirect object might be a deep understanding of this kind of situation. The actions then may be characterized by a combination of observations, asking questions and studying literature about crises and practice. The *what* and *how* aspects are intertwined and impossible to separate in a real learning process. As a basis of research, Marton and Booth argue that they can be studied one at a time. In my research, I focused on the *how* dimension. This means that I have tried to analyse what actions and indirect objects the students were describing in the narratives. I did not analyse the direct objects; that is to say, the direct learning. In order to reason about the *how* aspect, I have found that I needed to incorporate the students' concepts about a direct object. I designated this as a 'possible learning object'.

According to Marton and Booth, the basis of learning is to experience something. A necessary starting point for learning is the discernment of an object. The learner has to discern the object in its environment, the context, and to be able to 'see' it and 'experience' it in terms of a learning object. This discernment requires a structure, the parts and boundaries of the object, and a meaning, attached to the object. What we discern depends on our pre-understanding (conceptions, attitudes, knowledge). Basic to this view of learning is that learning is always contextual. Learning is experiences related to situations and phenomena. This is expressed in the following quote:

> That nobody can experience a phenomenon in the absence of a situation is strongly intuitive. That a situation can be experienced only in terms of that which transcends it, follows from our ability to make sense of the here and now only through the experiences which precede it. The here and now is experienced in terms which link it with the past and reflect experienced similarities, differences or both. We refer to the wholeness of what we experience to be simultaneously present as a *situation*, whereas we call entities that transcend the situation, which link it with other situations and lend meaning to it, *phenomena.*
>
> (Marton and Booth 1997: 83)

The concepts I used in my analysis and that I discuss here are *what, how,* acts, indirect object, direct object, discernment and structural and referential aspects. They were systematically applied to and interpreted in relation to the students' narratives.

Findings

The analysis of the students' narratives using concepts from this theoretical perspective reveals some interesting aspects. Four indirect objects distinguished by different characteristics appeared. Two of them were related to learning the content and two related to the educational situation. In the next section I discuss the indirect objects and actions concerning the content. The two indirect objects related to the framework of the educational programme have been presented elsewhere (Silén 2003). One of the latter indirect objects is directed towards apprehending the demands the students believe the system places on them. The other indirect object is directed towards planning and structuring their learning situation. These two indirect objects can be characterized by responsibility and independence – that is, their own choices and decisions – but might also turn into the opposite: dependence.

The indirect object of understanding

One indirect object concerning the content related to the students' attempts to understand and handle the situations with which they were confronted. Their actions, the choices they made in their learning process as they tried to reach their 'possible' direct objects (goals), were similar to those that would be chosen to take a deep approach in learning. The concept of understanding means different things for the students, from being able to translate words to having insights into complex relationships. The objective of being able to perform in and handle a situation connected to being a nurse varies from simple skills up to informed awareness integrated in the actions of nursing. These actions appear in the way the student uses or wishes to use different learning situations, like the work in the base group, assignments, seminars and lectures. The students' actions in the ward and their studies for an examination also reflect these intentions, the indirect objective being to be able to handle the situation.

The indirect object of discernment on a meta level

The second indirect object is related to the indirect object of understanding. The actions are very similar, but the intention is qualitatively different. It appears that the students have the intention to master the discernment of meaningful situations and phenomena within the study programme and the context of nursing. This discernment concerns a comprehensive level, a meta level of the content. In the following quotations, two students describe their thoughts about and choices of learning objects:

The things we are studying at the moment ... they are really about things one should be able to apply when one becomes a nurse. Some things we studied before, OK, they were 'nursing things', but some of them were difficult to connect to the nursing profession ... but now, I'm studying this because I realize I can use it as a nurse. (Stina)

I have learned more from one semester to another how to study ... Perhaps I have learned more about an appropriate level for my studies ... In the first and second semester, I studied a subject in depth, and then I realized ... well, no, this is probably not so relevant for me as a future nurse. The area was relevant but I had studied too deep ... it is impossible to remember and it was not what is discussed in a ward. (Lilian)

This process of discernment involves the students making choices and decisions about 'possible learning objects'. Their intentions are to find out if certain phenomena and situations are important and significant when it comes to the actual professional domain. They also try to find out in what aspects they are relevant and the underlying reasoning for making that kind of decision. They pose and try to answer questions like: what structure might a learning object have, what constitutes the whole, what are the parts and how are they related, what is incorporated and what is not? Questions concerning the referential aspects are also present. What is the meaning of the object, what makes it relevant in this context? The students try to discern and understand the structure and meaning of the context of nursing related to other professions and different subjects involved. They also try to discern the relationship between theoretical studies and practical nursing work. This includes a search to understand the educational framework in relation to what they experience in the practical part of their education:

CS: You think that you have learned quite a lot during the semester?
Student: Yes, I have been able to apply what I know in a way I couldn't do before. To be aware of the relationship, like the one about the heart and the blood vessels ... I read about it the previous semester, but now I have seen it in reality, like in the emergency ward ... I can get it together in another way now ...

They compare their conceptions with different kinds of sources, like peers, facilitators, lecturers, nurse models and literature. The intention is to visualize and create a picture of 'possible learning objects', understand what they mean and decide whether they are a part of their education and their future professional domain. Their aim is to understand what the professional domain means on a meta level. This indirect object is to some extent a prerequisite of the indirect object of understanding, described above. The students have to make choices and decisions about what they believe is important to understand and handle as nurses, as a starting point for the learning process connected to their intention to understand. This discernment is an active part of the students' learning process, they think about it and they want to understand the underlying structures and references of their discernment in the context of becoming nurses:

> CS: When you make choices about what to study ... how do you think about it?
>
> *Student:* Well, I try to think like this. For example, about diabetes ... I thought hyperglycaemia and ketoacidosis, they must be important. It is a very serious condition for the patient. ... but when it comes to different drugs used to treat ulcers ... perhaps that is something that I can learn more about when I come across a situation where this comes up.

As described above, the students use different strategies (actions) to achieve the indirect object of discernment on a meta level. Actions related to discernment are characterized by the students' own activity, initiative and search for opportunities to reflect and cooperate. The base group is a forum for choices, priorities and judging the relevance of studying a possible content. Together, students try to find the outlines and meaning of situations and phenomena and their relevance in a wider perspective. The students listen to each other, try to interpret the reality-based situations and are very concerned about formulating questions that can guide their studies. A student says the following about the work in the base group:

> It is important to discuss what you have studied and if you have questions. It works quite well I think [in the group]. You get feedback about your own studies. You can hear what others have chosen to study, and you can bring up your thoughts and discuss things you have found unclear. (Astrid)

The learning resources the students use are scrutinized in different ways: the relevance of the source, how to make delimitations based on the information given, finding out about structures, what appears to be essential, what reappears as important and what the connections are between different sources. In this process, the students use peers and the base group and look for signs from the educational framework (objectives, assignments, exams):

> In the base group, you discuss questions arising from your own studies ... There are different things you find important and the same thing is dealt with differently in different books. (Moa)

> I read about diabetes in *Medical Care and Specific Nursing Care* and *Internal Medicine* ... I also borrowed *Clinical Nurse*, I think that one is worth its weight in gold, it deals with nursing care in a natural way. (Ellen)

Students consider lectures an important factor in their attempt to discern 'possible learning objects'. The characteristics of the actions are different from the processing in the base group and the students search for and scrutinize learning resources. Lectures seem to provide the students with 'possible learning objects' without the need for the students to consider and judge their relevance. They are regarded as credible sources for not missing important elements and guidance for how much detail they need to study. The students use them in a learning process that leads to their ability to discern, but in which they are not very active themselves. A student says about lectures:

> I take a lot of notes during lectures. They [the lectures] can show the appropriate level for the studies ... usually they do. When I study, I use them to check the level ... this is what I am supposed to know. (Kristina.)

The practical part of the education seems to be very important for actions connected to the indirect object of discerning on a meta level. The events the students take part in and what they observe are used as references for judging the relevance of meaningful 'possible learning objects'. Even so, the students' discernment of learning objects in practice is much less complicated compared with the situations processed in the base groups. The students meet nurses who perform what they themselves want to be able to do. This makes it possible for them to compare their thoughts with a concrete context directly and they get instant feedback if they act. If the students believe that they get the same messages from the nurses and the representatives of the study programme, they use them to increase their confidence as regards being able to discern on a meta level. If not, they seem to judge the nurses' versions as more reliable.

I would argue that the intention of becoming aware of and judging 'possible learning objects' is not only a starting point for learning, but also emerges as part of a significant learning process. This learning process might lead to learning outcomes representing metacognitive knowledge and metacognitive awareness of the professional domain and related contexts. Boekaerts (1997) builds on studies carried out by Flavell (1987) and describes metacognitive knowledge of a domain (discipline, subject) as an important prerequisite of self-regulation in learning. She describes metacognitive knowledge as attitudes, convictions and values concerning the content within a domain. Metacognitive knowledge also includes ability, skills and conceptions about the core and objectives. The meta level of discernment might lead to metacognitive awareness of the structure of a discipline/subject, a profession and/or a community of practice.

Conclusion

The focus for this chapter has been on the 'discovery' of a dimension in learning that I believe has not been highlighted before in connection with problem-based learning. I have described a meta level of discernment that comes to the fore in the students' narratives about being learners in a problem-based learning context. The students consider the structures and meanings of their professional domain. They do so in order to grasp what they need to learn. In so doing, they inquire into the content of different subjects, searching for facts they consider necessary in their learning to become nurses. In this process they also try to sort out the borders of their own area in relation to other professions. They compare their conceptions of being a nurse to other professions and related contexts.

The source of the students' actions and conceptions is their experience of facing the challenge to be responsible and independent in their learning process. The metaphor for this has been described as the dialectic relationship between chaos and cosmos. The experiences of the dialectic relationship between frustration and stimulation make the students consider the educational context of which that they are a part. On the basis of the students' feelings that the learning objects are very indistinct, they try to figure out for themselves what the 'possible' learning objects might be. Through active participation, making choices, judging relevance and forming positions, they try to understand the characteristics of the professional domain.

Apart from relevance being a driving force in learning (see Marton and Booth 1997), my analysis shows that the ability to judge relevance also appears to become a learning object for the students. The students' intention to discern on a meta level is based on judgements of relevance. The students describe how they try to gain insight and judge whether there are meaningful relations between what they study and the profession or a special subject. They themselves feel that they ought to discern and make choices about what they need to learn to become nurses. They compare the objectives of their courses, assignments and exams with the pictures they get of the work of nurses in the field.

If the boundaries and the meaning of subjects or a profession were well structured and presented by authorities on subjects (in lectures, for example) or in the profession, this inquiry into a meta level might never occur. The students would not have to think about and elaborate on it and they might take the choices made by the authorities for granted. It is the uncertainty about what to study that creates the indirect object of discernment on a meta level. A balance between uncertainty and the feeling of being able to handle the situation is very important. Otherwise, the frustration of not knowing what to study might instead turn into dependence and cue seeking (Silén 2001, 2003).

Note

1 'A scholarship of teaching is not synonymous with excellent teaching. It requires a kind of "going meta" in which faculty frames and systematically investigates questions related to student learning' (Hutchings and Shulman 1999: 13).

Part 4

Comparative Issues

This final part of the book explores some of the comparative issues related to problem-based learning. There has been a wealth of studies that have sought to compare a range of different issues and concerns in the field of problem-based learning. These range from comparisons about student capabilities and student performance through to more recent discussions about students' experiences and disciplinary differences. Much of the early work on comparisons relating to problem-based learning explored the similarities and differences between lecture-based learning and problem-based learning. However, although we do offer one such comparison in Chapter 12, by Bowe and Cowan, we also focus here on a comparison in the use of problem-based learning in terms of disciplinary differences in Chapter 13, by Hutchings and O'Rourke. We then compare tutors' experiences in Chapter 14, examining the extent to which the discipline where problem-based learning has been placed impacts on the way problem-based learning is played out in practice.

The early comparative work such as that undertaken by Coles (1985) and Newble and Clarke (1986) used the Approaches to Studying Inventory developed by Entwistle to verify that problem-based learning students were more likely to use deep approaches to learning than surface approaches. Such studies have focused on the nature of student learning and, in particular, the idea that some styles of learning are preferred over others by students. What follows is an assumption that if we design curricula in ways that fit with a variety of styles, then this may help to improve students' achievement within a programme. In more recent years there has been critique of learning inventories that decontextualize learner and learning (for example, Savin-Baden 2000a; Haggis 2002), and that focus on particular characteristics of the learner rather than the person themselves. Haggis (2002) has suggested that, over time, the huge focus by the academe on the notion of deep and surface approaches to learning (from the study by Marton and Säljö 1984) has resulted in assumptions being made that this study had described a highly significant set of relationships about how students learn. This has led to the promotion of types of learning environments that are expected to enhance deep approaches to learning; and in many cases this has meant the adoption of problem-based approaches. Although learners may change their approach according to their conception of the learning task, there is still an assumption that deep approaches are somehow necessarily better.

Many authors continue to suggest that problem-based learning promotes deep approaches (as opposed to surface or strategic approaches) to learning, the underlying assumption being that this is necessarily a good thing. There does appear to be some conflict around the notion of developing a deep approach, in that approaches are difficult to change and in many instances surface approaches can result in very successful learning. Other studies have compared the effectiveness of problem-based and traditional curricula on developing lifelong learning skills. Several of these studies have specifically looked at clinical performance as a demonstration of these skills, and in most cases, problem-based learning students performed better than traditional learning students (Albanese and Mitchell 1993; Vernon and Blake 1993). Students who acquired knowledge in the context of solving problems were more likely to use it spontaneously to solve new problems than individuals who acquired the same information under the more traditional methods of learning facts and concepts through lectures (Bransford *et al.* 1989). In addition, it has been suggested that students in problem-based learning environments developed stronger clinical competencies, although the differences were small and non-significant (de Vries *et al.* 1989). Furthermore, Moore *et al.* (1994) reported a statistically significant difference on an ethics problem-solving task undertaken with Harvard medical students. Another study conducted on a nutrition and dietetics course found that problem-based learning students perceived they developed stronger thinking and problem-solving skills than traditional learning students (Lieux 1996).

The interest in disciplinary differences in the use of problem-based learning is still largely under-researched in this field, but there is growing interest. Disciplinary culture tends to exert a strong influence on both students' learning and curricula design, since curricula are established on existing understandings about the nature of knowledge and how it should be organized. Thus many tutors often have stronger allegiances to their disciplines than they have to their institutions and to other tutors on campus. This is in part because of the professionalization of tutors, who have become so specialized in their fields that they may well have more in common with their counterparts in other countries than with individuals at home. Culture affects teaching practices and thus learning and assessment differ depending upon the nature of the discipline. For example, mathematics and other related subjects tend to focus on general problem-solving and the need for correct answers. At first glance it may seem that a shift to problem-based learning will not be difficult. However, Bowe and Cowan have reported that the shift from problem-solving to problem-based learning in physics was a complex disciplinary shift for both tutors and students. In addition, in the professions, it is easy to picture what kind of problem a professional might face, so it is not a huge leap to develop a problem.

In their chapter Bowe and Cowan present the findings of a formative evaluation of a problem-based learning programme in physics. The evaluation was used to determine the effects on the learning process of important elements of the course, namely the curriculum design, induction, assessment and problems. The evaluation strategy of generating immediate findings thus allowed the problem-based learning tutors to make significant enhancements to the course, without delay, thus benefiting the current cohort. The findings of the study illustrate that it is important to have a clear understanding of the distinction between learning via problem-*solving* and problem-*based* learning. In engineering and physics the use of problem-solving learning is well established. In this method the students are first presented with the material, usually in the form of a lecture; and are then given sheets of 'problems' to solve. These problems are narrow in focus, test a restricted set of learning outcomes, usually do not assess other key skills and call for a concentration on the mastery and use of standard algorithmic procedures. The evaluation indicates that problem-based learning can be successfully introduced into the first year of undergraduate study if it is facilitated correctly and if the tutors are aware that the students are only in the early stages of developing as self-directed learners.

In English literature, collaborative learning may be fairly common, so the shift to using problem-based learning is often easier, but the models of group work and problems management suggested by proponents such as Barrows and Tamblyn (1980) may also seem too restricting for those accustomed to flexible learning patterns where critique is central to disciplinary learning. Yet the growth in the use of problem-based learning has arguably been slower in arts and humanities, perhaps because of the challenges of adapting the classical model to these subjects. Certainly Hutchings and O'Rourke's work as presented in Chapter 13 here suggests that 'literary studies is essentially a discursive, open-ended, critically contested, responsive and creative subject that challenges students and encourages them to find their own intellectual pathways.' In their chapter Hutchings and O'Rourke examine how existing problem-based learning paradigms may be adapted to suit the needs of disciplines not associated with problem-based learning practices, taking literary studies as its principal example. It undertakes a philosophical study into the extent to which the nature of the subject, the problems appropriate to it and the kinds of students who are attracted to study it may affect the problem-based learning process. The chapter evaluates the implementation of problem-based learning over a three-year period in the delivery of selected literary studies courses in the Department of English and American Studies at the University of Manchester.

The findings indicate that any imposition of a rigid structure in terms of specific responsibilities within the groups was counter-productive in the context of the discipline. Students' stories illustrated the findings, in that the students themselves rejected the constraints imposed by such defined roles as those suggested by the literature; for example, the whole-group problem-based learning processes as developed by the University of Maastricht (Netherlands) and McMaster University (Canada).

In the final chapter we bring together two pieces of research that explored tutors' changing roles and relationships in the context of problem-based learning. In particular we examine the impact of discipline-based pedagogy on staff and the changes that staff experienced as they became expert facilitators. Surprisingly few studies have focused on tutors' outcomes or experiences with problem-based learning. Studies conducted by Major and Palmer (2002a) showed that tutors who move from traditional teaching to a problem-based learning environment do change their knowledge levels in several important ways. For example, they change their views of themselves as teachers, shifting away from an authoritarian perspective. In addition, facilitators change their views of their students, coming to accept them as peers and professionals. Facilitators change their knowledge of their fields, starting to see inter- and intra-disciplinary connections of which they had been unaware previously. Finally, they change their knowledge of instructional methods and strategies, expressing the value of educational techniques such as scaffolding.

It is interesting to note that tutors who are familiar with problem-based learning favour it over other methods. For example, Dahlgren *et al.* (1998) found that tutors' perceptions of their roles influenced their levels of satisfaction: tutors who perceived themselves as supporters, those who emphasised the responsibilities of the students and those who spent more time on group process were all more satisfied with the problem-based learning experience than those who instead viewed themselves as directors.

Thus, although there has been increasing interest and research into staff experiences of problem-based learning in the past ten years, there has been little examination of the impact of the discipline on the way problem-based learning is implemented and enacted. In this final chapter we use interpretive meta ethnography to integrate the findings of two qualitative studies that explored staff experiences of problem-based learning in the same discipline. The findings indicate themes relating to changes in role perception through the process and experience of becoming facilitators, shifts in views about the nature of power and control in the learning environment, and the impact of the discipline on the way problem-based learning is played out in practice. We suggest that future inquiry is needed into: the impact of staff pedagogical knowledge in problem-based learning; what it is that is meant by learning, and by whom; and the changes in disciplinary constructions when problem-based learning is being used.

12

A Comparative Evaluation of Problem-based Learning in Physics: A Lecture-based Course and a Problem-based Course

Brian Bowe, with John Cowan

Introduction

In 2001 I engaged in collaborative action research in order to design, implement and evaluate a first year physics problem-based learning course. The research included formative evaluation and reflection that informed all decisions pertaining to any subsequent developments. In order to evaluate this course both quantitative and qualitative data were collected and John Cowan, as external evaluator, helped to conduct a comparative study with a lecture-based course. The aim of this research was to address the problems of decreasing student numbers in science and student retention, and to develop a course that would attract students to physics by providing a supportive student-centred learning environment in which students could learn in context and develop as self-directed learners.

Background

Physical science education currently faces a crisis as each year fewer students choose to pursue science in undergraduate studies (Irish Government 2002). This has led science educators in tertiary education to take a critical look at what and how is taught (Institute of Physics 2001). Since 1999 the School of Physics in the Dublin Institute of Technology (DIT) has been critically analysing its pedagogical strategy, leading to a reconsideration of teaching and assessment practices. This has led to staff awareness of the importance and potential of student-centred and active learning, and specifically to the development and introduction of a physics problem-based learning course in 2001.

Although the reasons for changing to problem-based learning were primarily pedagogical, another factor was the increased importance that industry was putting on the key skills whose development is inherent in the problem-based learning process. The effects of fewer students choosing to pursue physics at all levels of education have also led to a reduction in students' academic qualifications entering tertiary level, followed by poor attendance in lectures, lack of motivation and high dropout rates.

The problem-based learning course was developed to address these problems and make the subject more appealing to entrants. However, in changing our whole approach to teaching and learning, we had to ensure that the course standard and quality was maintained. The primary bene-factors of this innovation had to be the students, and its success had to be measured in terms of their learning and learning experiences. Therefore the course team developed an evaluation strategy that concentrated on the students, their knowledge and their skill-based learning outcomes. This strategy, which was both formative and summative, included a comparative evaluation of the problem-based learning course and a parallel lecture-based course. This chapter charts the development and implementation of the problem-based learning physics course and describes the evaluation process and initial findings.

In September 2001 the School of Physics in DIT launched a problem-based learning first year physics course in the degree in applied sciences (Bowe 2001a). From the onset there was great interest from other teachers within DIT, and from physics educators outside DIT. In October 2001, John Cowan agreed to act as an external evaluator, and has contributed to this chapter in that role.

The physics problem-based learning course

In May 2001 the problem-based learning team began the process of developing the problem-based learning physics course. There were a number of pedagogical questions that needed to be addressed early in the process; for instance, the issues of content coverage and subject and practical work integration. The course team also decided against integrating the topics within physics and so kept mechanics, optics and so on separate from one another, since these subjects' students were inexperienced in problem-based learning and some also had no prior physics knowledge.

Other than the move to problem-based learning, the most significant change made was to the assessment strategy. This had comprised summative tests and examinations. However, as the problem-based learning team was aware of the vital role of the hidden curriculum (Margolis 2001) in driving the learning and actually determining what is 'covered' by the student, particular attention was paid to the assessment strategy. The team was also aware that the assessment methodologies could determine whether students would choose a surface or deep learning approach (Marton *et al.* 1984). The assessment strategy attempts to encourage the latter, includes both formative and summative methods and allows for extensive feedback.

Research (Taylor and Burgess 1995) has shown that students starting a problem-based learning course for the first time are at different stages of readiness for self-directed learning. It was believed they would benefit from an induction course that highlighted: the lecturers' expectation for self-directed learning; the role of the facilitator; the principles and practices of learning in groups; and issues of time management. In order to address these findings, an induction programme was developed in the School of Physics that introduced and explained the problem-based learning rationale and philosophy, the teaching methodology, assessment strategies and the learning resources that were available to the students. Further workshops were arranged throughout the year to deal with group dynamics and assessment.

Research carried out in Maastricht University (Gijselaers 1996) showed that the most important elements for a successful problem-based learning course were the problems and the tutors. In designing the problems for this course, the team started by listing the intended learning outcomes, and then developing appropriate problems that would stimulate the students to achieve those outcomes. The first year physics syllabus is covered by approximately 30 problems that are 'real' and engaging, place the group in a 'professional' role and require the students to make assumptions and approximations and to deal with omitted information.

In the problem-based learning activity itself, a typical group size is six students; and at the start of the year each group will have a tutor observing the process and acting as facilitator. The students are usually presented with one trigger problem per week, and have two or three two-hour problem-based learning group sessions to work on these with (initially) a tutor present. The students are also expected to work on their individual tasks outside class time. At first the idea of a physics problem with no one correct answer or solving strategy inhibits the students' learning. The process at first seems very chaotic and confusing to them, and to new tutors, but it is by working through this introductory stage that the students develop a purposeful approach to problem-based learning, and hence develop a real understanding of the subject.

The students stay in the same groups for up to seven weeks, so it is important that the ground rules will address any problems they may have. For each problem they delegate (in rotation) roles of chair and recorder before they begin the problem. Initially the students use the 'four columns' technique where they list the facts, ideas, learning issues and tasks (Barrows and Tamblyn 1980).

After a few problems the students become more aware of their roles and of the expectations the tutors have of them as individuals and as group members. The group is continuously assessed and the students are given regular feedback. A complete set of assessment criteria for the group process was developed at the outset, and includes such factors as the individual level of contribution, peer-teaching, questioning and completion of group-assigned tasks. Based on these criteria, each student is given a mark by the tutor for their work and these marks are supported with extensive feedback.

Collaborative assessment is introduced about halfway through the academic year. The students attend a workshop where the rationale and objectives of self-assessment are explained, followed by a negotiation of the assessment criteria. From this point on, after each problem, each student is required to self-assess their own contribution to the group process and award a reasoned mark, a justification for that mark, explain where they lost marks and describe what they will do differently in the next problem session. The tutors also continue to award a mark with feedback, and the average of these two marks goes towards the summative assessment.

Upon completion of a problem, the group produces a report or gives a presentation, both of which have detailed assessment criteria. This continuous assessment and feedback process is designed to assist student learning and promote deep learning. To augment this process, a WebCT on-line learning resource centre was developed, which includes on-line tutorials, assignments, quizzes, individual students' feedback pages, calendar, noticeboard and details of the laboratory project programme (Bowe 2001b). The feedback from both the formative and summative assessments is provided through the WebCT site. The students are also required to complete regular on-line multiple-choice quizzes as part of the overall continuous assessment. There is also an end of year examination that is open book, and involves the testing of the students' abilities to problem-solve, as well as their understanding of the physics concepts.

Evaluation

The problem-based learning team had to ensure that the new course's quality matched that of the old. However, the enhancement of the provision through the introduction of other learning outcomes was also felt worthy of attention and recognition. Therefore, the team developed an evaluation strategy that concentrated on the students' experiences and the total effects the course had on the students' knowledge and skill-based learning outcomes.

Formative evaluation (George and Cowan 1999) should be an essential step in any curriculum development process, as it is necessary to enhance and develop the course systematically and comprehensively. The evaluation was a comparison between aims, objectives and learning outcomes on the one hand, and the reality of student learning and development on the other. However, as this innovation had made substantial changes in the school's traditional pedagogical approach, there was also a particular need for formative evaluation in order to discover areas where improvements could still be made to improve the learning process and environment. In this case the changes in approach had apparently also led to new and valuable learning outcomes not associated with lecture-based teaching. It was therefore necessary to evaluate thoroughly – for the purpose of identifying, and determining the extent of, these new learning outcomes and to identify their scope and means of further enhancement. It was also the team's purpose to obtain reliable and triangulated data that would inform their decisions for refinement, and minimize the occurrence of intuitive and subjective decision-making.

Before the problem-based learning development, the school's approach concentrated on the assimilation of content, and the learning outcomes therefore centred on knowledge of the principles and concepts, and their application in routine computations. In the problem-based learning approach, the emphasis has changed to the application of these principles and concepts, and to genuine if modest problem-solving. To evaluate the students' learning experience, the team depends on a sound assessment strategy. It was decided that the fulfilment of the learning outcomes that are physics-content specific could be evaluated through the use of traditional assessments, such as individual examinations. These could also be used to compare the levels of fulfilment between the problem-based learning and the lecture-based courses. However, the team envisaged deeper conceptual understanding and new physics learning outcomes arising due to the nature of the student-centred learning. The evaluation would first have to identify these enhanced outcomes before the team could properly assess the extent to which they were fulfilled. There was also the issue of the development of personal and professional skills, which are also assessed or otherwise identified through, for instance, interviews.

Evaluation strategy

As mentioned in the introduction, the evaluation strategy formed part of an overall action research plan. The aim of this research was to develop a new physics course, that would provide a supportive student-centred learning environment. The action research devised certain aspects of the course, such as assessment and teaching methodologies, and evaluated their effects on the students' learning experience. From analysis of this evaluation and reflection on both staff and tutor activities, subsequent changes were made to the course in order to enhance and develop it further. This was a cyclic process in that the formative evaluation was repeated through the first year of the course. The evaluation combined both qualitative and quantitative research methods in order to triangulate the data so as to ensure the credibility of the conclusions. The evaluation strategy aimed to ascertain the effects problem-based learning has on the students, their learning and their learning experience, in terms of effective professional and personal development.

The methods of data collection used were questionnaires, interviews, focus groups, examination results, attendance records and the course documentation itself. It also involved a comparative study of a lecture-based course and the problem-based course. Specifically, the evaluation strategy comprised the following:

1. Evaluation by an independent *external evaluator.* This encompassed consideration of data derived under the headings 'comparison of performances', 'alignment matrices' and 'student evaluation and feedback', as well as the observations to which reference has already been made, and interviews with problem-based learning and traditional students.
2. *Comparison of performances* with those on a traditional lecture-based course, based upon outcomes covered within the traditional course. This part of the evaluation should confirm adequacy of coverage of the learning outcomes realized in the lecture-based course.
3. Compilation and analysis of an *alignment matrix* (Biggs 1999; Cowan 2002). On advice from the evaluator in May 2002, the problem-based learning staff team decided to compile and compare alignment matrices. In these matrices, learning outcomes, assessment and its rationale, and the facilitation of this learning are expected to match each other in a pedagogically sound manner. Thus the outcomes, assessment and teaching practices should be compatible, as a mismatch can lead to confusion, misdirection and poor learning. This investigation should also serve to check on the problem-based learning coverage, identifying explicit and implicit outcomes that featured within the problem-based learning provision, enabling checks on the coverage there as well as of the traditional outcomes. The learning outcomes of the problem-based learning course were identified as subject specific content and skills, personal development and the development of key skills, such as the ability: to work in, and effectively manage, groups; to present and communicate knowledge; to retrieve and critically analyse information; and to formulate a problem-solving strategy.
4. *Student evaluation and feedback.* This source of data, coupled with the evaluator's interviews, should enable a sound picture to be assembled of the nature and quality of the learning experience for the problem-based learning students. As one of the main reasons for developing the problem-based learning course had been to deal with the problem of motivation and lack of interest, we also compared attendance and application and, from the interviews, the level of interest in not only the physics but, more importantly, the students' own learning. Students were asked to fill out questionnaires midway through the year and at the end of the year. The questionnaires consisted of qualitative open-ended questions, as well as quantitative multiple choice and rank order questions. The two questionnaires contained a number of identical questions relating to aspects of the problem-based learning process,

such as group dynamics, assessment and their learning resources. This made it possible to see if student perceptions or opinions changed during the year. The analysis of the questionnaire data was used to inform the questions used in the interviews at the end of the year.

Before the problem-based learning course was launched, first year science students were lectured alongside computer science students for the physics element. When the pilot was launched, the computer science students remained on the lecture-based course while the science students began the problem-based learning physics course. These two groups of students had very similar profiles in terms of age, prior knowledge of physics, gender and academic qualifications.

Findings

Observations and interviews

In December 2001, the evaluator (who had played no part in the planning and delivery of the course) visited the School of Physics to view all course documentation, talk to staff and students involved in both the problem-based learning and lecture-based course, and observe groups in action. The purpose of this was mainly to get an initial impression of the course, to inform the subsequent research methods and to compare the students from both courses in terms of motivation and satisfaction. As the course was then only three months old, the staff team was keen to gain initial feedback that could lead to improvements.

Analysis of the data from the various sources found that, despite identical syllabi, the learning outcomes of the problem-based course appeared to be considerably in advance of those of the lecture-based course, because of the way the material was presented, since student learning through the analysis and resolution of problems resulted in a deeper understanding of the material. The problem-based course also developed problem-solving skills, and its assessment strategy forced students to consider what they were doing and how they were contributing to the group process, thus developing group and communication skills. It was also very clear that at this early stage student motivation and satisfaction in the problem-based course were high, and that they were well resourced, and appreciated the thought that had gone into this aspect of planning and provision. During the induction process, and in a subsequent workshop, the staff team had paid particular attention to the assessment strategy. Analysis showed the assessment scheme and its judgements were strongly endorsed by the students. It also showed that the problems were not too restrictive; they enabled progress with open-ended problem-solving and deep conceptual understanding – within a tight time scale – while providing enough structure to ensure progress.

The evaluator returned in May 2002. Together with a member of the

School of Physics staff who had had no involvement with the problem-based learning course, he interviewed students individually. The purpose of the interviews was to obtain further information regarding the nature of the learning experience within the problem-based learning course, and to compare that with the experience of an admittedly small sample of traditionally taught students. The findings of these interviews were summarized by the evaluator, with careful emphasis on the nature of the experience for problem-based learning students, highlighted where this had appeared either noteworthy or in contrast to that reported by the traditionally taught students.

The interviews consisted of qualitative questions regarding the students' perceptions and opinions of physics, their learning, the learning environment and the course structure. They provided the opportunity to evaluate the students' communications skills, their ability to articulate their opinions and their motivation and enthusiasm for physics and learning. Analysis of the interview data by the evaluator led to the following conclusions:

1. The problem-based learning students exhibited, in interviews, discussions and group working, a liveliness and articulateness that was noteworthy. Questioned about this, the students were keenly aware that the activities of the problem-based learning course had led to significant development in their interpersonal and communication skills.

2. The motivation and enthusiasm of the problem-based learning students for their course experience emerged naturally, without the matter being raised. Clearly they enjoyed their learning, though they did not deny that it was at times 'tough'.

3. Understanding of concepts had developed through the group activities, and was retained so effectively that the students did not anticipate having to revise physics for the exams with anything like the intensity in their other, traditionally taught, courses.

4. The perceptions that problem-based learning and traditionally taught students expressed of the nature of physics as a discipline were fairly similar.

5. The problem-based learning students saw their activity, and the abilities that they developed and could subsequently use and display, as essentially in the area of problem-solving. The traditionally taught students, in contrast, described learning expressed as the ability to deal with algorithmic questions of a fairly standard form.

6. The problem-based learning students spoke of lecturers who provided very little in the way of instructional input, other than at the outset on method, and on the occasions when a group was well and truly bogged down, or going off in a totally wrong direction. They described, although they did not use the term, a facilitative style of teaching.

7. The problem-based learning students made much use of resources from the Internet and otherwise. The traditionally taught students relied much more on lecture notes and handouts.

8. Problem-based learning students stressed the importance of the group: of group roles, of the linking in of individual learning, and of responsibility for the learning of the others in the group.
9. The problem-based learning students were aware of maturing markedly over the year. They spoke without prompting of this, persuasively identifying not only the ways in which they had developed but the part that their problem-based learning activity had played.
10. A refreshing element in discussions with the problem-based learning students was their awareness, in their own terms, of the practical pedagogy that was contributing to their development.

A complementary analysis by the course team of questionnaire data and reporting back from students expresses many of these points. Analysis showed that the problem-based learning students are more motivated, have a 100 per cent class retention rate (defined as completing the year), as compared with 66 per cent for the traditionally taught students, and are more willing to interact with the teaching staff. The students found the problem-based learning course to be fun, interesting, challenging and motivating and wondered why problem-based learning was not used more extensively. The major problems they had were related to group work and their inexperience of working in groups. They were unsure about coping with conflict and students failing to undertake assigned tasks.

Comparisons of end-of-year performance

To date it is the team's and the evaluator's experience that problem-based learning suits first year physics students of all abilities, regardless of prior knowledge. The pass rates in problem-based learning physics at the end of first year were very high and a marked improvement on previous years, even though performance was assessed in an open book examination that the students found very challenging, because they were faced with complex problems that they had not seen before. Two external physics educators both said this open book paper was very difficult, and certainly more difficult than traditional papers. In the open book examination, the students cannot rely on memorization but instead have to use their problem-solving abilities, analytical skills and understanding of the physics concepts.

In addition, the problem-based learning students achieved much higher scores than their counterparts when both were given the same hour-long traditional examination. The initial evaluation thus shows that the problem-based learning students exceed the lecture-based students in their understanding of physics concepts, their achievement in standard physics tests, the development of their key skills and their ability to work in groups.

The alignment matrices

As data from the questionnaires, interviews and focus groups were analysed, it was possible to complete a full list of learning outcomes for the course. The alignment matrix was used to ensure that there were compatible teaching practices and assessments for all the learning outcomes. The interviews in particular highlighted learning outcomes such as those relating to communication or interpersonal skills that were not previously mentioned in the course documentation. The alignment matrix allowed the staff team to ensure that both the expected and newly identified learning outcomes were being explicitly taught and were part of the formative assessment strategy, and also made it possible to compare the learning outcomes, teaching practices and assessment strategies of both the traditional and problem-based courses. As suspected, analysis and comparison of the alignment matrices indicated coverage within the problem-based learning course of the implicit, unlisted outcomes of the traditional provision; and of a considerable number of extra explicit and implicit learning outcomes, at a higher level in the cognitive and interpersonal domains.

Questionnaires and other opportunities for feedback

The questionnaires consisted of qualitative open-ended questions as well as quantitative multiple choice and rank order questions. The fact that the students completed two questionnaires at different times in the year made it possible to see whether student perceptions or opinions changed, which could then be explored in the interviews. Analysis of the questionnaires' data reinforced what had already been concluded from the interviews and focus groups. Analysis showed that students' motivation levels for physics were higher than those for other lecture-based subjects they attended. Students enjoyed the problem-based learning course, with comments such as 'having fun learning' being typical. This is important, as studies have shown that lack of student motivation is a key contributor to poor student retention in science in higher education (DIT Student Retention Office 2003). It was important to show that the students were enjoying the learning experience and therefore interacting with their learning resources. As it was insufficient to use attendance records to represent student motivation and application, many questions in both the interviews and questionnaires related to this. The students mainly attributed their high motivation to the type of problems ('the real-life problems are more interesting and challenging') and the group interaction and dynamics ('it's great learning from each other').

Discussion

This research has direct implications for the international physics education community. It challenges current teaching practices, in that this problem-based physics course not only achieves the same learning outcomes as those reportedly achieved in traditional courses but addresses the following challenges physics educators are currently facing.

- The problem-based learning physics course ensures student motivation by providing a supportive student-centred learning environment. One of the recommendations made by the Physical Science Task Force to the Irish Government (2002) is to increase recruitment to science, engineering and technology courses and to improve the teaching and learning experience within science departments. The underpinning rationale for this is that quality is a driver of participation, integration and retention.
- Due to the changes in recent student profiles, students are not always sufficiently developed as self-directed learners to deal with the traditional didactic teaching methodologies in higher education. In the physics problem-based learning course the students develop the necessary skills to become self-directed learners.
- Lifelong learning skills are important and need to be developed in science education (OECD 1998). The evaluation of the problem-based learning course shows that the development of these skills is inherent in this learning environment.
- The results of the evaluation show that the course is successful in developing generic skills such as problem-solving, critical thinking, interpersonal and intrapersonal skills, all of whose importance has been stressed by the National Council for Educational Awards in Ireland (NCEA 1999).
- Other reports form the view that traditional science education is outmoded and often leads to rote learning without deeper understanding (Millar and Osborne 1998; Sjöberg 2001). Triangulation of the research data described in this chapter shows that the students have attained a deeper understanding of the physics concepts.
- Present assessment strategies implemented in science curricula do not promote higher-order skills and can allow students to do well without engaging them in any meaningful way. The assessment strategy outlined previously, which is both formative and summative, was specifically designed to promote and reward higher-order skills and engage the students in the learning process.

The outcomes of this research are directly and immediately relevant to other educators designing problem-based learning physics courses, or institutes involved in implementing elements of problem-based learning into physics curricula.

Until recently there had been a reluctance to introduce problem-based learning into physics courses due to the expressed (but seldom substantiated) view that the students require a sound body of knowledge and mathematical skills before they can be considered equipped to engage with this process. In responding to such judgements, it is fair to comment that many critical physics educators assume (incorrectly) that problem-based learning simply involves presenting the students with problems. It is important to have a clear understanding of the distinction between learning via problem-*solving* and problem-*based* learning. In engineering and physics the use of problem-solving learning is well established. In this method the students are first presented with the material, usually in the form of a lecture, and are then given sheets of 'problems' to solve. These problems are narrow in focus, test a restricted set of learning outcomes, usually do not assess other key skills and call for a concentration on the mastery and use of standard algorithmic procedures. The students do not get the opportunity to evaluate their knowledge or understanding, or to explore different approaches, or to link their learning with their own needs as learners. They have limited control over the pace or style of learning and this method tends to promote surface learning of standard procedures rather than deep conceptual learning. In another discipline (structural mechanics) Brohn and Cowan (1977; also Cowan 1980, 1983) have shown the fundamental differences between what they have called qualitative and quantitative understanding of engineering phenomena. Cowan (1982) has subsequently shown from recorded protocols that the former, as developed by problem-based learning, calls for a much higher and deeper grasp of concepts.

In problem-based learning the students determine their learning issues and develop their unique approach to solving the problem. The members of the group learn to structure their efforts and delegate tasks. Peer teaching and organizational skills are critical components of the process. Students learn to analyse their own and their fellow group members' learning processes; and, unlike in problem-solving learning, must engage with the complexity and ambiguities of real life problems. It is ideally suited for the development of key skills, such as the ability to work in a group, problem-solving, critique, improving personal learning, self-directed learning and communication.

Conclusion

I believe that it has been shown in the School of Physics that problem-based learning can be successfully introduced into the first year of undergraduate study if it is facilitated correctly and if the tutors are aware that students are in the early stages of developing as self-directed learners. This course addresses the challenges facing physics education throughout the world, while ensuring that course quality is both maintained and enhanced.

Acknowledgements

I wish to thank the School of Physics staff who were involved in the development and implementation of this problem-based course, Dr Siobhan Daly, Dr Robert Howard and Dr Cathal Flynn, and also the school management for supporting my endeavours and making this innovation possible. Finally, special thanks go to DIT's Learning and Teaching Centre and Learning Technology Team for their invaluable input.

13

Medical Studies to Literary Studies: Adapting Paradigms of Problem-based Learning Process for New Disciplines

Bill Hutchings and Karen O'Rourke

Introduction

The project we have been engaged in over the past three years has been to implement problem-based learning in the delivery of selected literary studies courses in the Department of English and American Studies at the University of Manchester. The courses chosen for implementation in 2001–3 were two final year options (one on Samuel Johnson, one on eighteenth-century poetry), both taught solely by Bill and involving small groups of between 15 and 20 students. Our project therefore has necessitated a particular kind of educational change. We are adopting problem-based learning methods for a discipline that is completely different from those within which such methods were generated and have largely developed. With literary studies, we are dealing with an arts subject that is non-practical and non-vocational in any accepted sense of the term. The principles and practices established in those subject areas where problem-based learning activity is embedded have had to be subjected to a process of rigorous scrutiny to assess and evaluate their suitability for our discipline. Thus our project has become a revealing test of the extent to which existing problem-based learning methods, processes and paradigms are generic, applicable to all educational contexts, or need to be open to revision to meet the needs of essentially different subjects.

Methodology

The study has been carried out through intensive qualitative methods designed to elicit from students detailed responses to new processes of learning and to gauge the degree to which these processes have enabled a deeper engagement with the intellectual core of the discipline and the skills, both subject-centred and generic, required.

During the first year of the project (2000–1), Karen researched existing models of problem-based learning processes in a variety of disciplines and institutions, locally, nationally and internationally. She also observed a number of problem-based learning sessions in action, even taking part in some. At the same time, Bill continued to teach the two courses named above by traditional tutor-led seminar method. Karen observed these 'conventional' sessions in order to establish points of comparison, particularly in terms of student participation and learning, for the future problem-based learning courses. These data have proved useful for estimating the extent to which changes in learning experience have been the result of the change in processes. Towards the end of the first year of the project, we analysed the results of Karen's research and observations in order to assess the extent to which curriculum structures, the organization of problem-based learning sessions and problem paradigms were transferable to our new courses. Curriculum structure was largely dictated by faculty practice, but we perceived – and experienced – little difficulty in adaptation. The success of the processes and sessions researched and observed led us to attempt as close a fit as possible in our implementation. Our actual experience of implementation caused us to undertake some revision of our methods, as we set out in the section 'What problem-based learning processes are appropriate for literary studies?' It was, by contrast, immediately apparent that we needed to take a different approach to creating problems, as we explain in the section 'What is a "problem" in Literary Studies?'

The new problem-based learning courses required students to engage with three problems during a 12-week semester. The first problem led to oral presentations (in groups but with clearly defined individual contributions) and formative assessment only, so that students could familiarize themselves with new learning methods. The second problem culminated in a similar group oral presentation, but with summative as well as formative assessment. The third problem required the groups to produce written outcomes, again assessed both formatively and summatively. Students were given a choice of seven or eight distinct problems (choice of problem to be negotiated by the student groups), in each case allowing a free choice of the textual material to be covered. Thus there was no defined syllabus other than that defined by the course title. Approximately 70 students over two years have now graduated with one or (in a small number of cases) two problem-based learning courses forming part of their university experience.

Data gathered consisted of:

1. Video tapes and written notes taken during the sessions by Karen as part of her class observations. These provided records of how students dealt with the processes.
2. Peer feedback on presentations and written work. This was not used as part of formal assessment, but provided evidence of interactive learning of discipline-specific and generic skills.
3. Reflection by students on their experience of group work and the outcomes achieved. This provided material on processes, skills and knowledge acquired.
4. Focus group discussions. Students from both years' cohorts took part in focus groups with an independent facilitator who taped the sessions and provided us with anonymized transcripts of the recordings. Discussions covered the full range of the learning experience, processes, subject-specific skills and generic skills.

The discursive nature of the subject made discursive evidence both intellectually appropriate and relevant to the kinds of students taking the courses. We thus avoided questionnaire responses of the 'tick box' kind in favour of allowing students the opportunity to express themselves both orally and in written form. Students were thus more motivated to respond than is often the case with automated forms of feedback. We were enabled to gather a large amount of qualitative evidence, from which the illustrative quotations below are all taken.

Principles of problem-based learning

There have, of course, been many attempts to define the essential principles behind problem-based learning and the learning practices it engenders. What we seek to do here is to define a conceptual framework that will enable us to compare paradigms of problem-based learning with the nature of literary studies as a discipline and as a learning experience. Such a comparison will determine how far problem-based learning processes and their epistemological bases are aligned with principles underpinning the discipline of literary studies, and the extent to which our adoption of problem-based learning methods necessitates adaptation of its models.

The philosophical bases for problem-based learning lie in cognitive learning theories that derive from the writings of the American philosopher John Dewey. For Dewey, knowledge 'is a reflective or intellectual grasp of a situation, which grows out of, but is not identical with, experience' (Dewey 1916). Experience, because of its diversity, presents us with conflicts or problems that inquiry attempts, through analysis and the development of hypotheses, to modify or resolve. Inquiry is the means by which knowledge is pursued. Proper educational procedures are thus those that challenge the student to assess a situation analytically and critically, leading to proposed modes of responding to the problem. Knowledge is experimental, practical and active. These ideas have been most fully developed in later educational literature by Kolb (1984), and through the concept of situated learning as defined by Lave and Wenger (1991). However, the real roots of the theory lie deeper in time. The emphasis upon experience and experiment aligns the methodology with the strong line of empiricist philosophical thought that received its classic English statement in John Locke's *Essay Concerning Human Understanding* (1690). The continuing centrality of this scientific method (or experimental method, as the eighteenth-century Scottish philosopher David Hume called it) has recently been asserted afresh in Sokal and Bricmont's *Intellectual Impostures*. Their words reflect the cross-disciplinary nature of the basic principles:

> For us, the scientific method is not radically different from the rational attitude in everyday life or in other domains of human knowledge. Historians, detectives and plumbers – indeed, all human beings – use the same basic methods of induction, deduction and assessment of evidence as do physicists or biochemists.
>
> (Sokal and Bricmont 1998: 54)

The central principles of problem-based learning processes have been summarized by Kolmos (2002: 64), and may be defined thus:

- Learning is generated by the problem. This problem provides the starting point and suggests the direction for learning procedures. Students focus on choosing a method of enquiry/research by which a response to the problem and a presentation of outcomes may be formulated. These processes are more significant for the activity of learning than any notion of a 'solution', which propagates the – possibly – misleading idea that knowledge is certain, assured and unchanging (Margetson 1991).
- Learning is student-centred. It is the students themselves who work out processes and decide on and organize research activities. Tutors act as facilitators of this process, not as directors of it.
- Learning does not operate within boundaries of a subject or parts of a subject. It is a holistic process and therefore involves interdisciplinary learning in which students' research may move across traditional subject boundaries.
- Learning functions best and most convincingly within teamwork, or group work. This is partly because of the accepted nature of advanced research in most disciplines and partly because of the professional situations that most graduates will find themselves operating within.

These principles will be largely accepted by problem-based learning practitioners. Savin-Baden (2000a: 124–34) develops from the core principles of problem-based learning activity a framework for comprehending the underlying conceptual bases of learning through problem-based learning. She there proposes five models by which knowledge, learning and the role of the student operate within the broad pattern of problem-based learning. These models range from relatively controlled practices that assume an element of fixed knowledge to fully open-ended processes that contest the notion of knowledge as conventionally formulated. Her models may be linked to the above principles as follows:

- *Problem-based learning for epistemological competence.* Knowledge is here perceived as propositional; that is, a series of givens that students use to devise solutions to problems. The process has as its primary aim that of testing students' cognitive understanding. This is therefore close to conventional modes of 'problem-solving', where students use knowledge given to them by other methods to 'solve' new problems. This is the most limited model, though perhaps an essential first step, and is implicitly challenged by the first principle above.
- *Problem-based learning for professional action.* Here, the focus is on practical outcomes, students' acquisition of knowledge and skills that will equip them for the workplace. Problems are very much associated with real life situations. This model is implicit within the above principles of problem-based learning as they operate with applied disciplines, and is explicit in the fourth principle above.
- *Problem-based learning for interdisciplinary understanding.* The focus here is on using propositional and performative knowledge and skills in a way that breaks across boundaries of disciplines. This model therefore reflects the third of the above principles.
- *Problem-based learning for transdisciplinary learning.* This category adds a crucial element of understanding that disciplinary boundaries, though existing, are to a degree illusory. The frameworks of disciplinary boundaries can thus be viewed more critically as a means of understanding and testing them. Students become significantly independent in their outlook. This relates the third to the second principle above at an epistemological as well as practical level.
- *Problem-based learning for critical contestability.* This is the most radical model, developing the autonomy defined in the second principle above in the direction of full student autonomy. The very frameworks are here to be not just tested, but interrogated for their viability and deconstructed. Knowledge is embraced but also challenged, so that knowledge is actually constructed by students. Students therefore have to evaluate all knowledge, propositional and personal, on their own terms. A strong element of reflexivity is demanded in students' outlooks.

What is a 'problem' in literary studies?

Problems in medical sciences are readily generated from the practical and vocational nature of the discipline. This is not to deny the care that is still required in formulating the problems in relation to anticipated outcomes and the level of student experience. An example might be as follows:

Near Drowning

This incident took place in early Spring in Northern Europe. An eight-year-old boy, Henry, had been lying under water for more than 15 minutes. Fortunately, a passer-by succeeded in getting him out of the water. Mouth to mouth resuscitation was applied immediately. Everyone was astonished to notice that the boy was still alive. Later, Henry was on the intensive care ward of the local hospital and was said to be out of danger. According to his doctors he was expected to recover completely.

Problems in literary studies have to be artificially constructed, but similar demands are made on tutors formulating problems in making them appropriate for the student group. For example, we devised the following problem for the course in eighteenth-century poetry:

The English Tourist Board (ETB) is initiating a campaign to attract people back into the countryside after the 'foot and mouth' crisis. As part of this campaign, it is sponsoring an exhibition documenting visitors' responses to the English countryside through the ages. The exhibition is to be called 'The Eye of the Beholder: Landscape Description 1700–2000'.

The ETB is also sponsoring a booklet to accompany the exhibition. This booklet will present representative examples of landscape description from three centuries, together with commentary and notes. The booklet will be aimed at a wide public, but it is intended to be scholarly and informed. The ETB invites applicants for the post of compiler of the booklet to submit a specimen example(s) from the eighteenth century. Submissions should be in the range of 2500–3000 words including texts.

This assumes advanced skills of information retrieval, research and bibliographical procedures that would need to be 'taught' by a more contained problem than one that invited students to investigate the whole poetic output of a century. Students who tackle such a broad problem would need to be confident in finding their way quickly about primary sources.

Similarities with applied disciplines can go further. For example, many of the scenarios we have used reflect how the subject does relate to the external world in terms of the generic nature of skills in communication and creativity. Asking students to present proposals for a radio broadcast requires of them a sophisticated ability to recognize the appropriateness of diverse registers of language and to negotiate between different forms of media. The invitation to write a booklet for The Open University involves similar issues of language in a purely written form, together with complex issues of audience, intention and rhetoric. (See below for full text of these problems.)

What problem-based learning processes are appropriate for literary studies?

As in most problem-based learning curricula, students do not spend time passively listening to lectures but are expected to attend scheduled, facilitated 'tutorial group' meetings once a week, supplemented by as many non-timetabled meetings of their subgroup as deemed necessary by its members to work through the issues posed by a particular problem.

The problem-based learning literature and our observation of problem-based learning sessions in medicine, dentistry and biomolecular science reveal that typically there are certain functional roles within the student groups that may assist the problem-based learning process. Usually, the group elects a *chairperson* who will act as arbitrator and timekeeper and who will endeavour to keep the group focused on the task in hand. It is useful if somebody within the group makes brief notes during any discussions. This scribe often works closely with the chairperson to ensure that all group members' ideas are noted. It is recommended that these roles are periodically 'rotated' within the group, so that each member has an opportunity to experience different responsibilities.

Two well known paradigms of the whole-group problem-based learning process have been developed by the University of Maastricht (Netherlands) and McMaster University (Canada):

Maastricht's 'Seven Jumps'

1. Clarify terms and concepts that are not clear.
2. Define the problem.
3. Analyse the problem.
4. Formulate learning goals.
5. Agree about reporting back at next meeting.
6. Self-study – collecting additional information.
7. Reporting back, synthesis and checking newly acquired information.

McMaster's 'Eight Steps'

1. Explore the problem, create hypotheses, identify issues, elaborate.
2. Identify what you already know that is pertinent.
3. Identify what you do not know.
4. As a group, prioritize the learning needs, set learning goals and objectives and allocate resources. Members identify which tasks they will do.
5. Individual self-study and preparation. Return to group, share new knowledge effectively so that all the group learn the information.
6. Apply the new knowledge to the problem.

7. Assess the new knowledge, the problem solution and the effectiveness of the process used.
8. Reflect on the process. Elaborate on the problem.

Informed by the tried and tested methods outlined above, and having seen them working well in practice in our own institution, it seemed appropriate that we should develop a similar paradigm to support problem-based learning with our own literary studies students. In order to clarify where key subject-specific skills were being developed, we incorporated into this paradigm the specific range of skills outlined in the subject benchmarking statement and aligned them as shown in Figure 13.1.

To reiterate, literary studies is essentially a discursive, open-ended, critically contested, responsive and creative subject that challenges students and encourages them to find their own intellectual pathways. It became evident (as early as our second problem-based learning session) that any imposition of a rigid structure in terms of specific responsibilities within the groups would be counter-productive to what we were trying to achieve and in fact the students themselves rejected the constraints imposed by such defined roles. It is extremely difficult to participate verbally in a group discussion while scribing for that group, and our students resented any exclusion from such discussions, often abandoning the pen in frustration, only for it to be picked up later by another member of the group and then another. In a similar way, the role of chair was perceived by our students to be jarringly hierarchical and they invariably adopted a collective approach to time management and organization. The idea that one member of the group might monitor or even close down avenues of discussion, single-handedly delegate tasks or assume the role of 'leader' was never really on their agenda, although some did admit to giving it a try. For example, students explained:

> We tried to allocate roles – chair, scribe etc. – but I thought that was too rigid and could be detrimental.

> We didn't define roles, it was very organic ...

> This course has given me freedom ... a voice of my own.

> We scheduled meetings from the start. We all talked, gave input and had far too many ideas! Yet we managed to work, compromise and learn so much. We were all reliable and positive. Group effort was the key to the whole experience, it felt really like a group project.

Students valued autonomy and self-direction and developed further than our own pedagogical and disciplinary expectations. Thus, it was the very 'open-endedness' of the problem-based learning methodology that drew us to examine its compatibility with our subject in the first place, and so we quickly learned to trust students to forge working patterns that suited them as the kinds of people who were drawn to study English literature at university.

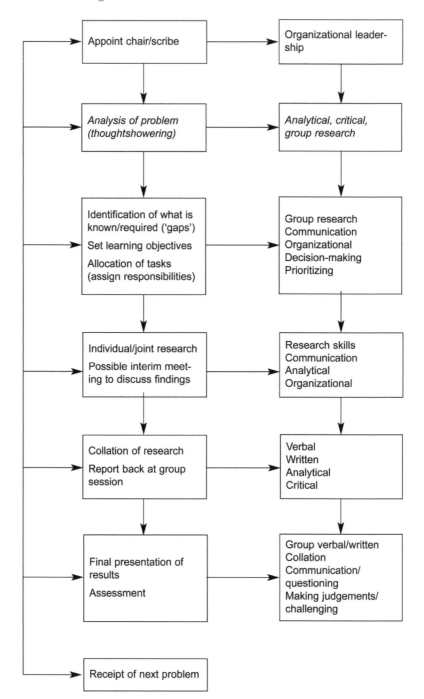

Figure 13.1 Problem-based learning process skills.

Conceptual models of problem-based learning and the discipline of literary studies

The principal question to be addressed is how far each of the conceptual models proposed by Savin-Baden is appropriate for learning in literary studies. Readers with some knowledge of the debates about literary studies that have reverberated through the academy over recent decades will be aware that conclusions about the essential principles of the discipline are always going to be controversial and subject to revision. We shall attempt to be as inclusive and non-judgemental as possible in this area. The subject benchmarking criteria published by the Quality Assurance Agency for Higher Education (2000) will be cited as key points of reference. We shall take each of the models in turn, aligning them with our experience of problem-based learning in literary studies as illustrated by quotations from student feedback and focus group commentary.

Epistemological competence has always been claimed as a central aim of traditional teaching. Thus it would seem that proponents of problem-based learning need simply to demonstrate that such methods do not reduce the levels of epistemological competence. However, student evaluations on the courses we have run provide evidence that levels might actually be increased, that students can actually end up with a sounder basis of knowledge. The principal reasons are as follows.

First, the process of cooperation (including feedback, presentations to whole group and exchange of materials) invites sharing and involvement in other groups' tasks, rather than the typical isolation, even selfishness, of traditional learning in our subject, in which the individual essay has always been regarded as the conventional outcome. Students explained:

> I learnt so much from working closely with others. Dispelled the somewhat arrogant belief that I can do OK on my own and made me (finally) concede that two (or more) heads are better than one.

> For the last three years you could have been sitting next to somebody who has so many good ideas and you never get the benefit of those ideas because you don't talk to each other. When you get into a [problem-based learning] group like this and people are talking, you really learn so much from one another. Ordinarily you're just learning from the tutor whereas if you're talking to other people it's like ... 'Well, what about this and what about that' ... and if you work with your group properly you learn fourfold. It works so much better.

> Peer feedback helped us to improve. You knew exactly what went well and what went wrong. It was quite hard to do at first because you didn't want to be too critical, but once you got into it and the more you did it the more it worked, became more critically constructive.

Second, traditional forms of examination invite 'question spotting', with the result that each individual student engages in selective learning. By contrast, the collaborative nature of problem-based learning encourages students to feel a sense of ownership over the entire course and so all material being researched. For example, students argued:

> You learn to rely on your own resources more. For the exam my way of working was completely different than ever before ... I went away and found the readings and did stuff off my own back for the group and I was taking it in because I was interested in it and I wasn't just reading for the exam.

> It changes the degree into something interesting and useful as opposed to something which just shows the strength of your memory and how you perform in an exam.

> It allows the student to draw not only from tutors and written resources, but the learning experiences, methods and knowledge of peers. I have found this extremely useful.

> Throughout my university career I have felt I have only studied to fulfil the minimum criteria for a course but with problem-based learning I have worked not only for the requirements but for the benefit of a group.

Third, working on a problem involves a process of wider exploration (including into areas that are eventually discarded as far as the outcome of the problem is concerned) than is the case with a clearly defined, set question. Exploratory research, rather than picking from a set reading list, involves students in a less restricted approach to the relevance of knowledge to success in the course. Thus students reconceptualized their view of knowledge:

> Toying with and manipulating ideas is a more successful method than making your mind up and pursuing things blindly.

> I was surprised that there weren't any set texts.

> I always covered too much and ended up sorting ideas out at the last minute – fortunately it worked this time but I really want to give myself more time to reflect on things before I actually present them.

> All of us hold a key to loads of information, we are all sources of information as much as the tutor and the bookshelves. It taught me to trust and work with others.

This model might not carry with it those limitations identified above when applied to learning in literary studies. The subject may, therefore, be regarded as effectively fitting proper paradigms of problem-based learning.

Literary studies is not a vocational subject, and so *professional action* would seem to be an irrelevant consideration. However, some professional skills (in the loose sense of providing skills relevant to employment, rather than specific vocational training) have always been implicit in the learning outcomes. These include writing, critical/analytical and organizational skills. Problem-based learning enhances the professional aspects of the subject in two ways.

First, problem-based learning assists the process of making skills of potential vocational relevance more explicit. Such explicitness can be created in non-problem-based learning courses. For example, skills of oral communication can be developed by including these in assessment criteria in any course. However, problem-based learning, with its emphasis upon collaborative and open-ended research work, is a means of making such skills an integral part of the learning process. Thus problem-based learning is not a necessary condition for professional relevance, but often operates as a sufficient condition for professional skills to become inherent in a course. Students' stories illustrate this:

> Whilst the course is excellent at developing individual skills the group aspect is where it truly excels. The fact that students are encouraged to share their individual knowledge and expertise is enriching for all and knowing that people are relying on you is a great motivator and gives an insight into the group dynamics that I'm told are an essential part of 'real world' work.

> We had to do a reflection on how we had come together to do our last presentation – we were absolutely astounded at how much we had learnt! We just kept saying it was a learning process, we learnt so much about group skills and about the problem. Different people were using different talents within the group and each person brought something different to the group.

Second, skills are enhanced. For example, although organizational skills can be developed through any form of group work, appropriate problems can produce situations that allow students to demonstrate a deeper level of skills. One such problem requires students to produce material for a radio broadcast.

Advertisement

> BBC Radio 4 is planning a series of thirty-minute programmes on various arts. The aim is to address a number of fundamental questions. Among these might be: What is the nature of the art form? Why do/did artists produce these artefacts? How do/should readers/audiences respond to them? How much explanation do we need in order to understand them? How do we extend their appeal to a broad audience? We have already commissioned programmes on contemporary sculpture (to be presented by Antony Gormley), on installation art (to be presented by Tracey Emin), on baroque music (to be presented by

Christopher Hogwood) and on Jacobean drama (to be presented by Jude Kelly). We invite teams to present an oral version of a script for our planned programme on eighteenth-century poetry.

One group taking eighteenth-century poetry decided that the most effective way of producing an outcome would be to present a tape of its final version of the broadcast. The group reported in feedback that producing the finished product made exceptional demands upon the members in terms of time, arranging meetings outside sessions and preparing materials. The group was quite happy to have responded to these demands because of the satisfaction given by the outcome:

> In terms of time spent it has far exceeded my other courses and I, at first, resented the degree to which it had occupied me. Having now completed it I am able to appreciate the skills and experience that I have gained. As a naturally lazy student the emphasis on group work was useful for focusing my efforts and keeping me to deadlines.

> There really was no shirking the fact that individuals had to cooperate/ share ideas/discuss ideas. For the first time I actually spoke to fellow students. I learnt so much more than pursuing only my own line of thought. All of a sudden I had multiple points of reference rather than just the tutor or me ...

Interestingly, then, the principle of problem-based learning practice that seems at first to have the least degree of transferability to literary studies can be seen to be unexpectedly appropriate. This suitability is generally at the level of generic transferable skills, although it is worth noting that we have observed at least one unanticipated match between a specific problem and the workplace. This relates to a student who took part in the English Tourist Board problem that we cited above. She found herself within months of graduating being interviewed for a job as a tour guide for an eighteenth-century stately home and her ability to talk about her work on the problem proved timely.

Interdisciplinary understanding and transdisciplinary learning are actually inherently more appropriate for literary studies than for many areas within which problem-based learning commonly operates. History, art history, philosophy, theology and sociology intersect with many traditional and modern interpretive and theoretical approaches to the study of literature. So much is this the case that the subject benchmark as defined by the Quality Assurance Agency for Higher Education actually includes 'recognition of the multi-faceted nature of the discipline, and of its complex relationship to other disciplines and forms of knowledge' among its criteria for subject knowledge. Such interdisciplinarity is reinforced by the current tendency to see literature within a broader context of cultural products, such as films. It is quite common for literary texts such as the novels of Jane Austen, Henry James and E. M. Forster to be examined alongside film versions of them. Such studies examine the interface between generic transformations and the resultant influence on reader response, raising such questions as the effect experience of a later film version has on readers' interpretations of the original text. A student will be expected to think about the interpretive blurring of boundaries consequent upon the production of these cultural artefacts. Thus both these models are entirely appropriate for adaptation to a literary studies course, whether or not it is taught through problem-based learning.

Problem-based learning may support investigation of these issues by allowing students a greater freedom to introduce interdisciplinary approaches. What problem-based learning certainly can do is to invite students' presented outcomes to invoke a range of cross-disciplinary skills. For example, the English Tourist Board problem cited earlier was approached by one group through a pictorial method, with eighteenth-century visual representations of scenery being set alongside eighteenth-century poetic depictions of similar types of landscape. This raised interesting cross-disciplinary issues to do with how different media represent landscape. Issues of layout and design come into the format of this and other problems, so introducing a practical interdisciplinary test.

Another of our problems presented students with issues of educational methodology as well as layout.

Creating a course

The Open University is setting up a new undergraduate course (level 2) on eighteenth-century literature. Its aim is to introduce students to a representative selection of set texts, chosen to reflect the range of literature of the period and to raise and address the problems that modern readers from a diversity of backgrounds have in approaching the literature of a past age. The teaching is conducted largely through distance learning, and it is therefore essential that the course is supported by effective course material. Each booklet is to focus on one prose or poetry text, or extracts from a long prose work, or a small selection of short poems. You have been commissioned to produce one such booklet on an appropriate work by Samuel Johnson. The format of the booklets is up to the presenters, but should operate according to the following principles:

- No prior knowledge of the author's work is to be assumed on the part of the students.
- No prior experience of the literature of the period is to be assumed on the part of the students.
- Students must be assumed to come from a diversity of backgrounds, social and cultural.
- Students will have successfully passed the Arts Foundation course (level 1), which introduces them to critical methods and the range of

approaches to literature, but they cannot be expected to have addressed the particular problems that your choice of text presents.

• The material should focus on critical and interpretive issues, in order to allow students to engage with the important literary issues in the work(s). All biographical material will have been presented in another introductory booklet.

The Open University course team asks you to make an oral presentation of the script for your booklet as part of the scrutiny and editorial process.

The final model, that of *critical contestability*, is arguably also inherent within literary studies in a way that is not always the case in disciplines commonly taught through problem-based learning. In our application of problem-based learning, we have removed many of the frameworks on which courses are conventionally constructed. These include prescribed reading lists of secondary, critical material, set books and tutor-determined curriculum. The result is a removal (or at least a diminution) of the conventional hierarchical model, whereby the tutor takes the leading role in establishing the conceptual and interpretive parameters of the course. Instead, there is a focus on students finding their own way through issues. Problem scenarios set up a series of possible, intellectually valid pathways, some of which may not even have been envisaged by the tutor when constructing the problem. The variety of such pathways reflects the open-ended nature of the subject.

Students of literary studies

What is the nature of the student community attracted to literary studies? Of course, such a large number of people will inevitably present as much diversity as similarity. But our experience shows that there are some qualities that can be identified as common to most students of the subject. We might cite an interest in how language works; an interest in communication (both as receivers and deliverers); often a drive towards creativity (many students write themselves, whether in literary forms such as poetry or in professionally oriented forms such as student newspapers); an interest in how ideas and emotions are expressed; and, increasingly these days, a concern for the diversity of contemporary media.

These interests are clearly reflected in the subject benchmark statement from the Quality Assurance Agency for Higher Education (2000). The criteria for 'graduateness' in English include among key subject-specific skills: 'critical skills in the close reading and analysis of texts', 'rhetorical skills of effective communication and argument, both oral and written' and 'awareness of how different social and cultural contexts affect the nature of language and meaning'. Generic skills defined include 'the capacity to adapt and transfer the critical methods of the discipline to a variety of working environments,' 'the capacity for independent thought and judgement', 'the ability to comprehend and develop intricate concepts in an open-ended way which involves an understanding of purpose and consequences', 'the ability to work with and in relation to others through the presentation of ideas and information and the collective negotiation of solutions' and 'time-management and organisational skills'. These criteria reflect the nature of the subject as discursive, open-ended, critically contested, analytic, responsive and creative. Literary studies is not just a body of knowledge to be absorbed and regurgitated, although of course some fixed and essential knowledge is involved: Pope came after Milton, *The Waste Land* cites Shakespeare. Instead, the subject is an actively developing set of ideas, thoughts, emotions and communications. In a phrase, the 'acceptance of uncertainty' is at the core of the discipline. To re-read the principles of problem-based learning defined earlier and the models of problem-based learning process as described by Savin-Baden is to encounter, in another form, definitions of what it is to be an English graduate.

Conclusion

Our argument is that problem-based learning offers a method of learning that is close to the principles of literary studies as a discipline and as something experienced by students when they are working most creatively and imaginatively. This is intriguingly reflected by the way in which the most radical of Savin-Baden's models can actually be argued to be the closest to the heart of literary studies. The epistemological centre of the idea of applying problem-based learning paradigms to this subject area is that problem-based learning makes the 'teaching' process partake of the qualities of the discipline itself. If the study of literature is about response, critical and analytical engagement, discussion, disagreement, the need to agree on some outcomes while acknowledging the provisional status of such conclusions and the need to find an appropriate form for articulating these conclusions, then problem-based learning is the discipline's appropriate pedagogic form. The learning process we establish may, indeed, be more aligned with the nature of literary studies than with that of many other subjects that are already widely recognized as appropriate areas for problem-based learning.

14

Exploring the Impact of Discipline-based Pedagogy on Problem-based Learning through Interpretive Meta Ethnography

Maggi Savin-Baden and Kay Wilkie

Introduction

This chapter explores staff experiences of discipline-based pedagogy (teacher knowledge and beliefs about what to do and how to do it in their subject area), in the context of problem-based learning. There has been increasing interest and research into staff[1] experiences of problem-based learning in the past ten years but little examination of the impact of the discipline on the way problem-based learning is implemented and enacted. Furthermore, few researchers have integrated findings across qualitative studies that have explored staff experiences of problem-based learning. This chapter undertakes such a project but shifts away from quantitative forms of meta analysis and quasi-qualitative forms of meta analysis and instead adopts interpretative meta ethnography. The results of two studies that explored staff experiences of problem-based learning in the same discipline are reviewed and synthesized. The findings indicate themes relating to changes in role perception through the process and experience of becoming facilitators, shifts in views about the nature of power and control in the learning environment and the nature of the disciplinary knowledge on the way problem-based learning is played out in practice. We argue that future inquiry is needed into the impact of staff pedagogical knowledge in problem-based learning; into what it is that is meant by learning, and by whom; and for increased exploration into changes in disciplinary constructions when problem-based learning is being used.

Literature review

There has been increasing discussion about discipline-based pedagogy in the United Kingdom, particularly in the debates about the relationship between research and teaching. Jenkins and Zetter (2003) argue that disciplines shape the nature of pedagogy and such pedagogies reflect the practices and culture of the discipline. Thus teacher knowledge and beliefs about what to do, how to do it and under which circumstances can affect the way that students learn a particular subject matter. Shulman's (1986, 1987) work in the United States of America provides a framework for understanding teacher knowledge in which he describes several layers of teacher knowledge, including both subject knowledge and pedagogical knowledge. Subject or content knowledge comprises the theories, principles and concepts of a particular discipline. In addition to this subject matter knowledge, general pedagogical knowledge, or knowledge about teaching itself, is another important aspect of teacher knowledge. While subject knowledge and pedagogical knowledge are perhaps self-evident, Shulman (1986: 6) asks: 'why this sharp distinction between content and pedagogical process?' Somewhere between subject matter knowledge and pedagogical knowledge sits discipline-based pedagogy, what Shulman termed 'pedagogical content knowledge', which he describes as:

> the ways of representing and formulating the subject that make it comprehensible to others ... Pedagogical content knowledge also includes an understanding of what makes the learning of specific topics easy or difficult: the conceptions and preconceptions that students of different ages and backgrounds bring with them to the learning of those most frequently taught topics and lessons.
>
> (Shulman 1986: 9–10)

Yet one of the areas where we see the breaking down of disciplinary boundaries and the merging of subject knowledge and pedagogical knowledge for both staff and students is in problem-based learning.

Much of the research conducted in the area of problem-based learning has focused on student outcomes, but recently studies have begun to focus on staff experiences of the approach. Research indicates that using problem-based learning has an influence on staff members' perceptions of their teaching. For example, staff who are familiar with problem-based learning favour it over other instructional methods (Albanese and Mitchell 1993; Vernon and Blake 1993). In a study of problem-based learning staff roles, Dahlgren *et al.* (1998) found that tutors' perceptions of their roles influenced their levels of satisfaction with problem-based learning. What staff know, or think they know, about the discipline, the course and the students as learners affects their pedagogical choices (Martin *et al.* 2001; Major and Palmer 2002b). However, there remain questions about the kinds of personal and pedagogical transitions that are required when moving to a problem-based learning approach.

Research methods

Meta analysis remains rare among those using collaborative and interpretive inquiry, and few researchers have undertaken an integration of findings from these kinds of studies. Those that have, have tended either to impose the frameworks and values of quantitative systematic reviews on qualitative studies or to move towards the use of meta ethnography. The use of systematic reviews, of whatever sort, implies that the drawing up of a set of rules for 'systematically' reviewing evidence will necessarily make the process of the review and research transparent. Yet there are degrees of transparency and points beyond which it is not possible to go when undertaking such reviews. The difficulty with meta analysis that is not located in an interpretive tradition is the propensity to decontextualize material, thin descriptions and ignore methodological difference.

Thus, we set out to undertake an analysis and synthesis of findings from two different studies using interpretive meta ethnography. This approach adopts meta ethnography as defined by Noblit and Hare (1988) but firmly locates the management and synthesis of findings in interpretivism. However, we also argue against 'validity' as a position that we suggest has led us to meaningless and even questionable practice in interpretive research, and instead we argue for 'honesties' (following Stronach *et al.* 2002) – a category that allows us to acknowledge that trust and truths are fragile and, at the same time, enables us to engage with the messiness and complexity of data interpretation in ways that really do reflect the lives of our participants (Savin-Baden and Fisher 2002). Honesties as a concept allow us to acknowledge not only the cyclical nature of 'truths', but also that the nature of honesties is defined by people and contexts and also helps us to avoid the prejudice *for* similarity and *against* difference in data interpretation. The conventional clustering of data and ways of 'ensuring' validity often result in a kind of formula about how we 'do' validity and data interpretation. Instead we argue here for the presentation of difference and movement, and more transparent approaches to validity claims that help us to engage with the way our participants often tell contradictory stories so that they are 'caught between stories, split between grounding narrative that offer(ed) different versions of a professional self along with tangential manifestations of a personal self' (Stronach *et al.* 2002: 16). We believe there are a number of ways in which we can engage with honesties in the research process and we began by using four, as identified by Savin-Baden and Fisher (2002):

1. Situating ourselves in relation to our participants.
2. Voicing our mistakes.
3. Situating ourselves in relation to the data.

4. Taking a critical stance towards research.

These methods for establishing honesties have been used as the basis of an evaluation instrument that was developed and used by Savin-Baden and Major (2003) to identify studies that reflected these values. However, we have developed this further in order to reflect interpretive meta ethnography.

Table 14.1 Instrument for evaluating studies suitable for interpretive meta ethnography

	0 No mention	1 Some mention	2 Good mention	3 Extensive mention
Researcher(s) situated in relation to participants				
Mistakes voiced				
Researcher(s) situated in relation to the data				
Researcher(s) take a critical stance towards research				
Participant involvement in data interpretation				
Study theoretically situated				
Different versions of participants identities acknowledged				

Interpretative meta synthesis

The difficulty with synthesis in this kind of study is reflected by those who have already undertaken this kind of meta ethnography. For example, suggestions by Britten *et al.* (2002) and Jones (2003) were compelling but seemed to lack an interpretive stance. Britten *et al.* throughout the course of the exemplar systematically decontextualized the studies, privileged some themes and issues over others and tended to thin thick description, possibly in order to present their findings in an accessible tabulated format. Yet the original argument for meta ethnography (Noblit and Hare 1988) is that through interpretation and by acknowledging the positions of the researchers as interpretivists it is possible to recover the social and theoretical context of the research and thus reveal further noteworthy findings.

Thus we synthesized data by interpretive comparison and inductive analysis. Rather than starting with raw data (to which we did have access), we began with predetermined themes and the description that we as authors had chosen to include to illustrate the themes. Several themes crossed over to both studies and some themes were relabelled to account for differences between the studies, but we stayed as true as possible to the original themes. However, because we believe that forcing all data into common themes results in questionable research practices, we retained issues that diverged, pointing out differences.

The contexts of the studies

The first study was undertaken in a newly formed School of Nursing and Midwifery, within a faculty of medicine at a university that we refer to as Curbar University. A new problem-based programme was designed with the aim of improving integration with practice and the development of critique in students. The research was therefore undertaken with a group of over 20 of the staff, between 1998 and 2002, who were from diverse backgrounds in the field of nursing and midwifery. Collaborative and narrative inquiry were used because they allowed for the development of collaborative relationships with the participants of the inquiry while also inviting reflexivity and critique. Data were collected through one-to-one in-depth interviews, informal discussions, e-mail discussion and post-interview reflections. These staff initially defined themselves as nurses, midwives, lecturers, clinical teachers and demonstrators in clinical skill laboratories. Such diverse roles with different philosophies prompted pedagogical conflict for the staff involved in their transition from and across their roles in the process of becoming facilitators.

The second study explored the perceived and actual facilitation roles in problem-based learning adopted by a group of 18 nursing lecturers. This study was undertaken in a School of Nursing and Midwifery at a university we refer to as Kingarth. This school had been created from two existing colleges of nursing and midwifery in the final phase of the transfer of nurse/midwife education into a higher education institution that had no nursing department prior to the integration. As the two existing programmes differed considerably, a completely new programme was written. This programme utilized problem-based learning as a major teaching strategy. Although all of the participants possessed a formal teaching qualification, none had had experience of problem-based learning. The study examined the transitions that occurred in espoused theories and theories-in-use as the lecturers new to problem-based learning became more experienced in facilitation. Data collection included audio recordings of problem-based learning sessions, interviews with facilitators, field notes, student focus groups and facilitators' reflective diaries.

Findings

The findings presented in this section represent three different approaches to answering the basic research question: how does staff thinking change as a result of moving from a traditional teaching approach to problem-based learning? Three cross-data themes emerged, which were:

1. Changes in role perception.
2. Changed perspectives about the nature of authority and control.
3. Shifts in views about the nature of disciplinary knowledge.

Changes in role perception

Several changes in perception of tutor roles were evident with tutors from both studies. Exposure to the problem-based process increased the realization that facilitation required skills that were different from those used previously. The concept of tutors no longer being central to student learning raised many issues, including threats to self-esteem and fear of job loss. Staff experience of problem-based learning led them to realize that the concept of teacher-centrality in student learning had to be redefined before different skills could be put into practice. Further, exposure to problem-based learning brought recognition over time that the variation in student personalities and abilities, linked to the range of material, required facilitators to be flexible, adaptive, responsive and inclusive. The roles adopted by staff altered with increased experience of problem-based learning. They moved from 'directive conventionalist', an approach in which staff retained control over what the students learned and how the evidence of their learning was presented, to that of 'pragmatic enabler', an approach characterized by an emphasis on students developing the processes to foster their learning rather than on the memorizing of content.

From directive conventionalist to pragmatic enabler

Tutors in both the studies described initial transitions from lecturer to facilitator. To begin with, tutors saw themselves as novice facilitators whose role was to control and direct the team, fill in the gaps in the students' knowledge base and ensure that the course content was covered. Many participants expressed similar concepts about the facilitator role, emphasizing the student-centred nature of problem-based learning and the facilitator's role in 'encouraging' students to take responsibility for their own learning. Staff in both studies seemed to have an awakening as they gained more experience with the facilitator role. For example, Simon, a facilitator at Curbar, was involved in multiple forms of teaching and learning. He had been given the overall remit of implementing curriculum change towards problem-based learning, and at the same time was also implementing technological learning. His background in mental health nursing led him to believe that working and learning through a variety of approaches was useful and he assumed that as a facilitator he would not be particularly directive:

> I didn't think for a minute that my normal teaching style was going to be OK as a problem-based learning facilitator, but I thought like many others do, that I do a lot of those things anyway. I ask a lot of questions, but it isn't until you actually think about being a facilitator, it's not just about asking questions, it's about the type of questions that you ask. And are the questions that you ask sufficiently open and non-directive to allow your students to think about issues and to find direction for themselves? So that I think I was just surprised about how much of a change was required of me.

Simon realized that he needed to change his approach in order to offer students more autonomy; he saw the shift he needed to make as the difference between directing and guiding, and acknowledged that he was often directive.

Lorna, a tutor at Kingarth with many years' experience of teaching post-registration students, commented on how difficult it was to move from a position of being in control:

> I think I tried to fall back on what I already did. I found that quite difficult. Most of my work has been in post-reg and that's with small groups anyway. So it's a case of prompting and doing a bit more and teasing them out and getting them to speak a bit more. Sometimes it works and sometimes it doesn't. The first years ... I've still got to tell them a lot and I've got to watch that I don't start saying, you know ... 'What about this, that and the next thing.' So I try not to tell them too much but sometimes I tell them quite a bit.

Like Simon, Lorna recognized that direct information transmission strategies were inappropriate in problem-based learning sessions and that she needed to develop skills that supported students in finding out for themselves. However, there were staff who remained directive throughout the studies, as we demonstrate in the next theme.

Changed perspectives about the nature of authority and control

In both studies staffs' stances did influence their overarching approaches as facilitators, but what seemed to be pivotal was the way in which they 'positioned' or 'placed' themselves. Thus in this sense the notion of how tutors positioned themselves does not displace their pedagogical stance

(Savin-Baden 2000), but *overlays* it. This theme comprised three subthemes, all related to the notion of repositioning: repositioned to maintain control, repositioned to offer control and repositioned to relinquish control.

(Re)positioned to maintain control

Jack, a Curbar staff member, presented a picture of one whose values would initially seem to be repositioned but in fact the values in use illustrated a need to be in control of knowledge. Initially Jack argued that there was not enough flexibility within the nursing profession about what was to be valued and what counted as knowledge. He found it difficult to discuss problem-based learning separately from his perspective on life and saw students engaging with learning as a life process. Thus Jack argued that knowledge should be seen as something to be challenged and explored not only within the framework of the university, but also within practice, and across the culture of practice and higher education. However, a year later it became apparent that the views he had first verbalized were not espoused in the practices of problem-based learning he adopted:

> I try not to be directive although at times I say to the group, 'I think I'm taking my problem-based learning hat off for a few minutes is that OK?' so they know the difference, 'now I'm putting on my nursing lecturers hat', and I will throw something out to them which is possibly a gaping hole in their argument and they should have identified it, so I will give it to them. Now go back and play with that ball, and I'll put that problem-based learning hat back on again. I think I'm that kind of facilitator, not directive, give them a long lead, do a lot of listening, try to play the game they want to play as long as they look at the objectives of the problem-based learning, and they are heading in that direction.

His perception of himself as not being directive does not square with 'putting on my nursing lecturer's hat' so that he could supply students with the practical knowledge he felt they needed. Repositioning for control here is seen in the values that Jack demonstrated in practice – he did not want students to challenge the status quo, instead he wanted to ensure they were heading in the right direction and had acquired the right knowledge, skill and capabilities for practice.

Similar discrepancies between facilitators' espoused theories and theories-in-action were identified in the directive conventionalist group of facilitators in the Kingarth study. Andy, a lecturer with a background in adult nursing, described his approach to facilitation:

> Initially, to begin with, it's to get the group to gel. To facilitate their introduction to each other ... related obviously to what the PBL is about. [It's] more controlling in the earlier parts and as the group developed to step back and let them run a bit freer,

without intervening, to clarify issues. So I think a lot of it [facilitation] is bringing other people into involvement.

Andy indicated that although he recognized a need for control in the early experience of problem-based learning, this should decrease over time, with students being given more time to explore and clarify issues. In practice, Andy's concept of 'bringing people into involvement' translated into telling them what to do. He did not tolerate silence. In introductory sessions students were given less than two minutes to read and develop an understanding of the problem. If they had not started to discuss the material within this time, Andy would ask a convergent question based on his perception of the related issues. Several incidents, such as rearranging classroom furniture to face the lecturer and withholding part of the problem material, highlighted the controlling nature of Andy's approach. Although Andy believed that he was facilitating in a way designed to include students and give them freedom to develop their own learning, he continued to direct his team with regard to both content to be learned and the format for presentation.

(Re)positioned to offer control

Tutors also repositioned themselves in order to promote self-direction in students. However, although they offered control, sometimes they did not then give it to the students and at other times students chose not to take that control even though it was offered. Neil was a lecturer in mental health and adult nursing at Curbar. To begin with he felt that this was just because it was a change in teaching style, but later he valued it in terms of the challenges it brought for him personally and pedagogically. He explained:

> I don't know how to put it, you don't see yourself as a teacher, you don't see yourself as a lecturer, yours is a different role. You have expertise in the area that you work, but it's not teaching, you are not really here to do teaching, you are here teaching outside the frame. I find it rewarding in the way that you know, you see the student moving on, you see the student buzzing, you know, but in terms of me giving, that's one thing I don't know, what do I give?

In a later interview Neil still did not see himself as a teacher, but his position had moved towards seeing himself more in partnership with the students in the learning process:

> ... and quite a few times I have seen myself almost as the student, you know, I was learning from them and I wouldn't say that it was something that I found surprising, you know, because the way problem-based learning is ... and you know I would be picking up from them and sometimes afterwards ask them for copies of the pieces of work

they have presented which actually made them aware that you know, it's their work.

Neil repositioned himself both in relation to the teaching approach and in relation to the students. He saw himself as an enabler of learning and a learner.

Karen, a lecturer at Kingarth whose clinical background was in a variety of community settings, likewise believed that she had something to offer students, based on her own expertise. In comparison with the directive conventionalist approach's emphasis on the acquisition of content, Karen's approach was that of nurturing socializer, an approach that provided the students with a great deal of support while also seeking to instil in them the values and beliefs she believed made a 'good' nurse. Karen tried to explain:

> How much do you influence? ... Because it's not small group work. Where you can manipulate in a small group and say, 'right you do this, this and this', or 'you haven't done enough', or 'you must' ...

She attempted to apply these values to facilitation and to encourage students to adopt them. Karen suggested that she tried to influence her teams in some way. She talked about 'manipulating' the group, indicating that she used the teaching situation to her own advantage, to make students do what she wanted them to do. However, as she began to recognize that achieving this through problem-based learning required different tactics, her approach to influencing students' beliefs about clinical practice became one of giving examples of good practice to the students from the point of view of an 'experienced friend'. Peers, she claimed, were more influential than teachers. Although Karen sought to reposition herself as a friend and peer, in sessions she always contributed extensively to the discussion and almost always had the last word. This led one of the second year students in her group to comment:

> It's so annoying. It doesn't matter how much effort we put in, she [Karen]'s still got to add something. People think that they've covered everything but she always has to cap it with some story or other.

Although Karen attempted to offer students the opportunity to take charge, her many contributions discouraged students from taking control of their learning, as they felt that no matter how much effort they made, they would never meet Karen's expectations. Karen often became despondent and frustrated as she felt that students were not responsive and did not want to be nurtured. Her repositioning as friend and expert did not achieve her expected results.

(Re)positioned to relinquish control

Staff in this subtheme sought to encourage both collaborative and dialogic learning so that students developed their ability to use dialogue, discussion and prior experience to enhance their learning. Tutors' concerns here were in relinquishing control to students so that autonomy was not just espoused but was played out in practice. Sally, a Curbar tutor, had been working with postgraduate students for many years. She had described herself as a non-directive facilitator, but the accounts she offered of what she did indicated the dilemmas of being displaced in this context. For her, failing to point out gaps in knowledge was irresponsible and she was not prepared to wait to let students discover the gaps for themselves in the weeks ahead, in case they missed them and then that would be her fault (not theirs). Yet some two years later she was repositioned as someone who wanted to relinquish control and be a responsible facilitator:

> You still hear people saying, 'I have done all this preparation for this trigger, it took me hours to do this', and I am still saying to them, 'Why? You are not doing these triggers, your group is doing this trigger. Your job is there to try and help them see the way that they've got to go with it, and if you're preparing stuff it may not be what they need to know.'
> ... So I think be well prepared when you go into class, but only be prepared to facilitate the group, not be prepared to teach them what the trigger is telling them.

Christine was a tutor at Kingarth who began to change her approach to facilitation as she became aware of differences, first between different students' responses to the problems and subsequently between problem-based groups in general:

> Generally I try to stay as hands off as possible, but I do a bit of dabbling. You know, a wee bit of prompting, a bit of a clue, asking a quiet one to speak. I dabble more when they're new, but they soon learn ... Then, for the first time the team were quite irritable and I've never known them like that. They felt lost because they had no past experience of the problem topic and they were still uncomfortable with care pathways so they were downright irritable in that they were asking questions, 'I can't do this.' That's the first time I've had to actively intervene ... I've had to dabble ... and I don't like dabbling.

Christine identified that students new to problem-based learning required more help or 'dabbling' in the form of prompting or giving clues. She believed that as students became more familiar with the method, crystallized as a group and increased in confidence, they would require less direction from her as a facilitator. This had happened with her first problem-based group, who had responded well to her approach, requiring less 'dabbling' as the programme progressed. Christine had expected her next group to continue to require less intervention. This had happened until they encountered a problem that they found difficult. Nothing in their previous clinical, or indeed personal, experiences provided insight into how this problem should be tackled, so they looked to Christine for assistance. Christine was surprised by this. The group had been independent learners and now, in the third year of the programme, they were seeking help. On reflection Christine realized that the disjunction had been created by the problem. Although the group was now in the third year, the unfamiliarity of this problem made its members feel as they had done at the start of the programme. Their reaction was to return to the strategy that had worked in the early months of the programme: to seek guidance from the facilitator. Their facilitator, however, expected that the team would manage with only minimal support from her. This experience made Christine realize that the nature of problem could affect the type of facilitation required by the team. In the situation Christine felt that she could not simply revert to directive conventionalist mode, given the seniority of the team and their proven ability to be self-directed. The experience caused Christine to identify that she had repositioned herself to relinquish control and was no longer comfortable with asking direct questions and handing out information.

Shifts in views about the nature of disciplinary knowledge

Staff across the studies expressed new understandings of their disciplines. Simon explained his frustration with staff who believed that didactic teacher-centred approaches were the only way to produce good nurses, as they saw disciplinary knowledge as 'volume':

> Well, the rationale underpinning problem-based learning was explained to these people [the biological science lecturers] and they were – and attempts were made to engage them in dialogue about the rationale and the principles behind an alternative way of delivering biological science material ... The staff in that group operate on the belief that attendance at a lecture by a student equates with acquisition of that large body of knowledge, and they obviously believe that imparting that large body of knowledge to the student equates with learning.

For other staff, designing problem-based learning scenarios added to the depth of their knowledge in their content area, and frequently prompted changes in their ideas about how to teach the content of their discipline. The change in perspective frequently occurred in two ways, as a breaking down of artificial boundaries within the discipline and a breaking down of barriers across disciplinary areas. Staff comments highlighted another important outcome of the course redesign process: rather than relying on textbooks for the organizational structure of a particular area of content, they began to see the walls within the discipline break down. Another aspect highlighted by staff was the potential for problem-based learning to teach the cognitive processes inherent in many nursing actions. Clinical skills with a large psychomotor element, such as taking blood pressure or giving an injection, are often seen as being fairly straightforward to teach, if not to learn. Yet such capabilities require the understanding of supporting knowledge and theories. Capabilities that are perceived to be less psychomotor are often seen as being harder, such as individualized care planning. Yet problem-based learning points up the difficulties with dividing knowledge from skills and demonstrates that this division does not stand up to scrutiny; instead it is the questions we ask of students and the way knowledges are managed that enable or prevent the development of criticality in our students.

Staff who embraced problem-based learning commented that problem-based sessions were about nursing as a discipline in its own right. While the 'art and science' debate has reached a truce where there is agreement that nursing requires elements of both, arguments about what constitutes true nursing knowledge still rage. Nursing is still too often perceived as a collection of menial tasks, attached to knowledge borrowed from another discipline, such as biological or social science, which is perceived as having credence in its own right. As Simon raised, staff who taught from the perspective that knowledge was certain, in disciplines such as biological sciences, were reluctant to adopt problem-based learning. In contrast, tutors who valued nursing as a discipline in its own right saw in problem-based learning the opportunity to raise the status of nursing. While problem-based learning for some tutors resulting in the breaking down of artificial boundaries within the discipline and in breaking down barriers across disciplinary areas, it also provided opportunities for disciplinary knowledge to be reconstructed and redefined.

Discussion

The synthesis of these findings raises a number of issues, but in particular staff spoke of role transitions as challenges to their identity, suggesting that the discipline in which they taught affected the pedagogical options they believed they had about ways knowledge should be taught and learned. This in turn was affected by issues of personal and institutional power and control.

Staff in these studies re-examined their understanding of their role as a lecturer, of their students' roles as learners, of the structures of their disciplines and of their views of teaching. As participants reflected on their experiences, the combined effect of time, resources, support for risk-taking and collegial discussion presented an unusual gateway for the transformation of their pedagogical stances, knowledge and practice. The staff had received substantial institutional support yet many of them found self-management a complex task, while they were simultaneously helping students to manage their own transitions towards learning approaches that few had previously encountered. Although this was the case for the majority of staff in this study, there continued to be others who were not prepared to make shifts of any kind. However, facilitators valued support from each other and many commented that the support of other facilitators had been a major influence in adjusting to and then developing problem-based learning. Henkel (2000: 19) suggested that staff in this situation experience 'the complexities and tensions inherent in two major sources of identity, one local, visible and tangible, the other cosmopolitan, largely invisible and disembedded'; in short, their department and the university. From the synthesis of the two studies a third source of identity conflict emerged, namely that of professional identity. Thus the institutions in which academics are located and position themselves ensure that knowledge production and transmission occurs in particular ways that are acceptable to both the profession and the academics, while also sustaining the professional identities of academics.

The impact of the discipline on the pedagogy raises some interesting issues, including the application of approaches such as problem-based learning, how tensions between professional demands for competency and academic demands for criticality are resolved and the degree of willingness among staff to adopt a particular pedagogy, in this case problem-based learning.

Impact of the discipline on the model of problem-based learning

Problem-based learning may be perceived as a panacea approach that can be adapted to suit most disciplines. The form this adaptation takes will be influenced in some way by the discipline. Problem-based learning allows a marrying of issues related to discipline-based pedagogy and content. However, in such a combination, the staff perceptions of the discipline will impact on the model of problem-based learning adopted. Where there is departmental agreement about the nature of the discipline, then a single model may apply. From the result of our analysis, however, it is more likely that individual members of staff will have differing, rather then shared, disciplinary perspectives and therefore a variety of adaptations will occur even within the same module. One aspect that emerged from the studies was the relationship between staff expectations of the shifts that will occur as a result of implementing problem-based learning and the actual impact of the change. Staff at both Curbar and Kingarth expressed beliefs that introducing problem-based learning would bring about improved criticality and enhanced application of theory to practice. We have no findings relating to the impact of the change on student learning in either institution, although it is likely that the alteration of one element of discipline-based pedagogy will impact on the others.

Professional and pedagogical tensions

One of the tensions apparent in both studies was the conflict between the self-directed nature of problem-based learning and the competency-focused registration requirements of the Nursing and Midwifery Council (NMC). The NMC's forerunner, the United Kingdom Central Council for Nursing, Midwifery and Health Visiting (UKCC), had recommended problem-based learning as a strategy for nursing and midwifery programmes (UKCC 1999), stating that potentially it could reduce the theory–practice gap. Many tutors initially thought that the requirement for students to achieve fairly rigid, externally set competencies conflicted with the problem-based learning philosophy of allowing students to explore issues that they had identified for themselves. There was a sense of pragmatism related to contractual requirements to produce qualified practitioners for the health service. Added to the tensions was the realization that health care knowledge has a short life span. The study at Curbar identified that many tutors new to problem-based learning adopted 'gap filling' as a strategy. Filling the gaps allowed tutors to give students some degree of learning freedom, while ensuring that any perceived shortcomings were rectified, thus attempting to resolve the conflict between the pedagogy and the regulations. The control of student learning activity in the early stages of the Kingarth study may also be related to this tension. Tutors believed that students should have the freedom to identify their own learning, but in practice preferred to retain control. With time and experience, many of the Kingarth facilitators recognized that a balance could be achieved between the demands of the regulatory body and the principles of problem-based learning.

The impact of professional identity on problem-based learning

Both studies identified that the facilitator's sense of professional identity impacts upon the way that discipline-based pedagogy is played out in the classroom. A continuum appeared to exist between facilitators who had moved beyond professional boundaries to post-disciplinarity (Delanty 2001) at one pole, and staff who retained a confined view of the discipline at the other. Where staff positioned themselves on this continuum impacted on how, and indeed if, problem-based learning was adopted within the discipline. Staff who had a belief in nursing as an evidence-based discipline, and whose boundaries were blurred and overlapped with those of other health and social care professions, were more likely to develop facilitation styles which encouraged students to find out for themselves. Where staff held a professional identity in which nursing was perceived as nurturing and caring, tutors often attempted to role-model these characteristics for students in the problem-based groups. This approach may have enhanced feelings of engagement and belonging for students, but its impact on problem-based learning was to impede the development of self-directed learning and criticality, while reinforcing traditional stereotypes. A third group, whose view of nursing relied on the application of knowledge borrowed from other disciplines (for example, the biological science lecturers identified by Simon in the Curbar study), was resistant to problem-based learning. Their resistance appeared to stem from problem-based learning's potential to alter their local, visible and tangible identity within the school – that is, from 'teachers of biological science in nursing' to the more cosmopolitan 'lecturer' – and to present nursing as operating independently on several ever-changing levels rather than as a function of a clearly defined knowledge base.

Conclusion

Although we consider that discipline-based pedagogy requires more understanding and further unpacking, we believe, as Delanty suggests, that 'disciplinary boundaries are becoming blurred as multidisciplinarity becomes the norm and as the new phenomenon of "postdisciplinarity" takes over' (Delanty 2001: 3). Knowledge production is no longer sited just in academe but also takes place in hospitals, schools, communities and companies. What is not clear in the studies and discussions about discipline-based pedagogy is how it is that staff breach disciplinary restrictions and instead search for more interdisciplinary approaches. We suggest that research needs to be undertaken that examines the integrative character of discipline-based pedagogy, and in particular, those staff who have all selected a particular educational approach because they believe it best supports teaching within an interdisciplinary context.

Note

1 We use the terms tutor and staff interchangeably to reflect a member of the teaching staff in the university, usually denoted as 'staff' in the UK and as 'faculty' in the USA.

Epilogue

Maggi Savin-Baden and Kay Wilkie

Ending on the threshold

Problem-based learning is contested ground and the research presented in this book illustrates this position. Research into this approach remains complex and difficult largely because of the different ways it is implemented and enacted in various institutions in different countries by assorted staff. Yet such diversity demonstrates the versatility of problem-based learning for both staff and students and also indicates that it is a challenging approach because it generates disjunction and 'stuckness' in people's lives. The transitions that problem-based learning seems to prompt have been well documented elsewhere (Savin-Baden 2000a; Wilkie 2002) but we would like to develop this argument in order to provide a troublesome and challenging ending.

Meyer and Land (2003) have argued for the notion of a 'threshold concept', the idea of a portal that opened up a way of thinking that was previously inaccessible. Although initially Meyer and Land argued for such a concept being located as something distinct within a set of core material that university lecturers would teach, more recently (Meyer and Land 2004) they have broadened this to include concept staff experiences. An example of this might be that university staff who have used lecture-based methods experience disjunction when undertaking a diploma in learning and teaching that is taught using a problem-based approach. Further, they suggest that characteristics of threshold concepts are:

- Transformative: resulting in a significant shift in the perception of a subject or set of ideas.
- Irreversible: unlikely to reversed, thus the position that is reached ultimately may be rejected but not returned to.
- Integrative: illustrates how ideas or knowledge are linked together in ways that were not formerly apparent.

- Bounded: so that the new 'space' that has been entered has frontiers that border with other threshold concepts.
- Troublesome: difficult to teach, something that may be counter-intuitive or seem to be incoherent.

We suggest that problem-based learning is something that for many staff and students begins as such a threshold concept. However, we argue that it becomes a *threshold philosophy* for many people because of the impact it has on their lives as learners and teachers. Although we would be the first to acknowledge that engaging with problem-based learning can be costly personally and pedagogically we also believe that it is a powerful transitional process. For example, problem-based learning is often a difficult approach for staff and students to grasp because it challenges them to see learning and knowledge in new ways. Once they have entered the portal they very quickly move away from the idea that is necessarily foundation knowledge(s) and core concepts. However, what is problematic, but also vital, about the notion of a threshold concept is that preliminary variation exists. Meyer and Land (2004) begin by suggesting that when students find particular concepts difficult they are in a state of liminality. This state of liminality (something that is very much akin to forms of enabling and disabling disjunction; Savin-Baden 2000a) tends to be characterized by a stripping away of old identities, an oscillation between states and personal transformation. Preliminary variation is a means of distinguishing between 'variation in students' "tacit" understanding (or lack thereof) of a threshold concept' (Meyer and Land 2004). This, they argue, means that it may be possible to understand why some students approach and manage the threshold concepts, while others cannot. However, given the notion of preliminary variation, the questions remain: how do we decide what counts as a threshold concept and what does not, and who makes that decision? Perhaps we should also ask whether the use of problem-based learning reduces the instance of preliminary variations because of the shifts that are made away from a belief in core concepts and the idea that some knowledge is necessarily foundational to other knowledge. This may in turn result in students on problem-based programmes having fewer requirements for engaging with threshold concepts because problems are designed to engage students with issues connected with learning, life and the development of future (professional) identities.

Yet we suggest that if we see problem-based learning as a *threshold philosophy* then preliminary variation is vital to the realization that there may be different levels and issues at which stuckness occurs for staff and students. Reflecting on the chapters across this volume it possible to see such variations in studies about particular issues, the different experiences of staff and students and diversity across disciplinary use. Furthermore, in the context of the arguments for discipline-based pedagogy we suggest that problem-based learning acts as a catalyst in the shift away from the need to ground understanding about the relationship between the discipline and the pedagogy towards 'postdisciplinarity', a position where the professions, professional knowledge, the discipline and disciplinary boundaries become a contested conglomerate ... a place where everything is brought together with a view that blurred boundaries and transitions are part of the way life and learning is managed.

We began by producing this volume as a means of illustrating the variety, versatility and vagaries of problem-based learning. We wanted to demonstrate the kinds of research and possibilities that are available through this approach but as we draw it together we realize that perhaps we have done something different. Instead, we believe that this book presents research and practice, disciplinary differences and similarities, but it also shows that problem-based learning can be seen as a threshold philosophy that promotes not just transitions but transformation in the lives of learners, whether staff or students. For us, problem-based learning is a place where we continue to stand on the threshold; it remains the brink and the borderland for our practice-led research.

Bibliography

Albanese, M. A. and Mitchell, S. (1993) Problem-based learning: a review of literature on its outcomes and implementation issues. *Academic Medicine*, 68(1): 52–68.

Altheide, D. and Johnson, J. (1994) Criteria for assessing interpretive validity in qualitative research, in N. Denzin and Y. Lincoln (eds) *Handbook of Qualitative Research*. Thousand Oaks, CA: Sage.

Alvesson, M. and Sköldberg, K. (2000) *Reflexive Methodology: New Vistas for Qualitative Research*. London: Sage.

Andersson, T. (1997) Studenternas perpektiv på examination (The student's perspective on assessement). Paper presented to The Nordic Association for Educational Research congress in Göteborg, Sweden, 6–9 March.

Argyris, C. and Schön, D. A. (1974) *Theory in Practice: Increasing Professional Effectiveness*. San Francisco: Jossey-Bass.

Ashworth, P. D. (2003) Developing usable pedagogic research skills. Paper presented to 11th Improving Student Learning Symposium: Theory, Research and Scholarship, Hinckley, Leicestershire, 1–3 September.

Aune, B. P. (1995) The human dimension of organisational change. *The Review of Higher Education*, 18(2): 149–73.

Barab, S. and Landa, A. (1997) Designing effective interdisciplinary anchors. *Educational Leadership*, 54(6): 52–6.

Barnes, D. (ed.) (1976) *From Communication to Curriculum*. London: Penguin.

Barnes, D. (ed.) (1992) *From Communication to Curriculum*, 2nd edn. Portsmouth, NH: Boyton/Cook Publishers.

Barrett, T. (2001) Philosophical principles for problem based learning: Freire's concepts of personal development and social empowerment, in P. Little and P. Kandlbinder (eds) *The Power of Problem Based Learning*. Refereed Proceedings of the 3rd Asia Pacific Conference on problem-based learning, 9–12 December. Newcastle, Australia: Problarc.

Barrows, H. S. (1985) *How to Design a Problem-based Curriculum for Preclinical Years*. New York: Springer.

Barrows, H. S. (1986) A taxonomy of problem-based learning methods. *Medical Education*, 20: 481–6.

Barrows, H. S. (1988) *The Tutorial Process*. Springfield: Southern Illinois University School of Medicine.

Barrows, H. S. and Tamblyn, R. M. (1980) *Problem-based Learning: An Approach to Medical Education.* New York: Springer.

Beaty, L., France, L. and Gardiner, P. (1997) Consultancy style action research: a constructive triangle. *International Journal for Academic Development*, 2(2): 83–8.

Bensimon, E. M. and Neumann, A. (1993) *Redesigning Collegiate Leadership: Teams and Teamwork in Higher Education.* Baltimore: Johns Hopkins University Press.

Biggs, J. (1999) *Teaching for Quality Learning at University.* Buckingham: SRHE/Open University Press.

Biggs, J. (2003) *Teaching for Quality Learning at University: What the Student Does*, 2nd edn. Maidenhead: SRHE/Open University Press.

Bloom, B. (1956) *Taxonomy of Educational Objectives.* New York: Longmans Green.

Blumberg, P. (2000) Evaluating the evidence that problem-based learners are self-directed learners: a review of the literature, in D. Evensen and C. Hemlo (eds) *Problem-based Learning: Research Perspective on Learning Interactions.* Mahwah, NJ: Lawrence Erlbaum.

Blumer, H. (1986) *Symbolic Interactionism, Perspective and Method.* Berkeley: University of California Press.

Boaler, J. (1996) Learning to lose in the mathematics classroom: a critique of traditional schooling practices in the UK. *Qualitative Studies in Education*, 9(1): 17–34.

Boekaerts, M. (1997) Self-regulated learning: a new concept embraced by researchers, policy makers, educators, teachers and students. *Learning and Instruction*, 7(2): 161–86.

Boekaerts, M. (2001) Context sensitivity: activated motivational beliefs, current concerns and emotional arousal, in S. Volet and S. Järvelä (eds) *Motivation in Learning Contexts: Theoretical Advances and Methodological Implications.* Amsterdam: Pergamon Press.

Boler, M. (1999) *Feeling Power: Emotions and Education.* New York: Routledge.

Bolman, L. G. and Deal, T. E. (1997) *Reframing Organizations: Artistry, Choice, and Leadership*, 2nd edn. San Francisco: Jossey-Bass.

Boud, D. (ed.) (1985) *Problem-based Learning in Education for the Professions.* Sydney: Higher Education Research and Development Society of Australasia.

Boud, D. (ed.) (1988) *Developing Student Autonomy in Learning*, 2nd edn. London: Kogan Page.

Boud, D. (1990) Assessment and the promotion of academic values. *Studies in Higher Education*, 15(1): 101–11.

Boud, D. (1995) Ensuring that assessment contributes to learning, in *Proceedings, International Conference on Problem-based learning in Higher Education.* Linköping, Sweden, 24–27 September.

Boud, D. and Feletti, G. (eds) (1997) *The Challenge of Problem Based Learning*, 2nd edn. London: Kogan Page.

Boud, D. and MacDonald, R. (1981) *Educational Development through Consultancy.* Guildford: SRHE.

Bowe, B. (2001a) Teaching physics using problem-based learning. Paper presented to the Physics Discipline Network Workshop, University of Leeds, 12–13 September.

Bowe, B. (2001b) Developing and using an online resource to support students learning. Paper presented to Dublin Institute of Technology E-Learning Innovations Conference, 22 November.

Boyer, N. (2003) Leaders mentoring leaders: unveiling role identity in an international online environment. *Mentoring and Tutoring*, 11(1): 25–41.

Bransford, J. D., Franks, J. J., Vye, N. J. and Sherwood, R. D. (1989) New approaches to instruction: because wisdom can't be told, in S. Vosniadou and A. Ortany (eds) *Similarity and Analogical Reasoning*. New York: Cambridge University Press.

Bridges, E. (1992) *Problem-based Learning for Administrators*. Eugene, OR: ERIC Clearinghouse on Educational Management.

Bridges, E. and Hallinger, P. (1995) *Implementing Problem-based Learning in Leadership Development*. Eugene, OR: ERIC Clearing House on Educational Management.

Bridges, E. and Hallinger, P. (1996) Problem-based learning in leadership education, in L. Wilkerson and W. H. Gijselaers (eds) *New Directions for Teaching and Learning, Volume 68*. San Francisco: Jossey-Bass.

Bridges, E. and Hallinger, P. (1997) Using problem-based learning to prepare educational leaders. *Peabody Journal of Education*, 72(2): 131–46.

Bridges, E. and Hallinger, P. (1998) Problem-based learning in medical and managerial education, in R. Fogarty (ed.) *Problem-based Learning: A Collection of Articles*. Arlington Heights, IL: Skylight.

Britten, N., Campbell, R., Pope, C., Donovan, J., Morgan, M. and Pill, R. (2002) Using meta ethnography to synthesise qualitative research: a worked example. *Journal of Health Services Research Policy*, 7(4): 209–15.

Broersma, J. and Macdonald, R. (1998) Developments in problem-based learning: the students' perceptions of their learning. Paper presented to 10th Annual Conference of the European Association for International Education, Stockholm, Sweden.

Brohn, D. M. and Cowan, J. (1977) Teaching towards an understanding of structural behaviour. *The Structural Engineer*, 55(1): 9–17.

Brouwers, M. P. and Macdonald, R. (1996) Transition from a subject-oriented to a theme-oriented curriculum. Paper presented to 3rd International Educational Innovations in Economics and Business Conference, Orlando, Florida, USA.

Brown, R. and Gilman, A. (1960) The pronouns of power and solidarity, in P. Giglioli (ed.) *Language and Social Context*. Harmondsworth: Penguin.

Burgess, H. and Taylor, I. (2000) From university teacher to learning coordinator: faculty roles in problem-based learning. *Journal on Excellence in College Teaching*, 11: 83–96.

Burton, L. (1995) Moving towards a feminist epistemology of mathematics. *Educational Studies in Mathematics*, 28: 275–91.

Burton, L. (1999) The practices of mathematicians: what do they tell us about coming to know mathematics? *Educational Studies in Mathematics*, 37: 121–41.

Burton, L. (2000) Strangers in paradise? The construction of mathematics as a male community of practice. Paper given to the 5th symposium on Gender Research, The Nature of Gender – the Gender of Nature, Kiel, Germany, 10–12 November.

Burton, L. (2001) Research mathematicians as learners – and what mathematics education can learn from them. *British Educational Research Journal*, 27(5): 589–99.

Burton, L. and Haines, C. (1997) Innovation in teaching and assessing mathematics at university level. *Teaching in Higher Education*, 2(3): 273–93.

Cameron, D. (2001) *Working with Spoken Discourse*. London: Sage.

Candy, P. (1991) *Self-direction for Lifelong Learning*. San Francisco: Jossey-Bass.

Carr, W. and Kemmis, S. (1986) *Becoming Critical: Education, Knowledge and Action Research*. London: Falmer Press.

Case, J., Gunstone, R. and Lewis, A. (1999) Student perceptions of new approaches to teaching and assessment in an undergraduate chemical engineering course. Paper presented to 8th European Conference for Research on Learning and Instruction, Gotenborg, Sweden, 24–28 August.

Chapman, D. W. (2000) Designing problems for motivation and engagement in the problem-based learning classroom. *Journal on Excellence in College Teaching*, 11: 73–82.

Charlin, B., Mann, K. and Hansen, P. (1998) The many faces of problem-based learning: a framework for understanding and comparison. *Medical Teacher*, 20: 323–30.

Cock, S. and Pickard, P. (1996) An experiment in flexible learning – Foundation Maths. Unpublished manuscript, University of North London.

Cockrell, K. S., Caplow, J. A. H. and Donaldson, J. F. (2000) A context for learning: collaborative groups in the problem-based learning environment. *Review of Higher Education*, 23(3): 347–63.

Coles, C. R. (1985) Differences between conventional and problem-based curricula in their students' approaches to studying. *Medical Education*, 19: 308–9.

Conway, J. and Little, P. (2000a) *From Practice to Theory: Reconceptualising Curriculum Development for PBL*, Conference Proceedings, 2nd Asia Pacific Conference on Problem-based Learning. Temasek Centre for Problem Based Learning (http://www.tp.edu.sg/pblconference/Paper.htm). Accessed 30 October 2001.

Conway, J. and Little, P. (2000b) Adopting PBL as the preferred institutional approach to teaching and learning: considerations and challenges. *Journal on Excellence in College Teaching*, 11(2/3): 11–26.

Cordova, D. and Lepper, M. (1996) Intrinsic motivation and the process of learning: beneficial effects of contextualization, personalization and choice. *Journal of Educational Psychology*, 88(4): 715–30.

Coumeya, C.-A. (2001) Too little, too late?, in P. Schwartz, S. Mennin and G. Webb (eds) *Problem-based Learning. Case Studies, Experience and Practice*. London: Kogan Page.

Cowan, J. (1980) Quantitative and qualitative understanding of engineering phenomena, in Proceedings of Ingenieur Pädagogik, Vienna, September.

Cowan, J. (1982) Ascending order questions. *Civil Engineering Education (ASEE)*, 4(2): 7–9.

Cowan, J. (1983) How engineers understand. *Engineering Education*, 13(4): 301–3.

Cowan, J. (2002) What makes a successful education innovation? Paper presented to Teaching Physics at First Year Level Conference, Dublin Institute of Technology, 2 May.

Csikszentmihalyi, M. (1975) *Beyond Boredom and Anxiety*. San Francisco: Jossey-Bass.

Curtin, J. (2002) WebCT and online tutorials: new possibilities for participant interaction. *Australian Journal of Educational Technology*, 18(1): 110–26.

Dahlgren, L. O. (1990) *Undervisningen och det meningsfulla lärandet*. Linköpings universitet, Skapande vetande, rapport nr 16.

Dahlgren, M. A., Castensson, R. and Dahlgren, L. O. (1998) PBL from the teachers' perspective. *Higher Education*, 36(4): 437–47.

Dahllöf, U. (1967) *Skoldifferentiering och undervisningsförlopp (School Differentiation and Teaching Process)*. Stockholm: Almqvist and Wiksell.

Dahllöf, U. (1971) *Ability Grouping, Content Validity, and Curriculum Process Analysis*. New York: Teachers College Press.

Dahllöf, U. (1991) Towards a new model for the evaluation of teaching: an interactive process-centered approach, in U. Dahllöf, J. Harris, M. Shattock, A. Staropoli and R. in't Veld (eds) *Dimensions of Evaluation*. London: Jessica Kingsley Publishers.

Davies, W. K., Nairn, R., Paine M. E., Anderson, M. E and Oh, M. S. (1992) Effects of expert and non-expert facilitators on the small group process and on student performance. *Academic Medicine*, 67: 407–74.

Deci, E., Koestner, R. and Ryan, R. (2001) Extrinsic rewards and intrinsic motivation: reconsidered once again. *Review of Educational Research*, 71(1): 1–27.

Deci, E., Vallerand, R., Pelletier, L. and Ryan, R. (1991). Motivation and education: the self-determination perspective. *Educational Psychologist*, 26: 325–46.

De Corte, E., Geerligs, T., Lagerweij, N., Peters, J. and Vandenberghe, R. (1981) *Beknopte Didaxologie*. Groningen: Wolters-Noordhoff.

De Graaff, E. and Cowdroy, R. (2002) The best way to Rome: a paradigm for the assessment of excellent student performance, in *Proceedings of the ASEE 2002 Conference*, Montreal.

De Graaff, E. and Kruit, P. (1999a) Assessment of learning results in a problem-based physics course (geaccepteerd), in J. Daudt and O. Rompelman (eds) *What Have They Learned? Assessement of Students in Higher Education*. Brussels: SEFI.

De Graaff, E. and Kruit, P. (1999b) Enhancing student motivation in applied physics by means of a PBL module. Paper presented to the 5th international PBL conference 99, Montreal, 7–10 July.

De Grave, W., Dolmans, D. H. J. M. and van der Vleuten, C. P. M. (1998) Tutor intervention profile: reliability and validity. *Medical Education*, 32: 262–8.

De Grave, W., Dolmans, D. H. J. M. and van der Vleuten, C. P. M. (1999) Profiles of effective tutors in problem-based learning: scaffolding student learning. *Medical Education*, 33: 901–6.

Delanty, G. (2001) *Challenging Knowledge. The University in the Knowledge Society*. Buckingham: SRHE/Open University Press.

Denzin, N. (1997) *Interpretive Ethnography: Ethnographic practices for the 21st Century*. Thousand Oaks, CA: Sage.

Denzin, N. K. and Lincoln, Y. S. (eds) (1994) *Handbook of Qualitative Research*. Thousand Oaks, CA: Sage.

Des Marchais, J. E. and Chaput, M. (1993) Validation by network and Sherbrooke tutors of problem-based learning tasks, in P. A. J. Bouhuijs, H. G. Schmidt and H. J. M. van Berkel (eds) *Problem-based Learning as an Educational Strategy*. Maastricht: Network Publications.

De Vries, M., Schmidt, H. G. and de Graaf, E. (1989) Dutch comparisons: cognitive and motivational effects of problem-based learning on medical students, in H. G. Schmidt, M. Lipkin, M. W. de Vries and J. M. Greep (eds) *New Directions for Medical Education*. New York: Springer-Verlag.

Dewey, J. (1911) *How We Think*. New York: Prometheus Books.

Dewey, J. (1916) *Democracy and Education: An Introduction to the Philosophy of Education*. New York: Macmillan.

DIT Student Retention Office (2003) *Retention Rates amongst First Year Students in the Faculty of Science*. Dublin: Dublin Institute of Technology.

Dolmans, D. (1994) *How Students Learn in a Problem-based Curriculum*. Maastricht: Universitaire Pers Maastricht–III.

Dolmans, D. H. J. M. and Schmidt, H. G. (1994) What drives the student in problem-based learning? *Medical Education*, 28(5): 372–80.

Dolmans, D. H. J. M., Wolfhagen, I. H. A. P., Schmidt, H. G. and van der Vleuten, C. P. M. (1994a) A rating scale for tutor evaluation in a problem-based curriculum: validity and reliability. *Medical Education*, 28(6): 550–8.

Dolmans, D. H. J. M., Wolfhagen, I. H. A. P. and Snellen-Balendong, H. A. M. (1994b) Improving the effectiveness of tutors in problem-based learning. *Medical Teacher*, 16(4): 369–77.

Donald, J. (1997) *Improving the Environment for Learning: Academic Leaders Talk about What Works.* San Francisco: Jossey-Bass.

Duch, B. (1996) Problems: a key factor in problem-based learning. *Newsletter of the Center for Teaching Effectiveness (University of Delaware), About Teaching,* 49.

Duch, B., Groh, S. and Allen, D. (eds) (2001) *The Power of Problem-based Learning.* Sterling VA: Stylus.

Duek, J. (2000). Whose group is it, anyway? Equity of student discourse in problem-based learning (PBL), in D. Evensen and C. Hmelo (eds) *Problem-based Learning: A Research Perspective on Learning Interactions.* Mahwah, NJ: Lawrence Erlbaum.

Eccles, J., Wigfield, A. and Schiefele, U. (1998) Motivation to succeed, in W. Damon (ed.) *Handbook of Child Psychology, Volume 3.* New York: John Wiley.

Eco, U. (1984) *The Role of the Reader. Explorations in the Semiotics of Texts.* Bloomington: Indiana University Press.

Eisner, E. (1975) The perceptive eye: toward the reformulation of educational evaluation. Occasional papers for the Stanford Evaluation Consortium, Mimeo, Stanford University.

Elliott, J. (1991) *Action Research for Educational Change.* Buckingham: Open University Press.

Engel, C. H. (1997) Not just a method but a way of learning, in D. Boud and G. Feletti (eds) *The Challenge of Problem-based Learning.* London: Kogan Page.

Entwistle, N. and Marton, F. (1984) Att förändra uppfattningar av inlärning och forskning (Changing attitudes of learning and research), in F. Marton, D. Hounsell and N. Entwistle (eds) *The Experience of Learning.* Edinburgh: Scottish Academic Press.

Evans, R. (1996) *The Human Side of School Change: Reform, Resistance, and the Real-life Problems of Innovation.* San Francisco: Jossey-Bass.

Evensen, D. and Hmelo, C. (2000a) Problem-based learning: gaining insights on learning interactions through multiple methods of inquiry, in D. H. Evensen and C. E. Hmelo (eds) *Problem-based Learning: A Research Perspective on Learning Interactions.* Mahwah, NJ: Lawrence Erlbaum.

Evensen, D. and Hmelo, C. (eds) (2000b) *Problem-based Learning: A Research Perspective on Learning Interactions.* Mahwah, NJ: Lawrence Erlbaum.

Fairclough, N. (1992) *Discourse and Social Change.* Cambridge: Polity Press.

Fairclough, N. (2001) *Language and Power.* Harlow: Pearson Education.

Fairclough, N. (2003) *Analysing Discourse: Textual Analysis for Social Research.* London: Routledge.

Felder, R. (1996) Matters of style. *ASEE Prism,* 6(4): 18–23.

Festinger, L. A. (1957) *A Theory of Cognitive Dissonance.* Evanston, IL: Row, Peterson.

Fineman, S. (1993) Organizations as emotional arenas, in S. Fineman (ed.) *Emotions in Organizations.* London: Sage.

Fiske, J. (1982) *Introduction to Communication Studies.* London: Methuen.

Flavell, J. H. (1987) Speculations about the nature and development of metacognition, in F. E. Weinert and R. H. Kluwe (eds) *Metacognition, Motivation and Understanding.* Hillsdale, NJ: Erlbaum.

Frederiksen, N. (1984) The real test bias: influences of testing on teaching and learning. *American Psychologist*, 3: 193–202.

Freire, P. (1985) *The Politics of Education*. South Hadley, MA: Bergin and Garvey.

Fullan, M. (1982) *The Meaning of Educational Change*. New York: Teachers College Press.

Fullan, M. (1992) *Successful School Improvement*. Buckingham: Open University Press.

Fullan, M. (1997) Emotion and hope: constructive concepts for complex times, in A. Hargreaves (ed.) *Rethinking Educational Change with Heart and Mind*. Alexandria, VA: ASCD.

Fullan, M. and Hargreaves, A. (1991) *What's Worth Fighting For: Working Together for Your School, Strategies for Developing Professionalism in Your School*. Hawthorn, Victoria: Australian Council for Educational Administration.

Gadamer, H.-G. (1960) *Wahrheit und Methode*. Tübingen: J. C. B. Mohr.

Garfinkel, E. (1967) *Studies in Ethnomethodology*. Englewood Cliffs, NJ: Prentice Hall.

Garrison, D. R. (1997) Self-directed learning: toward a comprehensive model. *Adult Education Quarterly*, 48(1): 18–33.

Geertz, C. (1973) Thick descriptions: towards an interpretive theory of culture, in *The Interpretation of Cultures: Selected Essays*. New York: Basic Books.

George, J. W. and Cowan, J. (1999) *A Handbook of Techniques for Formative Evaluation*. London: Kogan Page.

Gibbs, G. (1992) *Improving the Quality of Student Learning*. Bristol: Technical and Educational Services.

Giddens, A. (1984) *The Constitution of Society: Outline of the Theory of Structuration*. Cambridge: Polity Press.

Gijselaers, W. H. (1996) Connecting problem-based practices with educational theory, in L. Wilkerson and W. Gijselaers (eds) *Bringing Problem-based Learning to Higher Education: Theory and Practice*. San Francisco: Jossey-Bass.

Gijselaers, W. H. (1997) Effects of contextual factors on tutor behaviour. *Teaching and Learning in Medicine*, 9(2): 116–24.

Gijselaers, W. H., Templelaar, D. T. and Keizer, P. K. (eds) (1995) *Educational Innovation in Economics and Business Administration: The Case of Problem-based Learning*. Boston: Kluwer Academic.

Gitlin, A., Siegel, M. and Boru, K. (1989) The politics of method: from leftist ethnography to educative research. *Journal of Qualitative Studies in Education*, 2(3): 237–53.

Glaser, B. and Strauss, A. L. (1967) *The Discovery of Grounded Theory, Strategies for Qualitative Research*. Chicago: Aldine.

Goleman, D. (1998) *Working with Emotional Intelligence*. London: Bloomsbury.

Grabinger, S. and Dunlap, J. (2000) Rich environments for active learning: a definition, in D. Squires, G. Conole and G. Jacobs (eds) *The Changing Face of Learning Technology*. Cardiff: University of Wales Press.

Greenbaum, T. L. (2000) *Moderating Focus Groups: A Practical Guide for Group Facilitation*. Thousand Oaks, CA: Sage.

Greene, J. (1994) Qualitative program evaluation: practice and promise, in N. K. Denzin and Y. S. Lincoln (eds) *Handbook of Qualitative Research*. London: Sage.

Grundy, S. (1982) Three modes of action research. *Curriculum Perspectives*, 2(3): 23–34.

Guba, E. and Lincoln, Y. (1981) *Effective evaluation*. San Francisco: Jossey-Bass.

Guilbert, L. and Ouellet, L. (1999) *Étude de cas. Apprentissage par problèmes*. Montreal: Presses de l'Université du Québec.

Gynnild, V. (2001) Læringsorientert eller eksamensfokusert? Nærstudier av peda- gogisk utviklingsarbeid i sivilingeniørstudiet (Oriented towards learning or focused on exams? A close up study of educational development in the engi- neering faculties). Thesis, Norwegian University of Science and Technology, Trondheim.

Habermas, J. (1984) *The Theory of Communicative Action, Volume 2, System and Lifeworld: A Critique of Functionalist Reason.* Boston: Beacon Press.

Habermas, J. (1996) *Between Facts and Norms.* Cambridge: Polity Press.

Hager, P. and Butler, J. (1994) Problem-based Learning and paradigms of assess- ment, in S. E. Chen, R. M. Cowdroy, A. J. Kingsland and M. J. Ostwald (eds) *Reflections on Problem-based Learning.* Sydney: Australian Problem Based Learning Network.

Hager, P., Gonczi, A. and Athanasou, J. (1994) General issues about assessment of competence. *Assessment and Evaluation in Higher Education,* 19(1): 3–16.

Haggis, T. (2002) Exploring the 'black box' of process: a comparison of theoretical notions of the 'adult learner' with accounts of post graduate learning experi- ence. *Studies in Higher Education,* 27(2): 207–20.

Haith-Cooper, M. (2000) Problem-based learning within health professional edu- cation: what is the role of the lecturer? A review of the literature. *Nurse Education Today,* 20: 267–72.

Hak, T. and Maguire, P. (2000) Group process: the black box of studies on problem- based learning. *Academic Medicine,* 75: 769–72.

Hall, S. (1980) Encoding/decoding, in S. Hall, D. Hobson, A. Lowe and P. Willis (eds) *Culture, Media, Language.* London: Hutchinson.

Hammersley, M. and Atkinsson, P. (1995) *Ethnography: Principles in Practice,* 2nd edn. London: Tavistock.

Hannan, A. and Silver, H. (2000) *Innovating in Higher Education: Teaching, Learning and Institutional Cultures.* Buckingham: SRHE/Open University Press.

Hargreaves, A. (1992) Cultures of teaching: a focus for change, in A. Hargreaves and M. Fullan (eds) *Understanding Teacher Development.* London: Cassell.

Hargreaves, A. (1997) Rethinking educational change: going deeper and wider in the quest for success, in A. Hargreaves (ed.) *Rethinking Educational Change with Heart and Mind.* Alexandria, VA: ASCD.

Hargreaves, A. (1998) The emotional practice of teaching. *Teaching and Teacher Education,* 14(8): 835–54.

Henkel, M. (2000) *Academic Identities and Policy Change in Higher Education.* London: Jessica Kingsley Publishers.

Hochschild, A. R. (1983) *The Managed Heart: The Commercialization of Human Feeling.* Berkeley: University of Cambridge Press.

Hockings, C. (2003) Swimming against the tide. Unpublished PhD thesis, University of Birmingham School of Education.

Hoel, T. L. (1995) Elevsamtalar om skriving i vidaregående skole. Responsgrupper i teori og praksis (Student conversations about writing in upper secondary school. Response groups in theory and in practice). PhD thesis, University of Trondheim, ALS-skrift 3 I and II.

Hogan, K. and Pressley, M. (eds) (1997) *Scaffolding Student Learning: Instructional Approaches and Issues.* Cambridge, MA: Brookline Books.

Holliday, A. (2002) *Doing and Writing Qualitative Research.* London: Sage.

Holub, R. C. (1984) *Reception Theory: A Critical Introduction.* London: Methuen.

Houston, K., Rogers, P. and Simpson, A. (1997) Teaching mathematics as a way of life, in C. Rust (ed.) *OCSLD, Proceedings: Improving Student Learning through the Discipline*, 7th international symposium. Oxford: Oxford Brookes University.

Hutchings, P. and Shulman, L. S. (1999) The scholarship of teaching: new elaborations, new developments. *Change*, 31(5): 11–15.

Institute of Physics (2001) *Physics: Building a Flourishing Future*. Report on the Inquiry into Undergraduate Teaching. London: IOP Publishing.

Irish Government (2002) *Report of the Task Force on the Physical Sciences: Report and Recommendations*. Dublin: Irish Government Publications.

Jacobsen, D. Y. (1997) Tutorial processes in a problem-based learning context: medical students' reception and negotiations. Thesis, Norwegian University of Science and Technology, Trondheim.

Jacobsen, D. Y. (2002) Kommunikasjonsprosesser i problembaserte læringsgrupper (Communication processes in problem-based learning groups), in K. H. Lycke (ed.) *Perspektiver på problembasert læring* (*Perspectives on Problem-based Learning*). Oslo: Cappelen akademisk forlag.

Jank, W. and Meyer, H. (1997) Didaktikens centrala frågor, in M. Uljens (ed.) *Didaktik-teori, reflektion och praktik*. Lund: Studentlitteratur.

Järvelä, S. (2001) Shifting research on motivation and cognition to an integrated approach on learning and motivation in context, in S. Volet and S. Järvelä (eds) *Motivation in Learning Contexts: Theoretical Advances and Methodological Implications*. Amsterdam: Pergamon Press.

Jeffrey, B. and Woods, P. (1996) Feeling deprofessionalised: the social construction of emotions during an OFSTED inspection. *Cambridge Journal of Education*, 26(3): 325–43.

Jenkins, A. and Zetter, R. (2003) *Linking Teaching and Research in Departments*. York: LTSN Generic Centre.

Johansson, B. (1975) *Aritmetikundervisning. En rapport om en datainsamling* (*Teaching Arithmetic. A Report from a Data Collection*), PUMP-projektet 9. Göteborg: Pedagogiska Institutionen, Göteborgs universitet.

Jonassen, D., Peck, K. and Wilson, R. (1999) *Learning with Technology: A Constructivist Perspective*. Columbus, OH: Merrill Prentice Hall.

Jones, K. (2003) Mission drift in qualitative research or moving toward a systematic review of qualitative studies, moving back to a more systematic narrative review (http://users.wbs.ac.uk/group/ceehd/home/mission_drift). Accessed 14 January 2004.

Jørgensen, M. and Phillips, L. (2002) *Discourse Analysis as Theory and Method*. London: Sage.

Jung, I., Choi, S., Lim, C. and Leem, J. (2002) Effects of different types of interaction on learning achievement, satisfaction and participation in web-based instruction. *IETI*, 39(2): 153–62.

Kandlbinder, P. and Mauffette, Y. (2001) Perception of teaching by science teachers using a student-centred approach, in P. Little and P. Kandlbinder (eds) *The Power of Problem Based Learning*. Newcastle: PROBLARC.

Katz, G. (1995) Facilitation, in C. Alavi (ed.) *Problem-based Learning in a Health Sciences Curriculum*. London: Routledge.

Kelson, A. and Distlehort, L. (2000) Groups in problem-based learning (PBL): essential elements in theory and practice, in D. Evensen and C. Hemlo (eds) *Problem-based Learning: A Research Perspective on Learning Interactions*. Mahwah, NJ: Lawrence Erlbaum.

Kemmis, S. and McTaggart, R. (1981) *The Action Research Planner*. Geelong, Australia:

Deakin University Press.

Kemmis, S. and McTaggart, R. (eds) (1988) *The Action Research Planner*, 3rd edn. Geelong: Deakin University Press.

King, S. and Cottrell, J. (1997) Collaborative change to a context directed model of problem based learning (CDL) curriculum. Paper presented to the 1997 Biennial PBL Conference, Brisbane.

Kirkpatrick, D. L. (1975) *Techniques for Evaluating Programs, Parts 1, 2, 3 and 4, Evaluating Programs.* Alexandria, VA: ASCD.

Kirkwood, G. and Kirkwood, C. (1990) *Living Adult Education: Freire in Scotland.* Buckingham: Open University Press.

Knowles, M. (1970) *The Modern Practice of Adult Education. Andragogy versus Pedagogy.* Chicago: Follet.

Knowles, M. (1975) *Self-directed Learning. Guide for Learners and Teachers.* Toronto: Prentice Hall.

Kolb, D. A. (1984) *Experiential Learning: Experience as the Source of Learning and Development.* Englewood Cliffs, NJ: Prentice Hall.

Kolmos, A. (2002) Facilitating change to a problem-based model. *International Journal for Academic Development,* 7(1): 63–74.

Koschmann, T., Glenn, P. and Conlee, M. (1997) Analyzing the emergence of a learning issue in a problem-based learning meeting. *Medical Education Online,* 2(2) (http://www.utmb.edu/meo).

Larochelle, M., Bednarz, N. and Garrison, J. (eds) (1998) *Constructivism and Education.* Cambridge: Cambridge University Press.

Lave, J. and Wenger, E. (1991) *Situated Learning: Legitimate Peripheral Participation.* Cambridge: Cambridge University Press.

Lieux, E. M. (1996) A comparative study of learning in lecture versus problem-based format. *About Teaching,* 50: 25–7.

Lincoln, Y. and Guba, E. (1985) *Naturalistic Inquiry.* London: Sage.

Lincoln, Y. and Guba, E. (2000) Paradigmatic controversies, contradictions and emerging confluences, in N. Denzin and Y. Lincoln (eds) *The Qualitative Research Handbook.* London: Sage.

Little, P. (1990) Problem-based learning: educational change for a changing world. Paper presented to the ANZAAS Congress, Hobart, Tasmania.

Lundgren, U. P. (1972) *Frame Factors and the Teaching Process. A Contribution to Curriculum Theory and Theory on Teaching.* Stockholm: Almquvist and Wiksell.

Lundgren, U. P. (1977) *Att organisera omvärlden – en introduktion till läroplansteori* (*Organizing the Environment – An Introduction to Curricular Theory*). Stockholm: Liber Förlag.

Lundgren, U. P. (1996) Utbildningspolitik och utbildningsplanering – personliga reflektioner (Educational policy and educational planning – personal reflections), in C. Gustavsson (ed.) *Pedagogikforskarens roll i utbilningsplanering* (*The Role of the Educational Researcher in Educational Planning*). Uppsala: University of Uppsala.

McDonald, J. and Gibson, C. (1998) Interpersonal dynamics and group development in computer conferencing. *American Journal of Distance Education,* 12(1): 6–24.

Macdonald, R. (1996) Foreign students studying in English in the Netherlands: a challenge/problem and possible solution, in C. Rust (ed.) *Improving Students' Learning through Course Design.* Oxford: Oxford Centre for Staff and Learning Development.

Macdonald, R. (1997) The impact of a move to theme or problem-based learning on students' perceptions of their learning, in C. Rust (ed.) *Improving Students as Learners*. Oxford: Oxford Centre for Staff and Learning Development.

Macdonald, R. (1998) Problem-based learning: the student perspective, in *Proceedings of the Annual Conference of the Higher Education Research and Development Society of Australasia*, Auckland, New Zealand.

Macdonald, R. (2001) An evidence-based approach to improving the learners' experience of problem-based learning, in *Proceedings of the Third Asia-Pacific Conference on Problem-based Learning*, University of Newcastle, Australia.

McFalls, E. L. and Cobb-Roberts, D. (2001) Reducing resistance to diversity through cognitive dissonance instruction: implications for teacher education. *Journal of Teacher Education*, 52(2): 164–72.

McInnis, C. (2000) Changing academic work roles: the everyday realities challenging qualities in teaching. *Quality in Higher Education*, 6(2): 143–53.

Macintyre, C. (2000) *The Art of Action Research in the Classroom*. London: David Fulton Publishers.

MacKinnon, M. (1999) CORE elements of student motivation in problem-based learning. *New Directions for Teaching and Learning*, 78 (Summer): 49–58.

Major, C., Cortis, T., Netherton, J., Harris, J. and Brymer, J. (1999) Supporting pedagogical change: a case study of the Samford PBL initiative. Paper presented to the 5th International PBL Conference, PBL: A Way Forward, Montreal, Canada.

Major, C. H. and Palmer, B. (2002a) Faculty knowledge of influences on student learning. *Peabody Journal of Education*, 77(3): 137–61.

Major, C. H. and Palmer, B. (2002b) Influences of implementing problem-based learning on faculty pedagogical content knowledge. Paper presented at the Annual Meeting of the American Educational Research Association, New Orleans.

Marchais, J. (1999) A Delphi technique to identify and evaluate criteria or construction of problem-based learning problems. *Medical Education*, 33: 504–8.

Margetson, D. (1991) Why is problem-based learning a challenge?, in D. Boud and G. Feletti (eds) *The Challenge of Problem Based Learning*. London: Kogan Page.

Margetson, D. (1993) Education, pedagogy and problem-based learning, in A. R.Viskovic (ed.) *Research and Development in Higher Education, 14*. Sydney: Higher Education Research and Development Society of Australasia.

Margetson, D. (1994) Current educational reform and the significance of problem-based learning. *Studies in Higher Education*, 19(1): 5–19.

Margetson, D. (1996) Beginning with the essentials: why problem-based learning begins with problems. *Education for Health*, 9(1): 61–9.

Margetson, D. (1997) Wholeness and educative learning: the questions of problems in changing to problem-based learning. Paper presented to the International Conference on Problem-based learning, Uxbridge, UK, September.

Margetson, D. (1998) What counts as problem-based learning? *Education for Health*, 11(2): 193–201.

Margetson, D. (2000) Reality, value and the future of problem-based learning. A keynote paper presented to the Second International Conference on Problem-based Learning in Higher Education, Linköping, Sweden, 17–20 September.

Margolis, E. (ed.) (2001) *The Hidden Curriculum in Higher Education*. New York: Routledge.

Martin, E. (1999) *Changing Academic Work: Developing the Learning University*. Buckingham: SRHE/Open University Press.

Martin, E., Prosser, M., Trigwell, P., Lueckenheusen, G. and Ramsden, P. (2001). Using phenomenography and metaphor to explore academics' understanding of teaching matter and teaching, in C. Rust (ed.) *Improving Student Learning, Volume 8.* Oxford: Oxford Centre for Staff and Learning Development.

Marton, F. and Booth, S. (1997) *Learning and Awareness.* Mahwah, NJ: Lawrence Erlbaum.

Marton, F., Hounsell, D. and Entwistle, N. (eds) (1984) *The Experience of Learning.* Edinburgh: Scottish Academic Press.

Marton, F. and Säljö, R. (1984) Cognitive strategies in learning, in F. Marton, D. Hounsell and N. Entwistle (eds) *The Experience of Learning.* Edinburgh: Scottish Academic Press.

Mason, J., Burton, L. and Kaye, S. (1982) *Thinking Mathematically.* Bath: Addison-Wesley.

Mason, R. (1998) Models of online courses. *ALN Magazine,* 2(2) (http://www.aln.org/alnweb/magazine/vol2_issue2/Masonfinal.htm). Accessed on 20 September 1999.

Maudsley, G. (1999) Roles and responsibilities of the problem based tutor in the undergraduate medical curriculum. *BMJ,* 318: 657–61.

Mauffette, Y. and Poliquin, L. (2001) Problem-based learning in science education: a curriculum reform in biology at the University of Quebec in Montreal. *Problem-based Learning Insight,* 4(1): 1–5.

MER (2002) http://www.kvalitetsreformen.dep.no.

Meyer, J. H. F. and Land, R. (2003) Threshold concepts and troublesome knowledge (1): linkages to ways of thinking and practising within the disciplines, in C. Rust (ed.) *Improving Students' Learning: Improving Student Learning Theory and Practice – Ten Years On.* Oxford: Oxford Centre for Staff and Learning Development.

Meyer, J. H. F. and Land, R. (2004) Threshold concepts and troublesome knowledge (2): epistemological and ontological considerations and a conceptual framework for teaching and learning. *Higher Education.*

Mezirow, J. (1981) A critical theory of adult learning and education. *Adult Education,* 32: 3–24.

Miflin, B. M. and Price, D. A. (2001) Why does the department have professors if they don't teach?, in P. Schwartz, S. Mennin and G. Webb (eds) *Problem-based Learning. Case Studies, Experience and Practice.* London: Kogan Page.

Millar, R. and Osborne, J. (eds) (1998) *Beyond 2000: Science Education for the Future.* London: King's College, School of Education.

Minichiello, V., Aroni, R., Timewell, E. and Alexander, L. (1995) *In-depth Interviewing: Principles, Techniques, Analysis,* 2nd edn. Melbourne: Longman.

Mioduser, D. and Nachmias, R. (2001) WWW in education, in H. Adelsberger, B. Collis and J. Pawlowski (eds) *Handbook of Information Technology for Education and Training.* Berlin: Springer-Verlag.

Moore, G. T., Block, S. D., Briggs, S. C. and Mitchell, R. (1994) The influence of the New Pathway curriculum on Harvard medical students. *Academic Medicine,* 69: 983–9.

Moust, J. H. C. and Schmidt, H. G. (1994) Comparing students and faculty as tutors: how effective are they?, in P. A. J. Bouhuijs, H. G. Schmidt and H. J. M. van Berkel (eds) *Problem-based Learning as an Educational Strategy.* Maastricht: Network Publications.

Murray, I. and Savin-Baden, M. (2000) Staff development in problem-based learning. *Teaching in Higher Education,* 5(1): 23–7.

NCEA (1999) Conference on Skills Shortages in Science-based Industries in Ireland, January, Dublin.

Neville, A. J. (1999) The problem-based learning tutor. Teacher? Facilitator? Evaluator? *Medical Teacher*, 21(4): 393–401.

Newble, D. I. and Clarke, R. M. (1986) The approaches to learning of students in a traditional and an innovative problem-based medical school. *Medical Education*, 20: 267–73.

Newman, M. (2003) Prospective, blind, randomized controlled trial of PBL compared to 'traditional' teaching (http://www.hebes.mdx.ac.uk/teaching/Research/PEPBL/menu.htm). Accessed on 22 September 2003.

Nias, J. (1996) Thinking about feeling: the emotions in teaching. *Cambridge Journal of Education*, 26(3): 293–306.

Nias, J., Southworth, G. and Yeomans, R. (1989) *Staff Relationships in the Primary School: A Study of Organizational Cultures.* London: Cassell.

Noblit, G. W. and Hare, R. D. (1988) *Meta-ethnography: Synthesizing Qualitative Studies.* Newbury Park, CA: Sage.

Noll, V. H. (1961) *Introduction to Educational Measurement.* Boston: Houghton Mifflin.

Norman, G. and Schmidt, H. (1992) The psychological basis of problem-based learning: a review of the evidence. *Academic Medicine*, 67(9): 557–65.

Norman, G. and Schmidt, H. (2000) Effectiveness of problem-based learning curricula: theory, practice and paper darts. *Medical Education*, 34: 721–8.

Norman, G. R., Vleuten, C. P. M. and van de Graaff, E. (1991) Pitfalls in the pursuit of objectivity: issues of validity, efficiency and acceptancy. *Medical Education*, 25: 119–26.

Norris, N. (ed.) (1977) Safari: theory and practice. Paper 2, CARE, University of East Anglia.

Oakley, A. (1981) Interviewing women: a contradiction in terms, in H. Roberts (ed.) *Doing Feminist Research.* London: Routledge and Kegan Paul.

OECD (1998) *Educational Policy Analysis.* Paris: Organisation for Economic Co-operation and Development.

Pajares, F. (1996) Self-efficacy beliefs in academic settings. *Review of Educational Research*, 66: 543–78.

Paris, S. and Turner, J. (1994) Situated motivation, in P. Pintrich, D. Brown and C. Weinstein (eds) *Student Motivation, Cognition and Learning.* Hillsdale, NJ: Elbaum.

Patton, M. Q. (1987) *How to Use Qualitative Methods in Evaluation.* London: Sage.

Patton, M. Q. (1990) *Qualitative Evaluation and Research Methods*, 2nd edn. Newsbury Park, CA: Sage.

Potter, J. and Wetherell, M. (1987) *Discourse and Social Psychology. Beyond Attitudes and Behavior.* Newbury Park, CA: Sage.

Prosser, M., Trigwell, K. and Taylor, P. (1994). A phenomenographic study of academics' conceptions of science learning and teaching. *Learning and Instruction*, 4: 217–31.

Putnam, L. L. and Mumby, D. K. (1993) Organizations, emotion and the myth of rationality, in S. Fineman (ed.) *Emotion in Organizations.* London: Sage.

Quality Assurance Agency for Higher Education (2000) English Subject Benchmark (http://www.qaa.ac.uk/crntwork/benchmark/benchmarking). Accessed 5 December 2003.

Ramsden, P. (1984) The context of learning, in F. Marton, D. Hounsell and N. Entwistle (eds) *The Experience of Learning.* Edinburgh: Scottish Academic Press.

Ramsden, P. (1992) *Learning to Teach in Higher Education.* London: Routledge.

Ramsden, P. (2003) *Learning to Teach in Higher Education*, 2nd edn. London: Routledge.

Rando, W. C. and Menges, R. J. (1991) How practice is shaped by personal theories, in R. Menges and M. Svinicki (eds) *College Teaching: From Theory to Practice*. San Francisco: Jossey-Bass.

Reason, P. and Rowan, J. (1981) Issues of validity in new paradigm research, in P. Reason and J. Rowan (eds) *Human Inquiry: A Sourcebook of New Paradigm Research*. New York: John Wiley.

Reeve, J., Bolt, E. and Cai, Y. (1999) Autonomy-supportive teachers: how they teach and motivate students. *Journal of Educational Psychology*, 91(3): 537–48.

Renzetti, C. and Lee, R. (eds) (1993) *Researching Sensitive Topics*. London: Sage.

Ricoeur, P. (1986) *Time and Narrative, Volume 2*. Chicago: University of Chicago Press.

Rubin, H. and Rubin, I. (1995) *Qualitative Interviewing: The Art of Hearing Data*. London: Sage.

Ryan, G. (1993) Student perceptions about self-directed learning in a professional course implementing problem-based learning. *Studies in Higher Education*, 18(1): 53–63.

Sacks, H. (1984) On doing 'being ordinary', in J. M. Atkinson and J. Heritage (eds) *Structures of Social Action: Studies in Conversation Analysis*. Cambridge: Cambridge University Press.

Sadlo, G., Piper, D. W. and Agnew, P. (1994) Problem-based learning in the development of an occupational therapy curriculum, part 1. The process of problem-based learning. *British Journal of Occupational Therapy*, 57(2): 49–53.

Säljö, R. (2000) *Larande I praktiken: ett socuokultuellt perpektiv*. Stockholm: Prisma.

Savin-Baden, M. (2000a) *Problem-based Learning in Higher Education: Untold Stories*. Buckingham: SRHE/Open University Press.

Savin-Baden, M. (2000b) Facilitating problem-based learning: the impact of facilitator's pedagogical stances. *Journal on Excellence in College Teaching*, 11(2/3): 97–111.

Savin-Baden, M. (2001) (Dis)placed academics? Staff experiences of role change in the context of problem-based learning, in British Educational Research Association, Annual Conference, Leeds, 14–15 September.

Savin-Baden, M. (2003) Disciplinary differences or modes of curriculum practice? Who promised to deliver what in problem-based learning? *Biochemistry and Molecular Biology Education*, 31(5): 338–43.

Savin-Baden, M. and Fisher, A. (2002) Negotiating 'honesties' in the research process. *British Journal of Occupational Therapy*, 65(4): 191–3.

Savin-Baden, M. and Major, C. (2003) Fractured worlds and shattered pedagogies: Exploring the relationship between innovative approaches to learning and innovative methods of pedagogical research. Paper presented to Research, Scholarship and Teaching, changing relationships? Society for Research into Higher Education Annual Conference, Royal Holloway, University of London, 16–18 December.

Schmidt, H. G. (1993) Foundations of problem-based learning: some explanatory notes. *Medical Education*, 27: 422–32.

Schmidt, H. G. and Moust, J. H. C. (2000a) Towards a taxonomy of problems used in problem-based learning curricula. *Journal on Excellence in College Teaching*, 11: 57–72.

Schmidt, H. G. and Moust, J. H. C. (2000b) Factors affecting small-group facilitatorial learning: a review of research, in D. H. Evensen and C. E. Hmelo (eds)

Problem-based Learning: A Research Perspective on Learning Interactions. Mahwah, NJ: Lawrence Erlbaum.

Schoenfeld, A. H. (1988) When good teaching leads to bad results: the disasters of a 'well-taught' mathematics course. *Educational Psychologist*, 23(2): 145–66.

Schön, D. (1987) *Educating the Reflective Practioner.* London: Jossey-Bass.

Seely Brown, J., Collins, A. and Duguid, P. (1989) Situated cognition and the culture of learning. *Educational Researcher*, Jan/Feb: 32–42.

Shotter, J. (1993) *Conversational Realities: Constructing Life through Language.* London: Sage.

Shulman, L. (1986) Those who understand: knowledge growth in teaching. *Educational Researcher*, 15(2): 4–14.

Shulman, L. (1987) Knowledge and teaching: foundations of the new reform. *Harvard Educational Review*, 57(1): 1–22.

Silén, C. (2000) Between chaos and cosmos: about responsibility and independence in learning. Linköpings universitet, Department of Behavioural Sciences, doctoral thesis.

Silén, C. (2001) Between chaos and cosmos: a driving force for responsibility and independence in learning, in The power of problem based learning, PRO-BLARC, The 3rd Asia Pacific conference on PBL, University of Newcastle, Australia, 9–12 December

Silén, C. (2003) Responsibility and independence in learning: what is the role of the educators and the framework of the educational programme?, in C. Rust (ed.) *Improving Student Learning: Theory, Research and Practice.* Oxford: Oxford Centre for Staff and Learning Development.

Sjöberg, S. (2001) Science and technology in education: current challenges and possible solutions. Position paper presented to the informal meeting of Ministers of Education and Research in Uppsala, Sweden, 1–3 March.

Skinner, V., Winning, T. and Townsend, G. (2001) Using concept mapping to investigate changes in the organization and integration of students' knowledge to evaluate problem-based learning packages, in P. Little, and P. Kandlbinder (eds) *The Power of Problem Based Learning.* Newcastle: PROBLARC.

Sokal, A. and Bricmont, J. (1998) *Intellectual Impostures.* London: Profile Books.

Soucisse, A., Mauffette, Y. and Kandlbinder, P. (2003) Les problèmes: pivots de apprentissage par problème (AAP). *Res Academica*, 21(1): 129–50.

Stinson, J. and Milter, R. (1996) Problem-based learning in business education: curriculum design and implementation issues, in L. Wilkerson and W. Gijselaers (eds) *Bringing Problem-based Learning to Higher Education: Theory and Practice.* San Francisco: Jossey-Bass.

Stronach, I., Corbin, B., McNamara, O., Stark, S. and Warne, T. (2002) Towards an uncertain politics of professionalism: teacher and nurse identities in flux. *Journal of Educational Policy*, 17(1): 109–38.

Stufflebeam, D. L., Madaus, G. F. and Kellaghan, T. (eds) (2000) *Evaluation Models: Viewpoints on Educational and Human Services Evaluation.* Boston: Kluwer-Nijhoff.

Tanner, C., Galls, S. and Pajak, E. (1997) Problem-based learning in advanced preparation of educational leaders. *Educational Planning*, 10(3): 3–12.

Taylor, G. (1993) A theory of practice: hermeneutical understanding. *Higher Education Research and Development*, 12(1): 59–72.

Taylor, I. and Burgess, H. (1995) Orientation to self-directed learning: paradox or transition process. *Studies in Higher Education*, 20(1): 87–97.

Thayer-Bacon, B. J. (2000) *Transforming Critical Thinking.* New York: Teachers College Press.

Thomas, M. L., Snaddon, D. and Carlisle, S. (1998) 'When the talking starts': a framework for analysing tutorials. *Medical Education,* 32: 502–6.

Tipping, J., Freeman, R. F. and Rachlis, A. R. (1995) Using faculty and student perceptions of group dynamics to develop recommendations for PBL training. *Academic Medicine,* 70(11): 1050–2.

Tran, V. (1998) The role of the emotional climate in learning organisations. *The Learning Organisation,* 5(2): 99–103.

Trowler, P. and Cooper, A. (2002) Teaching and learning regimes: implicit theories and recurrent practices in the enhancement of teaching and learning through educational development. *Higher Education Research and Development,* 21(3): 221–40.

Trowler, P. R. and Knight, P. T. (2002) Exploring the implementation gap: theory and practices in change interventions, in P. R. Trowler (ed.) *Higher Education Policy and Institutional Change: Intentions and Outcomes in Turbulent Environments.* Buckingham: SRHE/Open University Press.

Uljens, M. (1997) *School Didactics and Learning.* London: Routledge.

United Kingdom Central Council for Nursing, Midwifery and Health Visiting (1999) *Fitness for Practice.* London: UKCC.

University of Sydney (1999) Student course experience questionnaire (http://www.itl.usyd.edu.au/SCEQ/sceqAbout.htm). Accessed 22 September 2003.

van Berkel, H. and Schmidt, H. G. (2000) Motivation to commit oneself as a determinant of achievement in problem-based learning. *Higher Education,* 40(2): 231–42.

van Berkel, H., Sprooten, J. and de Graaff, E. (1993) An individualized assessment test consisting of 600 items, in P. A. J. Bouhuijs, H. J. Schmidt and H. J. M. van Berkel (eds) *Problem-based Learning as an Educational Strategy.* Maastricht: Network publications.

van der Vleuten, C. P. M., Norman, G. R. and de Graaff, E. (1991) Pitfalls in the pursuit of objectivity: issues of reliability. *Medical Education,* 25: 110–18.

Vernon, D. T. A. (1995) Attitudes and opinions of faculty tutors about problem-based learning. *Academic Medicine,* 70(3): 216–23.

Vernon, D. T. A. and Blake, R. L. (1993) Does problem-based learning work? A meta-analysis of evaluative research. *Academic Medicine,* 68(7): 550–63.

Verwijnen, G. M., Imbos, T., Snellen, H., Stalenhoef, B., Pollemans, M., van Luyk, S., Sprooten, M., van Leeuwen, Y. and van der Vleuten, C. P. M. (1982) The evaluation system at the medical school of Maastricht. *Assessment and Evaluation in Higher Education,* 7(3): 225–44.

Viau, R. (1999) *La motivation dans l'apprentissage francais.* Saint-Laurent, Quebec: Éditions du Renouveau Pédagogiques.

Vygotsky, L. S. (1962) *Thought and Language.* Cambridge, MA: MIT Press.

Vygotsky, L. S. (1978) *Mind in Society: The Development of Higher Psychological Processes.* Cambridge, MA: MIT Press.

Walberg, H. J. and Haertel, G. D. (eds) (1990) *The International Encyclopedia of Educational Evaluation.* Oxford: Pergamon Press.

Walker, R. (1978) The conduct of educational case studies: ethics, theory and procedures, in M. Hammersley (ed.) *Controversies in Classroom Research.* Milton Keynes: Open University Press.

Webb, G. (1996) *Understanding Staff Development.* Buckingham: SRHE/Open University Press.

Weil, S. (1999) Recreating universities for 'beyond the stable state': from 'Dearingesque' systematic control to post-Dearing systematic learning and enquiry. *Journal of Systems Research and Behavioural Science,* 16(2): 171–90.

Weiss, C. H., Cambone, J. and Wyeth, A. (1992) Trouble in paradise: teacher conflicts in shared decision-making. *Educational Administration Quarterly,* 28(3): 350–67.

Wenger, E. (1998) *Communities of Practice. Learning, Meaning and Identity.* Cambridge: Cambridge University Press.

Wesdorp, H. (ed.) (1979) *Studietoetsen en hun effecten op het onderwijs.* The Hague: Staatsuitgeverij.

Wetzel, M. (1996) Techniques in medical education: problem-based learning. *Postgraduate Medical Journal,* 72: 474–7.

White, H. (1995) Creating problems for problem-based learning. *Newsletter of the Center for Teaching Effectiveness (University of Delaware), About Teaching,* 47.

Wilkerson, L. (1996) Tutors and small groups in problem-based learning: lessons from the literature, in L. Wilkerson and W. Gijselaers (eds) *Bringing Problem-based Learning to Higher Education Theory and Practice.* San Francisco: Jossey-Bass.

Wilkerson, L., Hafler, J. P. and Liu, P. (1991) A case study of student-directed discussion in four problem-based tutorial groups. *Academic Medicine,* 66(9): 579–81.

Wilkie, K. (2002) Actions, attitudes and attributes: developing skills for facilitating problem-based learning. Unpublished PhD thesis, Coventry University.

Williams, R., MacDermid, J. and Wessel, J. (2003) Student adaptation to problem-based learning in an entry-level master's physical education programme. *Physiotherapy Theory and Practice,* 19: 199–212.

Winter, R. (1996) Some principles and procedures for the conduct of action research, in O. Zuber-Skerritt (ed.) *New Directions in Action Research.* London: Falmer Press.

Wlodkowski, R. (1999) *Enhancing Adult Motivation to Learn: A Comprehensive Guide to Teaching All Adults,* rev. edn. San Francisco: Jossey-Bass.

Wolcott, H. (1994) *Transforming Qualitative Data Description, Analysis and Interpretation.* Thousand Oaks, CA: Sage.

Index

The Society for Research into Higher Education

The Society for Research into Higher Education (SRHE), an international body, exists to stimulate and coordinate research into all aspects of higher education. It aims to improve the quality of higher education through the encouragement of debate and publication on issues of policy, on the organization and management of higher education institutions, and on the curriculum, teaching and learning methods.

The Society is entirely independent and receives no subsidies, although individual events often receive sponsorship from business or industry. The Society is financed through corporate and individual subscriptions and has members from many parts of the world. It is an NGO of UNESCO.

Under the imprint *SRHE & Open University Press*, the Society is a specialist publisher of research, having over 80 titles in print. In addition to *SRHE News*, the Society's newsletter, the Society publishes three journals: *Studies in Higher Education* (three issues a year), *Higher Education Quarterly* and *Research into Higher Education Abstracts* (three issues a year).

The Society runs frequent conferences, consultations, seminars and other events. The annual conference in December is organized at and with a higher education institution. There are a growing number of networks which focus on particular areas of interest, including:

Access	FE/HE
Assessment	Graduate Employment
Consultants	New Technology for Learning
Curriculum Development	Postgraduate Issues
Eastern European	Quantitative Studies
Educational Development Research	Student Development

Benefits to members

Individual

- The opportunity to participate in the Society's networks
- Reduced rates for the annual conferences
- Free copies of *Research into Higher Education Abstracts*
- Reduced rates for *Studies in Higher Education*

- Reduced rates for *Higher Education Quarterly*
- Free online access to *Register of Members' Research Interests* – includes valuable reference material on research being pursued by the Society's members
- Free copy of occasional in-house publications, e.g. *The Thirtieth Anniversary Seminars Presented by the Vice-Presidents*
- Free copies of *SRHE News* and *International News* which inform members of the Society's activities and provides a calendar of events, with additional material provided in regular mailings
- A 35 per cent discount on all SRHE/Open University Press books
- The opportunity for you to apply for the annual research grants
- Inclusion of your research in the *Register of Members' Research Interests*

Corporate

- Reduced rates for the annual conference
- The opportunity for members of the Institution to attend SRHE's network events at reduced rates
- Free copies of *Research into Higher Education Abstracts*
- Free copies of *Studies in Higher Education*
- Free online access to *Register of Members' Research Interests* – includes valuable reference material on research being pursued by the Society's members
- Free copy of occasional in-house publications
- Free copies of *SRHE News* and *International News*
- A 35 per cent discount on all SRHE/Open University Press books
- The opportunity for members of the Institution to submit applications for the Society's research grants
- The opportunity to work with the Society and co-host conferences
- The opportunity to include in the *Register of Members' Research Interests* your Institution's research into aspects of higher education

Membership details: SRHE, 76 Portland Place, London
W1B 1NT, UK Tel: 020 7637 2766. Fax: 020 7637 2781.
email: srheoffice@srhe.ac.uk
world wide web: http://www.srhe.ac.uk./srhe/
Catalogue: SRHE & Open University Press, McGraw-Hill
Education, McGraw-Hill House, Shoppenhangers Road,
Maidenhead, Berkshire SL6 2QL. Tel: 01628 502500.
Fax: 01628 770224. email: enquiries@openup.co.uk
web: www.openup.co.uk

FOUNDATIONS OF PROBLEM-BASED LEARNING

Maggi Savin-Baden and Claire Howell Major

Despite the growth in the use of problem-based learning since it was first popularised by Barrows and Tamblyn (1980) in the first book on the subject, no text has examined the foundations of the approach nor offered straight-forward guidance to those wishing to explore, understand, and implement it. This book describes the theoretical foundations of problem-based learning and is a practical source for staff wanting to implement it.

The book is designed as a text that not only explores the foundations of problem-based learning and but also answers many of the often-asked questions about its use. It has also been designed to develops the reader's understanding beyond implementation, including issues such as academic development, cultural, diversity, assessment, evaluation and curricular models of problem-based learning.

Contents

*Acknowledgements – Prologue – **Part 1: Conceptual frames** – Delineating core concepts of problem-based learning – A brief history of problem-based learning – Problem-based learning and theories of learning – Curricula models – Cultural contexts of academe – **Part 2: Recurring themes** – What is a problem? – Learning teams – The role of students – The role of tutor – Staff support and development – Assessing problem-based learning – **Part 3: Broadening horizons** – Embracing culture and diversity – Programme evaluation – Sustaining problem-based learning curricula – Epilogue: Future imperative? – Glossary – Bibliography – Index.*

224pp   0 335 21531 9 (Paperback)   0 335 21532 7 (Hardback)

FACILITATING PROBLEM-BASED LEARNING: ILLUMINATING PERSPECTIVES

Maggi Savin-Baden

Interest in problem-based learning continues to flourish worldwide. To date there has been relatively little to help staff to examine the complex issues relating to facilitating the implementation of problem-based learning and the ongoing development of staff, students and the curriculum.

This book explores a broad range of issues about facilitation, in particular understandings of facilitation that have emerged from the author's recent research and ways of equipping and supporting staff in terrestrial and virtual contexts. It also questions how students are assessed and suggests ways of preventing plagiarism in problem-based learning. It examines what it might mean to be an effective facilitator and suggests ways of designing problem-based curricula that enhance learning.

Contents

176pp   0 335 21054 6 (Paperback)   0 335 21055 4 (Hardback)

PROBLEM-BASED LEARNING IN HIGHER EDUCATION: UNTOLD STORIES

Maggi Savin-Baden

'Problem-based learning is contested and murky ground in higher education. In her study, Maggi Savin-Baden clears the thickets, offering a bold ambitious framework and, in the process, gives us a compelling argument for placing problem-based learning in the centre of higher education as an educational project. It is a story not to be missed.' – Professor Ronald Barnett

'This is a challenging and very worthwhile read for anyone concerned with the future of higher education, and issues of teaching and learning. The metaphor of "untold stories" is powerfully explored at the level of staff and student experience of problem-based learning.' – Professor Susan Weil

Problem-based learning is becoming increasingly popular in higher education because it is seen to take account of pedagogical and societal trends (such as flexibility, adaptability, problem-solving and critique) in ways which many traditional methods of learning do not. There is little known about what actually occurs *inside* problem-based curricula in terms of staff and student 'lived experience'. This book discloses ways in which learners and teachers manage complex and diverse learning in the context of their lives in a fragile and often incoherent world. These are the untold stories. The central argument of the book is that the potential and influence of problem-based learning is yet to be realized personally, pedagogically and professionally in the context of higher education. It explores both the theory and the practice of problem-based learning and considers the implications of implementing problem-based learning organizationally.

Contents
Prologue – **Part one: A web of belief?** – *Problem-based learning underestimated* – *Missing elements* – **Part two: Problem-based learning: an unarticulated subtext?** – *Games of chess?* – *From rooks, pawns and bishops* – *Images and experiences of problem-based learning* – **Part three: Learning at the borders** – *Recognizing disjunction* – *Managing transition* – *As good as it gets?* – **Part four: Problem-based learning reconsidered** – *Critical perspectives on problem-based learning* – *Problem-based learning and organizational cultures* – *Epilogue* – *Glossary* – *Bibliography* – *Index.*

176pp   0 335 20337 X (Paperback)   0 335 20338 8 (Hardback)

RESEARCHING HIGHER EDUCATION
ISSUES AND APPROACHES

Malcolm Tight

This book couples an authoritative overview of the principal current areas of research into higher education with a guide to the core methods used for researching higher education. It offers both a configuration of research on higher education, as seen through the lens of methodology, and suggestions for further research.

Contents
Case studies and tables are separately listed after the main contents pages – Part I: Recently Published Research on Higher Education – Introduction – Journals – Books – Part II: Issues and Approaches in Researching Higher Education – Researching Teaching and Learning – Researching Course Design – Researching the Student Experience – Researching Quality – Researching System Policy – Researching Institutional Management – Researching Academic Work – Researching Knowledge – Part III: The Process of Researching Higher Education – Method and Methodology in Researching Higher Education – Researching Higher Education at Different Levels – The Process of Researching – References.

417pp   0 335 21117 8 (Paperback)   0 335 21118 6 (Hardback)

VIRTUAL LEARNING COMMUNITIES
A GUIDE FOR PRACTITIONERS

Dina Lewis and Barbara Allan

- What are the characteristics of a successful learning community?

- How are successful communities facilitated and maintained?

- What lessons can be learnt from existing learning communities?

- What type of learning community will suit your organisation or situation?

This user-friendly guide is written to help managers, professionals and learners, planning, facilitating or participating in online learning communities, as part of a structured learning programme, as an approach to continuous professional development, as a means of improving performance at work or as a dynamic approach to innovation and collaborative working.

The book is relevant to senior mangers with a responsibility for strategic planning and change management. This can include new work practices involving working in multi-professional teams across traditional boundaries. It aims to engage readers in identifying key issues in relation to their own work situation and prompts readers to find their own solutions

Virtual Learning Communities provides practical guidance and includes extensive examples, case studies and activities. It is key reading for those involved in e-learning courses, professional trainers and staff developers with a responsibility for CPD, and professionals involved in facilitating new approaches to group work.

Contents
List of tables – List of figures - Acknowledgements – Introduction to learning communities – Learning communities in the workplace – Using information and communications technology – The community lifecycle: Foundation and induction – The community lifecycle: Incubation – Community lifecycle: Improvement, implementation, closure or change – Participation in learning communities – Social learning – Time – Working in partnership – Community evaluation – References – Index.

224pp   0 335 21282 4 (Paperback)   0 335 21283 2 (Hardback)